Artificial Intelligence and Social Work

This book marries social work and artificial intelligence (AI) to provide an introductory guide for using AI for social good. Following an introductory chapter laying out approaches and ethical principles of using AI for social work interventions, the book describes in detail an intervention to increase the spread of HIV information by using algorithms to determine the key individuals in a social network of homeless youth. Other chapters present interdisciplinary collaborations between AI and social work students, including a chatbot for sexual health information and algorithms to determine who is at higher stress among persons with type 2 diabetes.

For students, academic researchers, industry leaders, and practitioners, these real-life examples from the USC Center for Artificial Intelligence in Society demonstrate how social work and artificial intelligence can be used in tandem for the greater good.

MILIND TAMBE is Helen N. and Emmett H. Jones Professor of Engineering and Founding Co-Director of the Center for Artificial Intelligence in Society at the University of Southern California. He is a fellow of Association for Advancement of Artificial Intelligence (AAAI) and Association for Computing Machinery (ACM), recipient of ACM/SIGAI Autonomous Agents Research Award, Christopher Columbus Fellowship Foundation Homeland security award, INFORMS Wagner prize in Operations Research, IJCAI John McCarthy Award, and others. He has contributed several foundational papers in AI in areas of intelligent agents and computational game theory, which have received best paper awards at major AI conferences including AAMAS, IJCAI, IAAI.

ERIC RICE is Associate Professor and Founding Co-Director of the Center for Artificial Intelligence in Society at the University of Southern California. An expert in community-based research and social network science and theory, he has spent the past several years working to merge social work science and AI to create solutions for major social problems such as homelessness and HIV. Since 2002, he has worked closely with homeless youth providers in Los Angeles and many other communities across the country to develop novel solutions to support young people across the nation who do not have a home, with the goal of ending youth homelessness.

Artificial Intelligence for Social Good

Artificial intelligence has a diversity of applications, many with social benefits. Books in this series will offer a multidisciplinary perspective on these applications, ranging from social work to health care to environmental sciences. Each book will survey the AI approaches to a particular societal problem and promising research directions, with case study examples.

This is the first book in this series.

Artificial Intelligence and Social Work

Edited by

MILIND TAMBE
University of Southern California

ERIC RICE
University of Southern California

CAMBRIDGE
UNIVERSITY PRESS

University Printing House, Cambridge CB2 8BS, United Kingdom

One Liberty Plaza, 20th Floor, New York, NY 10006, USA

477 Williamstown Road, Port Melbourne, VIC 3207, Australia

314-321, 3rd Floor, Plot 3, Splendor Forum, Jasola District Centre, New Delhi - 110025, India

79 Anson Road, #06-04/06, Singapore 079906

Cambridge University Press is part of the University of Cambridge.

It furthers the University's mission by disseminating knowledge in the pursuit of education, learning and research at the highest international levels of excellence.

www.cambridge.org
Information on this title: www.cambridge.org/9781108444347
DOI: 10.1017/9781108669016

© Milind Tambe and Eric Rice 2018

First published 2018
First paperback edition 2021

A catalogue record for this publication is available from the British Library

Library of Congress Cataloging in Publication data
Names: Tambe, Milind, 1965– editor. | Rice, Eric (Eric R. W.), editor.
Title: Artificial intelligence and social work / edited by Milind Tambe,
University of Southern California, Eric Rice, University of Southern California.
Description: Cambridge, United Kingdom ; New York, NY : Cambridge University
Press, 2018. | Series: Artificial intelligence for social good |
Includes bibliographical references and index.
Identifiers: LCCN 2018012813 | ISBN 9781108425995 (hardback : alk. paper) |
ISBN 9781108444347 (pbk. : alk. paper)
Subjects: LCSH: Social service–Technological innovations |
Artificial intelligence. | Social justice.
Classification: LCC HV40 .A79155 2018 | DDC 361.30285/63–dc23
LC record available at https://lccn.loc.gov/2018012813

ISBN 978-1-108-42599-5 Hardback
ISBN 978-1-108-44434-7 Paperback

Contents

6   Maximizing the Spread of Sexual Health Information in a
    Multimodal Communication Network of Young
    Black Women   93
    Elizabeth Bondi, Jaih Craddock, Rebecca Funke, Chloe LeGendre,
    and Vivek Tiwari

7   Minimizing Violence in Homeless Youth   119
    Ajitesh Srivastava, Robin Petering, and Michail Misyrlis

8   Artificial Intelligence for Improving Access to Sexual Health
    Necessities for Youth Experiencing Homelessness   136
    Aida Rahmattalabi, Laura Onasch-Vera, Orlando Roybal,
    Kien Nguyen, Luan Tran, Robin Petering,
    Professor Eric Rice, and Professor Milind Tambe

9   Know-Stress: Predictive Modeling of Stress among Diabetes
    Patients under Varying Conditions   153
    Subhasree Sengupta, Kexin Yu, and Behnam Zahiri

10 A Multidisciplinary Study on the Relationship between
    Foster Care Attributes and Posttraumatic Stress Disorder
    Symptoms on Foster Youth   169
    Amanda Yoshioka-Maxwell, Shahrzad Gholami, Emily Sheng,
    Mary Hemler, Tanachat Nilanon, and Ali Jalal-Kamali

11 Artificial Intelligence to Predict Intimate Partner Violence
    Perpetration   195
    Robin Petering, Mee-Young Um, Nazanin Alipourfard, Nazgol Tavabi,
    Rajni Kumari, and Setareh Nasihati Gilani

12 SHIHbot: Sexual Health Information on HIV/AIDS,
    chatbot   211
    Joshua Rusow, Jacqueline Brixey, Rens Hoegen, Lan Wei, Karan Singla,
    and Xusen Yin

13 Ethics and Artificial Intelligence in Public Health
    Social Work   231
    David Gray Grant

    Glossary   250
    Elizabeth Bondi and Mee-Young Um

    Index   255

Contributors

Nazanin Alipourfard
University of Southern California

Elizabeth Bondi
University of Southern California

Jacqueline Brixey
University of Southern California

Hau Chan
University of Nebraska–Lincoln

Jaih Craddock
University of Southern California

Rebecca Funke
University of Southern California

Shahrzad Gholami
University of Southern California

Setareh Nasihati Gilani
University of Southern California

David Gray Grant
Massachusetts Institute of Technology

Mary Hemler
University of Southern California

Rens Hoegen
University of Southern California

Nicole Immorlica
Microsoft Research

Ali Jalal-Kamali
University of Southern California

Albert Jiang
Trinity University

Rajni Kumari
University of Southern California

Chloe Legendre
University of Southern California

Michail Misyrlis
University of Southern California

Kien Nguyen
University of Southern California

Tanachat Nilanon
University of Southern California

Laura Onasch-Vera
University of Southern California

Robin Petering
University of Southern California

Aida Rahmattalabi
University of Southern California

Eric Rice
University of Southern California

Orland Roybal
California State University, Northridge

Joshua Rusow
University of Southern California

Subhasree Sengupta
University of Southern California

Emily Sheng
University of Southern California

Karan Singla
University of Southern California

Ajitesh Srivastava
University of Southern California

Milind Tambe
University of Southern California

Nazgol Tavabi
University of Southern California

Vivek Tiwari
University of Southern California

Luan Tran
University of Southern California

Mee-Young Um
University of Southern California

Lan Wei
University of Southern California

Bryan Wilder
University of Southern California

Hailey Winetrobe
University of Southern California

Darlene Woo
University of Southern California

Haifeng Xu
University of Southern California

Amulya Yadav
University of Southern California

Amanda Yoshioka-Maxwell
University of Southern California

Xusen Yin
University of Southern California

Kexin Yu
University of Southern California

Behnam Zahiri
University of Southern California

PART I

1

Merging Social Work Science and Computer Science for Social Good

Eric Rice and Milind Tambe

Artificial Intelligence (AI) is a ubiquitous part of our daily lives. Particularly and inextricably, AI is linked to our online lives. Your every click and post is being mined by increasingly sophisticated algorithms. Whenever you search for something online, AI is there. AI helps us more successfully navigate real-world traffic, not just online traffic. And because it helps us find information quickly or navigate city streets more effectively, it is easy to appreciate how AI can make our lives better sometimes. There are some in the tech world who view AI as a panacea, capable of solving any cognitive task given enough time, computing power, and rich enough data sets. As two authors who live in Los Angeles, where traffic is awful day and night, we certainly will not argue with some of the gains AI can bring to the daily life.

But AI is not always viewed with such a kind eye. Indeed, many in the scientific community as well as the general public are increasingly concerned about the negative impact AI may have on society. Some of these concerns, such as killer robots, may seem like dystopic science fiction fantasies, but weaponized drones guided by AI may not be so far-fetched. There are also genuine concerns over job loss, as some traditional white-collar jobs may be replaced by algorithms that are "happy" to perform dreary organizational tasks for a fraction of the cost of having a human being perform them. Furthermore, many ethicists, policy makers, pundits, and entrepreneurs with high influence in the tech world have begun to worry about the future of society, particularly when AI is applied in arenas where humans have traditionally made decisions, such as medicine and the law. We are also sympathetic to these fears and think that they need to be taken seriously.

This book, however, offers a third perspective. AI can be used to improve society and fight social injustice. From our perspective, the vast majority of the persons who currently benefit from AI are people who live with a certain

3

amount of privilege. Largely this is due to the fact that much of AI is wrapped up in the high-tech economy. Yet, many of the most impoverished parts of the world still struggle to obtain internet access. The digital footprints of homeless persons, for example, are far smaller than those of us who live in more affluent circumstances.

What we propose in this book is a radical shift in perspective. We dare you to imagine how AI can be used to benefit the disadvantaged. By bringing together social work scientists and computer scientists, we can tackle thorny, seemingly intractable social problems in brand-new ways. Consider this: If problems such as homelessness, HIV, gender discrimination, substance abuse, domestic violence, and suicide were easy to solve, then we would have solved those problems already. Right? But the reality is that many social problems are incredibly complex and require equally complex solutions.

The complexity of the world can rarely be explained by one single discipline. Solving complex problems with one discipline stands even less of a chance. We believe that much of the strength of our work rests in having created an intellectual space in which computer scientists and social work scientists are equal partners who bring unique knowledge and expertise to the table. From AI come new technologies and approaches, and from social work comes a deep understanding of human behavior and how to intervene effectively in society. As such, we see AI for social good as a new transdisciplinary intellectual space.

Motivations for Our Research

In some respects, this book is an introduction to the work at the University of Southern California (USC) Center for AI in Society (CAIS). This center is one of the first university-based centers focused on AI for Social Good. More importantly it is the first center to deliberately bring together computer science and social work science. CAIS is a joint venture between the Suzanne Dworak-Peck School of Social Work and the Viterbi School of Engineering. Our mission is to conduct research in Artificial Intelligence to help solve the most difficult social problems facing our world.

At CAIS, we seek to bring researchers from around the world to focus on how computer science can be used to solve social problems. This requires an engagement by social work science and computer science. As a field, AI has just begun to consider the role it can have in promoting social good. Similarly, social work has just begun to engage with computer science to enhance the impact of social work science. It is our intention to have the research emerging from this new intellectual space impact changes in national and international policy, enhance specific social programs, and move toward the creation of a new field of study that merges the technological expertise of engineering with the domain expertise of social work in solving seemingly intractable social problems.

There are many ways one can define social problems, but at CAIS we largely turn to three major sources of inspiration: the Grand Challenges of Social Work, the Grand Challenges of Engineering, and the Sustainable Development Goals of the United Nations. To learn more about these, we encourage you to explore the following web resources:

- Grand Challenges of Social Work (http://aaswsw.org/grand-challenges-initiative/)
- Grand Challenges of Engineering (www.engineeringchallenges.org/)
- United Nations Sustainable Development Goals (www.un.org/sustainabledevelopment/sustainable-development-goals/)
- United Nations Millennium Development Goals (www.un.org/millenniumgoals/environ.shtml)

The Grand Challenges of Social Work is a list of twelve challenges identified by the National Academy of Social Work to inspire social work practitioners and scientists in the twenty-first century. Progress made on any of these challenges will lead to important improvements in human well-being. Some of the challenges that we are particularly motivated by include issues such as ensuring healthy development for all youth, eradicating social isolation, ending homelessness, and harnessing technology for social good. Some of our projects, such as the HIV prevention program for homeless youth that we describe in detail in this book, draw inspiration from multiple challenges. That project in particular is inspired by the desire to harness technology for social good, end homelessness, and empower homeless youth to ensure healthy development for a group of youth who are often marginalized and discarded by mainstream society.

We also draw inspiration from some of the Grand Challenges of Engineering. Like the Grand Challenges of Social Work, the challenges identified by the National Academy of Engineering are for engineers in the field as well as engineering scientists. Two of the challenges we are particularly motivated by are advancing health informatics and securing cyberspace. We have a set of emerging projects that work with administrative data from health providers and social service providers. We are interested in helping build human–machine collaborative decision-making systems that can improve service delivery in both the health and social service fields. Likewise, we have a set of projects that have focused on public safety and security, both cyber and physical. Some concrete example projects include our collaborations with the US Coast Guard, the Transportation Security Administration, and different police departments. Here we have used AI for enhancing security resource optimization; these algorithms are in daily use for improving randomized patrol routines and allocation at major airports and ports around the United States, including New York, Los Angeles, and Boston. In some cases, such as the US Coast Guard patrols around the Staten Island Ferry in New York, they have radically altered the patrol patterns and resulted in improved effectiveness.

UN Sustainable Development Goals and UN Millennium Development Goals also help anchor the work of the center. We include these goals alongside the Grand Challenges for Social Work because we feel that those Grand Challenges have a domestic flavor, drawing primarily from issues that impact the United States and other developed nations. We doubt this was an intentional oversight, but at CAIS we are interested in issues that may impact the developing world, and emerging economies. We draw obvious inspiration from sustainable development goals such as good health and well-being, equality, no poverty, and decent work and economic growth, as well as millennium development goals such as eradicating extreme poverty, reducing child mortality, promoting gender equality and empowering women, and combating HIV/AIDS, malaria, and other diseases. But we also look to life on land and to ensuring environmental sustainability. We have actively explored the ways of using AI for environmental sustainability and conservation. Concrete ongoing projects include our continued work with nongovernmental organizations (NGOs) for wildlife conservation, including World Wildlife Fund (WWF), Wildlife Conservation Society (WCS), and PANTHERA to implement AI-based techniques for assisting rangers in the field. Here AI algorithms are used for predicting poacher activity, so that patrols can more effectively stop the poachers before they deploy their traps to kill animals. We hope to write a volume dedicated to work on AI for sustainability in the future.

There is a great deal of overlap across the Grand Challenges and Goals from which we draw our inspiration. Both Social Work and the United Nations prioritize fighting poverty, promoting equality, and ensuring healthy development for children. Both Engineering and the United Nations prioritize clean drinking water and improved health. What these challenges and goals share is a focus on improving lives for all people, especially underserved and marginalized populations throughout the United States and internationally. These set of goals provide important new directions for engineers and social workers. It is important to remember that these goals and challenges are not easy problems to tackle. In fact, a cynic could look at these lists and quickly dismiss most of the topics. If these were easy things to achieve, they would have been achieved already. What we have come to appreciate is that a merging of social work and engineering empowers each to be more effective in tackling these seemingly impossible challenges. We are not offering a panacea, but we are offering a new path. It is perhaps an unlikely path, but we hope that the contributions in this book will do much to demonstrate the potential we have come to see.

What Is Social Work

Since this book aims to speak to two very different audiences, social work scientists and computer scientists, a brief overview of just what happens in these two disciplines seems warranted. Unfortunately, a few paragraphs on the topics can hardly hope to do each discipline much justice. Moreover, such a short treatment will inevitably reflect our own personal stances within our respective disciplines. That said, we hope these next few paragraphs help you, our readers, to be grounded to some extent in the work of these two fields.

Social work is fundamentally an intervention-driven discipline. The historical roots of social work and its pioneers, particularly Jane Adams, Elizabeth Fry, and Mary Ellen Richmond, were first and foremost in improving the human condition, particularly for the disadvantaged. Over the past 100-plus years, social work has emerged as a practice and a science. Individual social workers work in a variety of settings. The most common are as members of child welfare agencies, community-based or nongovernmental organizations, as community organizers, and in policy-making organizations. What ties this work together is an overarching drive to fight inequality and to help all people live to their full potential. There has been and continues to be a fundamental focus on marginalized and disadvantaged groups within society and on assisting those communities and the individuals who are a part of those groups to thrive.

Social work science focuses on the complex causal forces that impact human life. Central to the discipline is an understanding of human well-being as existing in the nexus of micro-, messo-, and macro-level forces. When social work thinks about micro-level issues, the focus is on the psychology, biology, and even spirituality of individuals. Messo-level action is concerned primarily with the functioning of social networks and local communities. Macro-level issues are conceptualized as larger social forces, such as institutions and social norms. The science conducted by social work scientists happens at any of these three levels and often cuts across these levels.

Research conducted by social work scientists can take many shapes, but fundamentally there is always a focus on intervention and improving the lives of humans in need. Some of the goals of social work is specifically about the design and testing of new behavioral and/or mental health interventions. Social work scientists tend to want to create change in the world, and many are not happy to let their interventions be sequestered to university-based work. Thus, in recent years, there has begun to be a focus within the social work field on what is called implementation science, that, is the science of bringing evidence-based interventions to scale in communities.

Social work scientists also do a large amount of observational social science research. Much of this work is based on using statistical techniques to analyze survey data collected from a variety of populations, ranging from nationally representative samples to community-based samples of marginalized groups, such as homeless youth. There has been a recent turn toward using administrative data from social welfare and health care service settings as well. In addition, there are also qualitative methods, such as ethnographic work, focus groups, and individual open-ended interviews. But all of this work is in the service of intervention. Almost every article written by a social work scientist includes a discussion of how their finding impact intervention design or social policy change. Social work science is fundamentally a science of action.

What Is AI

There is no accepted definition of Artificial Intelligence, but generally speaking, we will consider AI to include computer systems (including robots) that perform tasks that require intelligence. From a discipline that the public knew almost nothing about a few decades ago, AI has grown into a discipline that is often in the news (arguably for the wrong reasons), and has led to national research strategies being developed in the United States and the United Kingdom.

Artificial Intelligence began in the late 1950s. Four scientists are generally considered to be the founding fathers of AI: Allen Newell and Herbert Simon of Carnegie Mellon University; John McCarthy of Stanford University, and Marvin Minsky of the Massachusetts Institute of Technology. Since those early years of optimism, AI has gone through its share of ups and downs; it is worthwhile taking a quick tour of these developments and understanding the roots of the discipline. The early years of optimism in AI were based on computer programs performing tasks that could be considered difficult for humans, such as playing chess, proving theorems, and solving puzzles. Early progress was dominated by use of logics and symbolic systems, heuristic reasoning, and search algorithms. If we are playing chess or proving a theorem, we do not face uncertainty in our reasoning steps: e.g., statements are either true or false; chess moves are deterministic. Accordingly, probabilistic reasoning and uncertainty did not play a major role in the field. Since interacting with the outside world was not a priority in these tasks, a program could reason about a situation in depth and then react.

Early years of optimism also focused on integrated AI systems that could combine sensory perception or computer vision, machine learning to autonomously learn from interactions of the AI system with the world, automated reasoning and planning to act in the world, possibly speech and dialogue in natural language, social interactions with humans and other entities, and so on. Such intelligent agents include robots, but can also be avatars in virtual worlds. This vision of AI involves gathering data from the world and machine learning to build a predictive model of how the world would evolve. However, it does not stop only at making predictions, but also includes planning and reasoning from first principles, i.e., providing prescriptions and taking actions in the world.

This optimistic period had reached its end in the 1990s, when AI research was accused of not living up to its promises, which led to a general cut in funding and interest in AI. Researchers realized that what was easy for humans (e.g., recognizing objects in images, understanding human speech as English words) turned out to be difficult for AI systems. As AI systems started interacting with the real world, there appeared a need for an entirely new set of tools to handle reasoning in the presence of uncertainty and to provide quick reactions to unanticipated events. These difficulties led to new quantitative tools from decision theory, optimization, and game theory being brought into AI. This period also coincided with an emphasis on fast reactive reasoning (rather than purely deep reasoning) in AI, particularly for robots interacting with the world; this was the beginning of the rise of a new AI, with the early symbolic AI approaches being called "Good Old-Fashioned AI" (or GOFAI).

With increasing computing power and the ability to gather large quantities of data, we now have reached yet another new era of AI. Machine learning using deep neural nets has led to significant new successes in tasks such as recognizing objects in images and natural language understanding. While these new approaches to machine learning have not penetrated all of the traditional areas of AI (e.g., planning and reasoning or social reasoning), this new era has brought significant new interest and investment from industry. It has also led to a mistaken perception among the general public that AI is only about machine learning and prediction, and that unless there are vast quantities of data, AI cannot function. Often not well understood is AI's ability to provide prescriptions, by reasoning through millions of possibilities based on millions of simulations from first principles of how entities may interact in the world. In our work described in Part II of this book, we often focus on this ability to plan interventions.

The Unlikely Partnership

AI and social work may seem like an unlikely combination or even a clashing set of disciplines. It turns out, however, that there are three major intellectual points of convergence between our individual research agendas, which make this a wonderful, albeit surprising, partnership.The research agendas embrace complexity in social settings. Likewise, both embrace uncertainty. And perhaps most importantly, both value praxis.

Eric Rice's research agenda has been rooted in the idea that the social world is a deeply complex place. The causes of social injustice are complex, and are the results of the intersections of historical oppression, contemporary societal structures, psychological issues, biological issues, and even spiritual issues. Much of his work prior to connecting with that of Milind Tambe focuses on the complexity of social networks and how the web of interconnections that surround people impact human well-being. Likewise, Tambe's research agenda is driven by complex real-world multi-agent system problems, an area of AI focused on social interactions. This area traditionally focuses on employing machine learning, planning, and reasoning in complex social environments involving interactions among humans, as well as between humans and AI (including software or robots).

In their research, both Tambe and Rice must wrestle with uncertainty. From the perspective of computer science modeling, the probabilistic nature of outcomes is par for the course, and techniques such as sequential decision-making and planning under uncertainty that we will discuss later are predicated on not knowing all of what happens in the world. Social work, likewise, has a deep understanding of the uncertainty of the social world. Human beings are not only complicated; they are idiosyncratic. Social work loathes "one size fits all" solutions and embraces understanding of not just what can be known but also what is not known.

But perhaps the greatest point of interconnection between Tambe and Rice's research agenda is a desire to implement solutions. Rice views social work science as fundamentally a science of intervention. Even when his scholarly articles focus on theory, methodological developments, or observational research, the intent is always to further the well-being of populations in need. Thus, among Rice's published work, there are articles that do not explicitly test new intervention strategies for homeless youth, but nearly all of these articles end with explicit discussions of how that particular piece of research may impact program development or policy change. Likewise, if you look at Tambe's publications, while some are more theoretical than others, focusing on the development of new algorithms, particularly over the past decade, all of this algorithmic work is explicitly focused on trying to assist in the solution of real-world problems.

New Science for Both Sides

Social work problems and AI may seem far apart, but we argue that, when brought together they engender powerful new science. We argue that AI for social good, or AI and social work, is a new intellectual space, because what has come from our collaborations is unique to both AI and social work. This is not just an issue of applying "out of the box" AI tools (as is the case sometimes when social scientists discover that new analytic techniques are available), nor is it an issue of doing typical social work interventions but with a technology enhancement (as is sometimes the case with mobile health technology projects). What we have created is a new intellectual space that is generative of innovative science from both the computer science and social work science perspective (Figure 1.1).

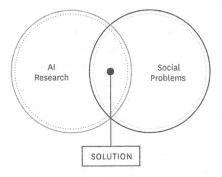

Figure 1.1 The USC Center for Artificial Intelligence in Society's approach to research

We can illustrate this point best in our work on HIV prevention for homeless youth. From the perspective of AI, influence maximization in the context of homeless youth networks introduced several new challenges for which algorithms did not exist. For example, traditional AI influence maximization algorithms, focused on domains such as product advertising, have relied on a "clean" data set of a social network (possibly downloaded from social media) without uncertainty. However, the social network of homeless youth is not downloaded from social media; rather, it is obtained from field observations of social workers, and may be full of uncertainty. Thus, we had to address new research challenges in influence maximization algorithms focused on reasoning with uncertainty in social networks and adapting to availability of new information reducing or adding to such uncertainty. Indeed, this research work has been lauded for its innovation with a number of awards at major AI conferences. Likewise, from the perspective of social work, working on diffusion-based interventions is common, but thinking about diffusion as a formal problem of influence maximization radically shifted the view of networks and actions of actors within those networks. And these innovations were not only significant from a scientific perspective but, as you will see in Chapter 4, made a real impact on the lives of homeless youth.

More generally, there are many new challenges in this interdisciplinary space that do not fit the traditional techniques of either field. As we discussed earlier, the new wave of AI has been driven by large data sets, massive computational power, and hence deep learning; this AI work has often focused on learning predictive models. The type of AI research required for this interdisciplinary space is often devoid of such convenient data sets. Indeed, we are often focused in low-resource communities that have incomplete and uncertain data. Often the massive computational power is in short supply; resources are very limited. Finally, we are often interested in going a step beyond prediction to prescription, to intervention. This style of AI research often calls for partnerships between humans and AI. For example, in our work on HIV prevention for homeless youth, humans are the ones responsible for interacting with homeless youth, whereas the AI programs focus on selecting which youth the social workers should interact with.

Similarly for social work, engaging in formal modeling of social processes in the context of AI allowed us to identify and solve intervention implementation challenges. As we discuss later in the book, peer-led HIV prevention programs have not always worked in all contexts. Part of this failure may have to do with who is picked to be a peer leader. The person who delivers the messages is as important as the messages being delivered. Two approaches to peer leader selection are typically used. Peer leaders are selected either based on attributes that seem to indicate they would possess the capacity to be a peer leader or by observing a population and selecting the most popular persons. Thinking about peer leader selection within the context of influence maximization, however, shifts the thought process toward the importance of interconnections within the community and the importance of groups of persons working in concert to enact social change. Even static network solutions such as the persons with the most connections to others were abandoned in favor of more dynamic solutions. This approach to intervention development and implementation of social programs is unique to this collaboration between social work and AI.

In addition to the new techniques discussed earlier, this interdisciplinary space also calls for support of new scientific traditions. AI research focuses on improving tools and techniques, and best papers in AI conferences provide technical breakthroughs in models, representations, algorithms, theorems and/or new analysis of algorithms or their theoretical or empirical behaviors. This is fast-paced research, with new breakthroughs coming fast and furious, and often easily evaluated with massive simulations or other evaluations on clean datasets. The focus is "inward," toward the technique. This scientific progress is exciting and obviously important. However, in our interdisciplinary space, it is important to go beyond the technical breakthroughs per se and measure their impact on society. What is required is a careful, patient, and detailed measurement of the pros and cons, benefits and deficits, conducted on the scale of human social interactions, potentially carried out over months. Such detailed understanding of impact of new proposed interventions is absolutely essential, but it is new to traditional AI. The result of such research is not new algorithms or new theorems – the staple of publications in AI – but detailed analysis of impact on society. This is clearly a new kind of science, one that requires nurturing. Similarly for social work, the process of intervention development from acceptability trials, to feasibility trials, to efficacy trials, and finally to effectiveness trials is an incredibly slow-moving process, one that typically takes more than a decade of work with a single new intervention program. We need new, more nimble ways of testing interventions in order to take advantage of the more fast-paced work of computer science. Perhaps something akin to beta-testing is needed for our work to keep pace with the emerging opportunities presented by collaboration with AI.

The Structure of the Book

This book has two sections: Part I focuses on our ongoing transdisciplinary research specifically around social issues such as homelessness and HIV risk. We focus on how AI can enhance the implementation of HIV prevention interventions for the homeless youth. Some of this work has been published in a series of papers at various international AI conferences including IAAI 2015, AAMAS 2016, AAMAS 2017 (two separate papers), as well as several workshop papers and *AI Magazine 2016*. We present a version of this work that is more accessible to an interdisciplinary audience rather than a purely AI audience. This work with homeless youth drop-in centers in Los Angeles illustrates that AI algorithms can actually significantly improve spreading of HIV prevention information among homeless youth. The work has received significant number of awards, including AAMAS16 best student paper, AAAI17 best video and best student video award, and a nomination for AAMAS17 best paper. This section also includes an overview of the social context of youth homelessness in the United States, provides an exploration of our first algorithmic solutions to peer-led HIV prevention models, "real-world" field tests of these algorithms with actual homeless youth in Los Angeles, and future thoughts about enhanced algorithmic techniques that rely on less extensive network data collection methods.

Part II of the book features seven aspirational chapters written by graduate students at USC. All of these chapters represent the work of transdisciplinary teams of students that include both social work and computer science graduate students working on a range of difficult social problems using cutting-edge techniques from AI to attempt to create new solutions to wicked social problems. These chapters were the product of a course that we co-taught in the spring of 2017 at USC called "AI for Social Good." The class included students from both social work and computer science, mostly PhD students with a handful of master's students. These chapters showcase many problems that can be tackled by this novel collaboration of AI and social work. The problems covered include interpersonal violence, intimate partner violence, sexual health information dissemination, posttraumatic stress, depression, and homelessness. The AI work includes machine learning techniques such as neural networks, decision trees, and Bayesian networks. There are also chapters that utilize sequential planning under uncertainty, the Uncertain Voter Model, and advances to the k-center problem. There is also an initial foray into natural language processing, with the creation of a Facebook bot to autonomously deliver sexual health information to sexual-minority youth. This section of the book concludes with a chapter on ethics of autonomous agents in the context of social work and public health interventions, written by a CAIS summer fellow who is a doctoral student in philosophy.

We end the book with a glossary of terms. Perhaps the most challenging aspect of AI for social work is that social work science and computer science both have very specific, technical, jargon-filled, academic languages. And these languages are not at all the same. Over the past few years we have learned that often we use different words to mean the same thing and the same word to mean different things. The word "objective" for an AI researcher is often framed in the context of an optimization problem, and implies a precise mathematical statement, as opposed to the objective that a social scientist may wish to achieve for, say, homeless youth in the real world. The "objective" of a real-world intervention is often something far more nebulous, such as to help prevent the spread of HIV among homeless youth. What a computer scientist calls a feature of a data set a social scientist would call a variable. And perhaps most frustrating, the difference in the word "model" in the context of computer science and social science is so different as to be comical, if it were not so disruptive at times. Because we have experienced the hard growth of trying to become bilingual, we share with you this glossary.

2

The Causes and Consequences of Youth Homelessness

Eric Rice and Hailey Winetrobe

In this chapter, we provide the social context and foundation for our work. "Have You Heard?" is a behavioral intervention that focuses on peer-led HIV prevention for homeless youth (Rice, Tulbert, et al., 2012). Our recent work has augmented this intervention by using the artificial intelligence algorithms HEALER and DOSIM to improve the implementation of this intervention. This chapter provides a broad overview of why this work is important, by discussing (1) the extent of youth homelessness, (2) the causes of youth homelessness, (3) the consequences of youth homelessness (particularly HIV infection), (4) the importance of social networks in the lives of homeless youth, (5) the complexity of working with networks of homeless youth, and (6) how and why AI- and network-based interventions for homeless youth are needed to increase the success of HIV prevention intervention implementation.

The "Have You Heard?" intervention, which utilizes HEALER and DOSIM, is designed to be delivered at homeless youth drop-in centers. These are often daytime programs providing food, clothing, hygiene supplies, and access to social workers who work with homeless youth to try to help them achieve stable, successful, independent lives (e.g., employment services, health care referrals, housing assistance) (De Rosa et al., 1999; Shillington, Bousman, & Clapp, 2011; Slesnick, Dashora, Letcher, Erdem, & Serovich, 2009). Drop-in centers tend to have very few barriers to youth (e.g., not mandating sobriety, regardless of mental health status), and as such, they have been shown to be the more successful route for engaging homeless youth compared to shelter programs, which often have many more restrictions (Slesnick et al., 2016). Moreover, drop-in centers are available to youth experiencing a range of home-lessness situations (e.g., couch surfing, temporary living programs, shelters, street-based), thus creating greater reach.

A systematic study of homeless youth in Los Angeles found that 78% of sampled youth accessed drop-in centers (even higher among youth recruited on the streets: 86%) (De Rosa et al., 1999). Moreover, homeless youth rank drop-in centers as easily accessible and are very satisfied with drop-in center services (De Rosa et al., 1999). Because the "Have You Heard?" intervention has been designed to be delivered in the context of these drop-in centers, much of the research we draw on in this chapter comes from work conducted by our team and others who sampled youth from such drop-in centers. This is not to say that work done by other research teams in other contexts (e.g., in shelters, outside of Los Angeles, or even outside of the United States) is unimportant. We focus primarily on the research on homeless youth drawn from this specific context to provide the most relevant background, describing the intervention participants' peers' demographic characteristics, histories, and behaviors.

The Extent of Youth Homelessness

We, most other researches, and homeless service providers define homeless youth as persons between the ages of 13 and 24 who are living on the streets, in emergency shelters or transitional living programs, or "couch surfing" (i.e., staying with friends, family, or strangers on a temporary basis) without the accompaniment of their parents or guardians. There is not a complete census of the number of homeless youth in the United States, though it has been estimated previously that there are approximately 1.6 million youth (7% of the youth population) in the United States who experience at least one night of homelessness each year (Ringwalt, Greene, Robertson, & McPheeters, 1998). (Currently, researchers at Chapin Hall at the University of Chicago are working to update this number [voicesofyouthcount.org].) Los Angeles, the setting for our research, is arguably the nation's capital for homeless youth. The 2017 point-in-time census of homeless individuals in Los Angeles County found 3,233 unaccompanied youth between the age of 13 and 24 sleeping on the streets or living in emergency shelters on any given day (Los Angeles Homeless Services Authority, 2018).

Homeless youth experience a variety of living situations. Based on our prior work with youth who access drop-in centers, we found that 31% were sleeping on the streets, 17% were staying in an emergency shelter, 7% were staying in a motel, and 44% were couch surfing (Rice, 2010). While the point-in-time census shows an alarming number of youth on the streets each night, it is invariably an undercount. The point-in-time count numbers always miss the 7% in motels and the 44% who are couch surfing, not to mention that the point-in-time count is a three-day snapshot of visibly homeless youth, which is not representative of the transience of youth who cycle in and out of homelessness. Moreover, couch surfing is the preferred strategy for coping with homelessness among this population, but it is not a stable form of housing and typically lasts anywhere from a few days to a few months, but is never a permanent housing solution.

It is important to understand that homelessness for youth is very cyclical. Following their first homeless experiences, 73% of youth exited homelessness within two years, but 49% cycled in and out of homelessness for those two years (Milburn et al., 2009). On average, homeless youth we surveyed in drop-in centers were 16.7 years old when they first experienced homelessness, but there was much variation in this number (standard deviation was 3.9 years) (Winetrobe, Rhoades, Rice, Milburn, & Petering, 2017). For most of these youth, homelessness dominated their lives. When asked to sum up their total time spent homeless, 66% of these youth reported more than two years of their lives, and only 13% reported less than six months (Winetrobe et al., 2017). While many youth at any point in time are couch surfing, 68% of youth report having slept on the streets, park, beach, or some other outdoor environment in the past year (Rice, Winetrobe, & Rhoades, 2013).

Homeless youth, despite their enormous numbers, are largely invisible to the world around them. Most of these youth do everything in their power to blend in with the world at large. The stereotype of homeless individuals pushing shopping carts or sleeping in "nests" of personal belongings does not apply to these youth. In our experience with homeless youth over the past 15 years, we would not recognize the vast majority as being homeless if we were to walk by them on the street. Frankly, if we did not know them personally from the drop-in centers where we conducted our research, they would be hidden from us, too. Yes, some homeless youth are identifiable, sitting on a corner with a cardboard sign, begging for spare change. However, in our experience, the vast majority of homeless youth we have known and worked with looked like any other teen or young adult walking down the street, albeit their shoes might have been a little more worn and their backpacks perhaps a little overstuffed. This invisibility is by design. A recent study of ours found that only 52% of the youth we surveyed answered "yes" to the question, "Do you consider yourself homeless?" (Winetrobe et al., 2017). These are teenagers and young adults who think of themselves first as teenagers and young adults, not homeless youth. They want to blend in; they do not want to be targeted because they are homeless. "Homeless" to them looks more like the older homeless adults who are entrenched in street life.

Causes of Youth Homelessness

Reasons for homelessness are often multidimensional. When we asked home-less youth at drop-in centers to check all of the reasons they felt were why they became homeless, they cited: being kicked/thrown out of home (42%), leaving home (33%), conflict with parents (26%), being evicted (16%), escaping abuse (physical: 10%, sexual: 6%) or violence at home (8%), financial problems (11%), released from jail (11%), their mental health (9%), their substance use (12%), aged out of foster care (7%), and sexual identity (4%) (Winetrobe et al., 2017). It is important to remember that one reason could be the direct/indirect consequence of another reason(s).

Thrown Out of Home/Run Away from Home

Research on homeless youth thoroughly documented the fact that most youth come from dysfunctional family backgrounds where households are consumed by parental substance abuse, neglect, and violence (e.g., Whitbeck & Hoyt, 1999). Our recent work documented that 44% of youth reported being physically abused as children, and 39% witnessed family violence in their homes (Petering, Rice, Rhoades, & Winetrobe, 2014). One multi-city study found that the majority (80%) of homeless youth were victims of physical abuse as children (Bender, Brown, Thompson, Ferguson, & Langenderfer, 2015). Sexual violence is an all too common experience in the lives of youth who become homeless. Our recent work has shown that 34% of female youth and 16% of male youth experienced sexual violence prior to becoming homeless (Harris, Rice, Rhoades, Winetrobe, & Wenzel, 2017). Many homeless youth are either thrown out of their home or they run away, making the difficult decision that life on the streets may be safer than life at home. Indeed, our recent work found that 42% of homeless youth reported being thrown out or kicked out of home, and 33% reported running away from home (Winetrobe et al., 2017).

Aging Out of Foster Care

Many youth who experienced violent or neglectful family situations were at some point removed from those homes by the child welfare system. Our drop-in center–based samples show that approximately 35% of the youth we encountered had a history of foster care system involvement (Yoshioka-Maxwell & Rice, 2017). These youth all experienced being removed from their family homes by the state because of reports of abuse or neglect perpetrated against them. When children are removed from their families by the child welfare system, they are placed with relatives, non-kin who may or may not adopt the child, or into group homes. These children are the responsibility of the state until they reach adulthood, which is typically defined as age 18, but has been recently extended to age 21 in some local jurisdictions, and can vary state to state. Unfortunately, for many children, these removals from home do not always lead to stable lives, as research has shown that between 11% and 36% of these children will experience homelessness, as youth who age out of foster care may not have a stable place to live following their last placement (Dworsky, Dillman, Dion, Coffee-Borden, & Rosenau, 2012).

Sexual- and Gender-Minority Youth

Forty-three percent of homeless youth accessing drop-in centers identify as lesbian, gay, bisexual, or transgender (LGBT) (Durso & Gates, 2012). LGBT youth face the usual turmoil of adolescence with the added burdens of social stigma and discrimination because of their sexual and/or gender identity, often without the support of peers, family, school, or social services (D'Augelli, Hershberger, & Pilkington, 1998; Savin-Williams, 1994). The consequences of this stigma, rejection, and isolation are many, including increased risk of substance use, depression, suicide, sexual risk taking, and homelessness (Savin-Williams, 1994). Recent data collected by our team (2012) in conjunction with the CDC's Youth Risk Behavior Survey, indicated that 37% of LGBT-identifying youth experienced at least one night of homelessness each year. Because of their sexual or gender identity, youth are thrown/kicked out of their home, or run away because of their family's rejection and/or abuse (Durso & Gates, 2012). Many LGBT youth run away from home because they perceive their community and/or family to be rejecting of their sense of self and/or to escape abuse. They desire to be accepted and safe in a community, thereby risking their life on the streets.

Travelers

A subpopulation of homeless youth known as travelers are an important part of a homeless youth social network. Travelers are youth who migrate from city to city by themselves or with friends after a short period of time (Um, Rice, Rhoades, Winetrobe, & Bracken, 2016; Winetrobe et al., 2017). One-third of homeless youth at Los Angeles drop-in centers identified as travelers and were less likely to consider themselves to be homeless (Winetrobe et al., 2017).

Moreover, travelers were more likely to binge drink, use marijuana, and inject illicit drugs (Martino et al., 2011; Um et al., 2016).

Typically, travelers stick together and are likely to be socially connected to one another. However, travelers will often learn about a particular city's resources and services by meeting "local" homeless youth. We found among Los Angeles area–drop-in center youth, that those who were connected to a traveling youth were more likely to use substances (Um et al., 2016). Because of their short residencies in a given city or at a particular drop-in center, it becomes more difficult to strategize appropriate social network–based interventions. Travelers contribute to the overall fluidity and evolution of homeless youth social networks, and are a prominent segment of the population to tap into for intervention delivery.

Consequences of Youth Homelessness

Experiences of Violence

Violence is a major consequence of life on the streets. In our recent work, more than half of the homeless youth had been in at least one fight during the previous year, and one-fifth sustained an injury during a fight that necessitated medical attention (Petering, Rice, & Rhoades, 2016). Violence in the context of romantic relationships is also prevalent. Approximately 38% of homeless youth in romantic relationships experienced some form of intimate partner violence in the previous year, the majority of which was bidirectional (26%); 7% reported being solely a perpetrator, and 5% reported being solely a victim (Petering, Rhoades, Rice, & Yoshioka-Maxwell, 2017). Sexual violence is also a major threat; 33% of girls and 26% of boys reported sexual assault victimization while homeless (Harris et al., 2017).

Mental Health

It should not come as a surprise that exposure to this much violence both before and after becoming homeless can take a toll on the mental health of homeless youth. Our recent work shows about 41% of homeless youth were likely suffering from posttraumatic stress disorder (PTSD). Reflecting the higher rates of sexual assault, more girls than boys reported symptoms of PTSD (Harris et al., 2017). Depression for homeless youth is often a consequence of being a victim of assault (Lim, Rice, & Rhoades, 2016). Moreover, homeless youth with histories of childhood abuse and assault while homeless were more likely to experience PTSD and depressive symptoms (Bender et al., 2015). In a cross-sectional, multicity study of homeless youth in the United States, Bender et al. (2015) found that 23% of the homeless youth they surveyed met diagnostic criteria for PTSD, and 31% for major depression. These are akin to rates found in a multisite, diagnostic study of homeless and runaway adolescents (Whitbeck, Johnson, Hoyt, & Cauce, 2004), which compared depression and PTSD prevalence rates among homeless youth to housed peers. Whitbeck et al. (2004) reported a lifetime prevalence of depression among homeless youth that was twice the rate in the same-age general population; PTSD prevalence among homeless youth was seven times the rate of their housed peers. Perhaps even more disturbing are the high rates of suicidal thinking and suicide attempts. Our most recent work found homeless youth's suicidal ideation and suicide attempts during the past year were 17% and 7%, respectively (Barr, Fulginiti, Rhoades, & Rice, 2017).

Substance Use/Abuse

Substance use is quite prevalent among homeless youth. Past-month substance use among homeless youth was quite high; 50% of homeless youth at drop-in centers in Los Angeles reported binge drinking (i.e., five or more alcoholic drinks in a row), 77% reported using marijuana, 25% reported using methamphetamine, 18% cocaine, 10% crack cocaine, and 12% reported using heroin (Rhoades, Winetrobe, & Rice, 2014). Past research demonstrated that homeless youth use substances to help them stay awake to protect themselves and their property (Christiani, Hudson, Nyamathi, Mutere, & Sweat, 2008) and to cope with mental distress and suicidality (Christiani et al., 2008; Kidd & Carroll, 2007). Additionally, homeless youth with foster care experiences (Hudson & Nandy, 2012; Nyamathi, Hudson, Greengold, & Leake, 2012), who were victims of abuse (Tyler & Melander, 2010), who are travelers, who engaged in survival sex (Walls & Bell, 2011), and who started using substances at a young age (Salomonsen-Sautel et al., 2008) were all more likely to be using while homeless. And the longer they were homeless, the more likely they were to use (Thompson, Bender, Ferguson, & Kim, 2015). Only 12% of homeless youth cited their own substance use as a contributing factor to their homelessness (Winetrobe et al., 2017). Some homeless youth come from families where substance use and abuse is common (McMorris, Tyler, Whitbeck, & Hoyt, 2002; Robertson, Koegel, & Ferguson, 1989), and thus large numbers began using drugs and alcohol at relatively early ages (Robertson et al., 1989). Our recent work has shown that 37% reported using alcohol and 35% reported using marijuana before age 13 (Rhoades et al., 2014). Mirroring the recent national trends of prescription opioid drug abuse (Compton, Jones, & Baldwin, 2016), 22% reported prescription drug misuse in the prior month, with opioids being the most commonly misused prescription drug category (Rhoades et al., 2014).

Contraception and Pregnancy

Many homeless youth are also at higher risk of pregnancy than most youth their age, and pregnancy among homeless youth may exacerbate youths' homelessness duration (Haley, Roy, Leclerc, Boudreau, & Boivin, 2004; Thompson, Bender, Lewis, & Watkins, 2008). Sixty-two percent of homeless girls reported ever having been pregnant, and 44% of males reported having ever impregnated someone (Winetrobe et al., 2013). One-fifth of Los Angeles area homeless youth reported having had a child, while 7% of homeless youth reported having their child(ren) stay with them (Rice et al., 2013).

Access to condoms and other contraception at drop-in centers, shelters, and other service agencies may increase effective contraception use, though only 36% of homeless youth reported using a condom at last vaginal sex (Winetrobe et al., 2013). In our recent study, one-third of homeless youth at drop-in centers reported accessing condoms within the previous month, and female homeless youth who accessed condoms within the previous month were less likely to have unprotected sex (Barman-Adhikari, Hsu, Begun, Portillo, & Rice, 2017). Additionally, male and female homeless youth who thought their street-based peers were using condoms were less likely themselves to engage in condomless sex (Barman-Adhikari et al., 2017).

Pregnancy among homeless youth may be a result of (1) sexual assault, (2) engaging in survival sex (i.e., trading sex for food, money, a place to stay), (3) a desire to become pregnant, or (4) an unintentional pregnancy because of lack of contraceptive use altogether or use of ineffective methods (Winetrobe et al., 2013). Female homeless youth use condoms because they are available more often and they also protect against sexually transmitted infections (STIs) (Ensign, 2001). Lack of access to other contraceptive methods may cause homeless youth to rely on other, less effective forms of contraception (e.g., withdrawal, rhythm method), and thus increase their chances of pregnancy.

Perhaps the greatest threat to the sexual health of homeless youth, however, is not pregnancy, but rather the risk of HIV and other STIs. Rates of HIV have been documented to be as high as 11.5% among homeless youth (Pfeifer & Oliver, 1997). Homeless youth are at extremely high risk for contracting HIV because of their risk and survival behavior, including sharing needles in the context of injection drug use, sex without condoms, and sex without condoms in the context of survival sex. Based on the data we collected as part of our National Institute of Mental Health-funded R01 study (Rice R01 MH093336), from 1,046 homeless youth between 2011 and 2013 in the Los Angeles area, we calculated the proportion of homeless youth who fall into different HIV risk categories: 6% were transgender, 24% were young men who have sex with men (YMSM), 16% injected drugs, 5% were YMSM who inject drugs, 16% were engaged in sex work, 60% had incarceration experiences, 6% were female youth who had partners who were YMSM or injection drug users, and 3% were HIV-positive persons (who thereby are at increased risk for transmitting the virus).

There is a fundamental need to identify new cases of HIV among homeless youth and link them to HIV treatment, not only for their own health but to also limit the spread of HIV. It is encouraging that 85% of homeless youth in Los Angeles County reported testing for HIV ever in their lifetimes, and 47% had a HIV test in the past 3 months (Ober, Martino, Ewing, & Tucker, 2012). The rates of current HIV testing, however, reveal key gaps in testing and treatment, especially for racial/ethnic minority and sexual minority youth. From our data we found that 33% of African American youth and 36% of Latino youth had not been tested for HIV in the past six months. Among female youth, 28% of African American female homeless youth and 23% of homeless Latinas had not been tested in the past 6 months. In addition, 19% of African American YMSM and 27% of Latino YMSM had not tested in the past 6 months (Rice, 2013). The Centers for Disease Control and Prevention recommend at least annual testing for HIV, and more frequent (i.e., every 3-6 months) among higher-risk groups, such as YMSM (Centers for Disease Control and Prevention, 2017).

Homeless youth are not engaged in regular testing, in part because they are not well engaged in health care service utilization of any kind (Winetrobe, Rice, Rhoades, & Milburn, 2016). This arises due to feeling discriminated against, disrespected, and stigmatized because of their homeless state (Christiani et al., 2008; Hudson et al., 2010; Martins, 2008; Wen, Hudak, & Hwang, 2007), and distrust with health care and other social service providers (Klein et al., 2000; Kurtz, Lindsey, Jarvis, & Nackerud, 2000). Moreover, homeless youth often lack adequate health insurance, transportation, and knowledge of how to navigate complicated health systems in order to receive care (Hudson et al., 2010). Homeless youth are less likely than other youth to seek help from traditional health care providers, choosing instead to rely on informal sources such as friends or relatives (Ensign & Gittelsohn, 1998) and the internet (Barman-Adhikari & Rice, 2011). In fact, we found that 61% of homeless youth reported ever looking for general health information online, and 23% searched specifically online for where to get an HIV test (Barman-Adhikari & Rice, 2011). It goes without saying that there is no guarantee that the health information found online is accurate; it requires specific assessment of the source.

The Importance of Social Networks

In Western developed nations, the normal developmental trajectory for adolescents has been well documented; from early to emerging adulthood, young people increasingly move toward independence and autonomy with the support and the relative influence of families, friends, and social institutions as socializing agents shifting over time (Arnett, 2000, 2001). By early adolescence, the role of family changes as the importance of peers and friends, as well as that of teachers and others in institutional settings, increases (Bauman, Carver, & Gleiter, 2001; Berndt, 1979). For homeless youth, being thrown out of home or running away from home exaggerates the process of engagement with peers and disengagement with family and further disenfranchises youth from their connections to pro-social institutions, such as school. The best developmentally focused models of this process are the Risk Amplification Model (RAM) (Whitbeck, Hoyt, & Yoder, 1999) and its augmentation, the Risk Amplification and Abatement Model (RAAM) (Milburn et al., 2009).

RAM asserted that the peer networks of homeless youth on the streets are largely comprised of other homeless adolescents, many of whom come from problematic backgrounds and engage in risky and/or deviant behavior (Whitbeck et al., 1999). When social networks are comprised largely of other deviant youth, the risks associated with living on the streets are magnified for individuals operating within those networks (e.g., McMorris et al., 2002; Rice, Milburn, & Monro, 2011). Negative peer influences in the street-based networks of homeless youth can be seen cutting across a wide spectrum of risk-taking behaviors, including violence (Petering et al., 2016), mental health (Fulginiti, Rice, Hsu, Rhoades, & Winetrobe, 2016), substance use (Barman-Adhikari, Rice, Winetrobe, & Petering, 2015; Yoshioka-Maxwell & Rice, 2017), and sexual risk-taking (Barman-Adhikari et al., 2017).

RAAM extended this thinking by recognizing that homeless youth networks are also a major source of resilience (Milburn et al., 2009; Rice, Milburn, & Rotheram-Borus, 2007). Research showed that the social networks of homeless youth were more heterogeneous (Johnson, Whitbeck, & Hoyt, 2005) than previously thought (Ennett, Bailey, & Federman, 1999; Whitbeck & Hoyt, 1999). Networks are not just limited to homeless peers, but also include relationships from youths' home communities, including relatives (Johnson et al., 2005; Rice et al., 2011), friends (Rice, 2010; Rice, Kurzban, & Ray, 2012), and non-familial adults (Rice et al., 2007; Rice et al., 2011). Furthermore, various dimensions and characteristics of heterogeneous social networks have differential effects on homeless youth. Homeless youths' social networks can and do include pro-social relationships that contribute to positive outcomes for the individual.

These pro-social relationships reduce homeless youths' risk behaviors and antisocial behaviors (Rice, 2010; Rice et al., 2007; Rice et al., 2011). This potential for positive influence can be seen across a wide spectrum of issues including improved mental health (Rice, Kurzban, et al., 2012), reduced substance use (Rice et al., 2011), and reduced sexual risk-taking (Rice, 2010; Rice, Monro, Barman-Adhikari, & Young, 2010). Most of these studies, however, point to peers from home and family as the major source of this pro-social influence. Fortunately for our interests in peer-led prevention interventions, this work also uncovered subtle, previously ignored positive impacts of homeless peers, particularly with respect to sexual health. While youth who were more deeply embedded in social networks of other street youth were less likely to be using condoms (Rice, Barman-Adhikari, Milburn, & Monro, 2012), being connected to condom-using peers who were also homeless was found to be associated with increased condom use (Rice, 2010).

HIV Prevention for Homeless Youth

At present, there is a dearth in peer-led interventions to improve health behaviors among homeless youth. A few limited interventions and evaluations that have been conducted produced mixed results. One study found that peer-based models were effective in increasing homeless youths' substance use knowledge and preventive behaviors (Fors & Jarvis, 1995), while another study found that although a peer-led intervention was effective in increasing HIV-related knowledge, it was ineffective in reducing sex risk and substance use behaviors among homeless youth (Booth, Zhang, & Kwiatkowski, 1999). Another program, YouthCare, included homeless youth staff in their outreach and HIV prevention education efforts; the result was an increase in HIV testing among homeless youth (Tenner, Trevithick, Wagner, & Burch, 1998). In addition to producing inconclusive results, these interventions are quite old.

Our recent research investigating homeless youths' social networks has shown that peers do play an important role in the HIV risk-taking and protective behaviors of homeless youth (Rice, 2010; Rice, Tulbert, Cederbaum, Barman Adhikari, & Milburn, 2012), and it has been suggested that a peer-based model for HIV prevention be developed for homeless youth (Rice, Tulbert, et al., 2012; Tenner et al., 1998). Peer-based models, such as Kelly's (1997) popular opinion leader model and Latkin et al.'s (2003) Self-Help in Eliminating Life-Threatening Diseases (SHIELD), may be particularly impact-ful strategies for homeless youth, due to the importance of social network engagement both to HIV risk-taking and protective behaviors. Creating an HIV prevention program that engages homeless youth peers as leaders has been shown to be acceptable (Rice, Tulbert, et al., 2012), but no work has demonstrated its feasibility to date.

There are many challenges associated with creating such intervention programs. Indeed, while peer-based models have been found to be effective in behavior change for the prevention of HIV in many contexts (Medley, Kennedy, O'Reilly, & Sweat, 2009), there have been some notable failures (Booth et al., 1999; The NIMH Collaborative HIV/STD Prevention Trial Group, 2010). Peer-based models are complex, involving not only careful, cul-turally tailored, norm-changing messaging but also the effective engagement of a diverse set of network contexts.

Identifying the right peer leaders is equally important to the intervention curriculum/program in order for the impact of a peer-based intervention to be successful. One method for choosing the right peer leaders is to select those who are in structurally advantageous positions in a social network (Schneider, Zhou, & Laumann, 2015; Valente & Pumpuang, 2007). Another method, as demonstrated in our prior work, is to select youth identified by agency staff and ethnographic methods who are pro-social in their behaviors to be peer leaders (Rice, Tulbert, et al., 2012). From a structural perspective, however, selecting peer leaders based on individual pro-social behaviors is an arbitrary selection process, and such an approach may result in selecting a set of peer leaders who are not well connected to the rest of the population (Schneider et al., 2015; Yadav et al., 2015).

Peer-led models for HIV prevention have rarely taken advantage of social network analytic methods to augment the implementation of these programs, despite the fact that networks are a crucial component of the Diffusion of Innovations Theory (Rogers, 1995) on which these interventions were built (e.g., Kelly et al., 1997; Latkin et al., 2003). As Schneider and colleagues (2015) suggested, perhaps one reason for the unsuccessful implementation of peer-based models is that the right persons were not engaged as the peer leaders. Some researchers suggest that those with high degree centrality (i.e., persons with the highest number of connections) or high betweenness (i.e., persons who bridge the most other pairs of actors in a network) could be viable solutions (Schneider et al., 2015; Valente & Pumpuang, 2007).

Why We Need Artificial Intelligence

We need artificial intelligence (AI) for two reasons. First, the static network solutions proposed by others (Schneider et al., 2015; Valente & Pumpuang, 2007) have limitations, especially among transient and frequently changing social networks, that dynamic selection algorithms can overcome. Algorithms that attempt to maximize overall potential influence are theoretically more likely to influence more people than static solutions that focus on particular structural characteristics of people in a network (see the simulation results in the chapters that follow). This becomes increasingly important as the size and complexity of the social networks increase. In the case of the homeless youth networks we worked with previously, we were often attempting to impact networks that had 150 to 300 youth at a particular time, who had several hundred connections among themselves (Barman-Adhikari, Begun, Rice, Yoshioka-Maxwell, & Perez-Portillo, 2016; Um, Rice, Rhoades, Winetrobe, & Bracken, 2016; Yoshioka-Maxwell & Rice, 2017).

Second, homeless youth networks are not only complex, but the instability of homeless youth social ties necessitates that we consider the uncertainty present in these networks. In our prior work, we attempted to interview the entire population of youth who accessed services over a one-month period at each of our two partner drop-in centers: My Friend's Place in Hollywood, CA and Safe Place for Youth in Venice, CA. We repeated these population, panel surveys every 6 months for 18 months. We found in Hollywood that, on average, 43% of the population remained stable over a six-month period of time (44% were included in panel 2 who were seen in panel 1, 42% who were included in panel 3 were seen in panel 2), and in Venice Beach, only 16% of the population remained stable over six months (18% stability to panel 2, 14% stability to panel 3) (Rice, 2013).

Homeless youth social networks are continually changing. New youth are constantly running away from home or being thrown out of their home and entering into street life. Youth are also exiting street life, finding either positive outcomes such as stable housing or negative outcomes such as becoming incarcerated. Some youth move to another neighborhood or city, and thus exit the local social network. Additionally, a subpopulation of travelers may integrate into a social network of homeless youth for a short period of time before moving on to another city. Such circumstances, along with changing relationships between homeless youth in networks, affect the fracture or formation of connections between homeless youth who stay in the network over time (Rice, 2013). To make matters even more complicated, the collection of network data from homeless youth in community settings always involves a certain amount of error (Petering et al., 2016; Rice et al., 2014; Yoshioka-Maxwell & Rice, 2017). Youth can forget whom they communicated with recently, and we as researchers can have difficulty identifying all the persons who youth may describe in their social networks. (See Brewer, 2000, for a review of these methodological issues.)

There are a large number of methods for collecting social network data. One of the most common field techniques is to utilize name generators: a question or a series of questions designed to elicit the naming of relevant social connections along some specified criterion (Campbell & Lee, 1991; Marsden, 2011). Typically, name generators are free-recall name solicitors. Respondents are given a prompt that defines some criterion, for instance, a category of persons such as "family," "friends," or types of social exchange relationships (e.g., "Who do you turn to for advice or support?"). Then respondents are asked to list as many people as they can. In some cases, an upper limit is given to the number of names that can be elicited. Most solutions to network recall begin with the understanding that a single-item free-recall name generator will be most subject to recall bias. Brewer and colleagues (Brewer et al., 2000; Brewer, Garrett, & Rinaldi, 2002) have extensively reviewed the topic and suggested and tested several viable solutions to the problem, including nonspecific prompting, reading back lists of names, semantic cues, multiple elicitation questions, and re-interviewing.

For our work, we chose to follow the solution of multiple elicitation questions. The following was read: "Think about the last month. Who have you interacted with? These can be people you interacted with in person, on the phone, or through the internet. These might be friends; family; people you hang out with/chill with/kick it with/ have conversations with; people you party with – use drugs or alcohol; boyfriend/girlfriend; people you are having sex with; baby mama/baby daddy; case worker; people from school; people from work; old friends from home; people you talk to (on the phone, by email); people from where you are staying (squatting with); people you see at this agency; other people you know from the street." Interviewers paused between each prompt to allow youth to nominate additional social connections before proceeding to the next prompt.

After youth finished nominating persons, attributes of each social connection were then collected, including first and last names, aliases, age, gender, race/ethnicity, visible tattoos, and whether the nominee was a client of the agency. In the paper-and-pencil version, attributes were entered into a spreadsheet on a laptop by the interviewer; in the iPad app version, responses were entered directly into the app by the interviewer.

A sociomatrix (or graph) was created linking participants in the sample. A directed tie from participant i to participant j was recorded if participant i nominated participant j in his or her personal network. Although directed network information was collected, the network information is intrinsically undirected (a person who interacts with another) and was treated in this fashion for the current analysis. The initial matrix creation depended on the information provided by each youth about their personal network members, and subsequent "matches" were made with other youth in the sample. Matches were based on name, alias, race/ethnicity, gender, approximate age, tattoos, and agency attendance. Two independent reviewers, who were part of the team collecting the field data, made match decisions for all alters who were between the ages of 13 and 39 years and not identified as agency staff.

A series of decision rules was derived from information that was available to make the match determination. Decisions were based on a series of algorithms that included (a) interviewer and recruiter field knowledge (through the compilation of field notes following each data collection period), (b) how well the ego knew the alter (i.e., relative, romantic partner, needle sharer, known for at least one year) and whether the alter was identified as a client, or (c) via an Access database and form that formulaically paired possible matches based on names, visible tattoos, and demographic characteristics. If two distinct youths were similar on all information, they were considered for the purposes of this research to be the same individuals. If two distinct youths matched on all information, presence of a third common tie in each personal network was used to assign the tie/edge. The independent reviewers' decisions were compared for agreement. Discrepant matches were discussed with the independent reviewers and a third reviewer who also served as an interviewer and recruiter during the data collection. Group consensus led to final match decisions.

It is not difficult to see that this protocol is not only extremely labor intensive but also subject to human error at several stages. Error is introduced by the memory and thus accurate collection of names and descriptors from youth (Brewer, 2000). Then, more error is introduced by the matching of youth to one another by research staff, particularly as not all identifying information collected from a given youth is sufficiently detailed or accurate in order to always disambiguate two different youths with similar names and appearances (e.g., two 20-year-old white youths named Cody who do not have distinctive visible tattoos). Our procedures involved multiple coders and interrater reliability checks, but we know this data is not a perfect representation of the social network of youth at a given time because of these unavoidable sources of error.

Thus, we need a peer selection procedure within large and complex networks of homeless youth (or other similarly composed networks), which can accurately account for the uncertainties we know to be present in this data. Enter AI.

References

Arnett, J. J. (2000). Emerging adulthood: A theory of development from the late teens through the twenties. *American Psychologist, 55*(5), 469

Arnett, J. J. (2001). Conceptions of the transition to adulthood: Perspectives from adolescence through midlife. *Journal of Adult Development, 8*(2), 133–143. doi:10.1023/a:1026450103225

Barman-Adhikari, A., Begun, S., Rice, E., Yoshioka-Maxwell, A., & Perez-Portillo, A. (2016). Sociometric network structure and its association with methamphetamine use norms among homeless youth. *Social Science Research, 58,* 292–308. doi:10.1016/j.ssresearch.2016.01.004

Barman-Adhikari, A., Hsu, H.-T., Begun, S., Portillo, A. P., & Rice, E. (2017). Condomless sex among homeless youth: The role of multidimensional social norms and gender. *AIDS and Behavior, 21*(3), 688–702. doi:10.1007/s10461-016-1624-2

Barman-Adhikari, A., & Rice, E. (2011). Sexual health information seeking online among runaway and homeless youth. *Journal of the Society for Social Work and Research, 2*(2), 89–103. doi:10.5243/jsswr.2011.5

Barman-Adhikari, A., Rice, E., Winetrobe, H., & Petering, R. (2015). Social network correlates of methamphetamine, heroin, and cocaine use in a sociometric network of homeless youth. *Journal of the Society for Social Work and Research, 6*(3), 433–457. doi:10.1086/682709

Barr, N., Fulginiti, A., Rhoades, H., & Rice, E. (2017). Can better emotion regulation protect against suicidality in traumatized homeless youth? *Archives of Suicide Research, 21*(3), 490–501. doi:10.1080/13811118.2016.1224989

Bauman, K. E., Carver, K., & Gleiter, K. (2001). Trends in parent and friend influence during adolescence: The case of adolescent cigarette smoking. *Addictive Behaviors, 26*(3), 349–361. doi:10.1016/S0306-4603(00)00110-6

Bender, K., Brown, S. M., Thompson, S. J., Ferguson, K. M., & Langenderfer, L. (2015). Multiple victimizations before and after leaving home associated with PTSD, depression, and substance use disorder among homeless youth. *Child Maltreatment, 20*(2), 115–124. doi:10.1177/1077559514562859

Berndt, T. J. (1979). Developmental changes in conformity to peers and parents. *Developmental Psychology, 15*(6), 608

Booth, R. E., Zhang, Y., & Kwiatkowski, C. F. (1999). The challenge of changing drug and sex risk behaviors of runaway and homeless adolescents. *Child Abuse & Neglect, 23*(12), 1295–1306. doi:10.1016/S0145-2134(99)00090-3

Brewer, D. D. (2000). Forgetting in the recall-based elicitation of personal and social networks. *Social Networks, 22*(1), 29–43. doi:10.1016/S0378-8733(99)00017-9

Brewer, D. D., Garrett, S. B., & Rinaldi, G. (2002). Free-listed items are effective cues for eliciting additional items in semantic domains. *Applied Cognitive Psychology, 16*(3), 343–358. doi:10.1002/acp.797

Campbell, K. E., & Lee, B. A. (1991). Name generators in surveys of personal networks. *Social Networks, 13*(3), 203–221. doi:10.1016/0378-8733(91)90006-F

Centers for Disease Control and Prevention. (2017, May 18). HIV testing. Retrieved from www.cdc.gov/hiv/testing/index.html

Christiani, A., Hudson, A. L., Nyamathi, A., Mutere, M., & Sweat, J. (2008). Attitudes of homeless and drug-using youth regarding barriers and facilitators in delivery of quality and culturally sensitive health care. *Journal of Child and Adolescent Psychiatric Nursing, 21*(3), 154–163. doi:10.1111/j.1744-6171.2008.00139.x

Compton, W. M., Jones, C. M., & Baldwin, G. T. (2016). Relationship between nonmedical prescription-opioid use and heroin use. *New England Journal of Medicine, 374*(2), 154–163. doi:10.1056/NEJMra1508490

D'Augelli, A. R., Hershberger, S. L., & Pilkington, N. W. (1998). Lesbian, gay, and bisexual youth and their families: Disclosure of sexual orientation and its consequences. *American Journal of Orthopsychiatry, 68*(3), 361

De Rosa, C. J., Montgomery, S. B., Kipke, M. D., Iverson, E., Ma, J. L., & Unger, J. B. (1999). Service utilization among homeless and runaway youth in Los Angeles, California: Rates and reasons. *Journal of Adolescent Health, 24*(3), 190–200. doi:10.1016/S1054-139X(99)00040-3

Durso, L. E., & Gates, G. J. (2012). *Serving our youth: Findings from a national survey of service providers working with lesbian, gay, bisexual, and transgender youth who are homeless or at risk of becoming homeless.* Retrieved from: http://williamsinstitute.law.ucla.edu/wp-content/uploads/Durso-Gates-LGBT-Homeless-Youth-Survey-July-2012.pdf

Dworsky, A., Dillman, K.-N., Dion, R. M., Coffee-Borden, B., & Rosenau, M. (2012). Housing for youth aging out of foster care: A review of the literature and program typology. Available at: https://papers.ssrn.com/sol3/papers.cfm?abstract_id=2112278

Ennett, S. T., Bailey, S. L., & Federman, E. B. (1999). Social network characteristics associated with risky behaviors among runaway and homeless youth. *Journal of Health and Social Behavior, 40*(1), 63–78. doi:10.2307/2676379

Ensign, J. (2001). Reproductive health of homeless adolescent women in Seattle, Washington, USA. *Women & Health, 31*(2–3), 133–151. doi:10.1300/J013v31n02_07

Ensign, J., & Gittelsohn, J. (1998). Health and access to care: Perspectives of homeless youth in Baltimore City, U.S.A. *Social Science & Medicine, 47*(12), 2087–2099. doi:10.1016/S0277-9536(98)00273-1

Fors, S. W., & Jarvis, S. (1995). Evaluation of a peer-led drug abuse risk reduction project for runaway/homeless youths. *Journal of Drug Education, 25*(4), 321–333. doi:10.2190/TU92-LX8W-G7FD-9LEM

Fulginiti, A., Rice, E., Hsu, H.-T., Rhoades, H., & Winetrobe, H. (2016). Risky integration. *Crisis: The Journal of Crisis Intervention and Suicide Prevention, 37*(3), 184–193. doi:10.1027/0227-5910/a000374

Haley, N., Roy, E., Leclerc, P., Boudreau, J. F., & Boivin, J. F. (2004). Characteristics of adolescent street youth with a history of pregnancy. *Journal of Pediatric and Adolescent Gynecology, 17*(5), 313–320. doi:10.1016/j.jpag.2004.06.006

Harris, T., Rice, E., Rhoades, H., Winetrobe, H., & Wenzel, S. (2017). Gender differences in the path from sexual victimization to HIV risk behavior among homeless youth. *Journal of Child Sexual Abuse, 26*(3), 334–351. doi:10.1080/10538712.2017.1287146

Hudson, A., & Nandy, K. (2012). Comparisons of substance abuse, high-risk sexual behavior and depressive symptoms among homeless youth with and without a history of foster care placement. *Contemporary Nurse, 42*(2), 178–186. doi:10.5172/conu.2012.42.2.178

Hudson, A., Nyamathi, A., Greengold, B., Slagle, A., Koniak-Griffin, D., Khalilifard, F., & Getzoff, D. (2010). Health-seeking challenges among homeless youth. *Nursing Research, 59*(3), 212

Johnson, K. D., Whitbeck, L. B., & Hoyt, D. R. (2005). Predictors of social network composition among homeless and runaway adolescents. *Journal of Adolescence, 28*(2), 231–248. doi:10.1016/j.adolescence.2005.02.005

Kelly, J. A., Murphy, D. A., Sikkema, K. J., McAuliffe, T. L., Roffman, R. A., Solomon, L. J., ... Kalichman, S. C. (1997). Randomised, controlled, community-level HIV-prevention intervention for sexual-risk behaviour among homosexual men in US cities. *The Lancet, 350*(9090), 1500–1505. doi:10.1016/S0140-6736(97)07439-4

Kidd, S. A., & Carroll, M. R. (2007). Coping and suicidality among homeless youth. *Journal of Adolescence, 30*(2), 283–296. doi:10.1016/j.adolescence.2006.03.002

Klein, J. D., Woods, A. H., Wilson, K. M., Prospero, M., Greene, J., & Ringwalt, C. (2000). Homeless and runaway youths' access to health care. *Journal of Adolescent Health, 27*(5), 331–339. doi:10.1016/S1054-139X(00)00146-4

Kurtz, P. D., Lindsey, E. W., Jarvis, S., & Nackerud, L. (2000). How runaway and homeless youth navigate troubled waters: The role of formal and informal helpers. *Child and Adolescent Social Work Journal, 17*(5), 381–402. doi:10.1023/a:1007507131236

Latkin, C. A., Sherman, S., & Knowlton, A. (2003). HIV prevention among drug users: Outcome of a network-oriented peer outreach intervention. *Health Psychology, 22*(4), 332

Lim, C., Rice, E., & Rhoades, H. (2016). Depressive symptoms and their association with adverse environmental factors and substance use in runaway and homeless youths. *Journal of Research on Adolescence, 26*(3), 403–417. doi:10.1111/jora.12200

Los Angeles Homeless Services Authority. (2018). *2017 Greater Los Angeles Homeless Count Results: Los Angeles County and Continuum of Care.* Retrieved from www.lahsa.org/documents?id=1873-2017-greater-los-angeles-homeless-count-presentation-los-angeles-county-and-continuum-of-care.pdf

Marsden, P. V. (2011). Survey methods for network data. *The SAGE Handbook of Social Network Analysis, 25*, 370–388

Martino, S. C., Tucker, J. S., Ryan, G., Wenzel, S. L., Golinelli, D., & Munjas, B. (2011). Increased substance use and risky sexual behavior among migratory homeless youth: Exploring the role of social network composition. *Journal of Youth and Adolescence, 40*(12), 1634–1648. doi:10.1007/s10964-011-9646-6

Martins, D. C. (2008). Experiences of homeless people in the health care delivery system: A descriptive phenomenological study. *Public Health Nursing, 25*(5), 420–430. doi:10.1111/j.1525-1446.2008.00726.x

McMorris, B. J., Tyler, K. A., Whitbeck, L. B., & Hoyt, D. R. (2002). Familial and "on-the-street" risk factors associated with alcohol use among homeless and runaway adolescents. *Journal of Studies on Alcohol, 63*(1), 34–43. doi:10.15288/jsa.2002.63.34

Medley, A., Kennedy, C., O'Reilly, K., & Sweat, M. (2009). Effectiveness of peer education interventions for HIV prevention in developing countries: A systematic review and meta-analysis. *AIDS Education and Prevention, 21*(3), 181–206. doi:10.1521/aeap.2009.21.3.181

Milburn, N. G., Rice, E., Rotheram-Borus, M. J., Mallett, S., Rosenthal, D., Batterham, P., ... Duan, N. (2009). Adolescents exiting homelessness over two years: The risk amplification and abatement model. *Journal of Research on Adolescence, 19*(4), 762–785. doi:10.1111/j.1532-7795.2009.00610.x

Nyamathi, A., Hudson, A., Greengold, B., & Leake, B. (2012). Characteristics of homeless youth who use cocaine and methamphetamine. *The American Journal on Addictions, 21*(3), 243–249. doi:10.1111/j.1521-0391.2012.00233.x

Ober, A. J., Martino, S. C., Ewing, B., & Tucker, J. S. (2012). If you provide the test, they will take it: Factors associated with HIV/STI testing in a representative sample of homeless youth in Los Angeles. *AIDS Education and Prevention, 24*(4), 350–362. doi:10.1521/aeap.2012.24.4.350

Petering, R., Rhoades, H., Rice, E., & Yoshioka-Maxwell, A. (2017). Bidirectional intimate partner violence and drug use among homeless youth. *Journal of Interpersonal Violence, 32*(14), 2209–2217. doi:10.1177/0886260515593298

Petering, R., Rice, E., & Rhoades, H. (2016). Violence in the social networks of homeless youths. *Journal of Adolescent Research, 31*(5), 582–605. doi:10.1177/0743558415600073

Petering, R., Rice, E., Rhoades, H., & Winetrobe, H. (2014). The social networks of homeless youth experiencing intimate partner violence. *Journal of Interpersonal Violence, 29*(12), 2172–2191. doi:10.1177/0886260513516864

Pfeifer, R. W., & Oliver, J. (1997). A study of HIV seroprevalence in a group of homeless youth in Hollywood, California. *Journal of Adolescent Health, 20*(5), 339–342. doi:10.1016/S1054-139X(97)00038-4

Rhoades, H., Winetrobe, H., & Rice, E. (2014). Prescription drug misuse among homeless youth. *Drug and Alcohol Dependence, 138*, 229–233. doi:10.1016/j.drugalcdep.2014.02.011

Rice, E. (2010). The positive role of social networks and social networking technology in the condom-using behaviors of homeless young people. *Public Health Reports, 125*(4), 588–595. doi:10.1177/003335491012500414

Rice, E. (2013). Substantial differences in risk behaviors of homeless youth in two large networks of homeless youth in Los Angeles. Paper presented at the American Public Health Association Annual Meeting, Boston

Rice, E., Barman-Adhikari, A., Milburn, N. G., & Monro, W. (2012). Position-specific HIV risk in a large network of homeless youths. *American Journal of Public Health, 102*(1), 141–147. doi:10.2105/ajph.2011.300295

Rice, E., Fulginiti, A., Winetrobe, H., Montoya, J., Plant, A., & Kordic, T. (2012). Sexuality and homelessness in Los Angeles public schools. *American Journal of Public Health, 102*(2), 200–201. doi:10.2105/ajph.2011.300411

Rice, E., Holloway, I. W., Barman-Adhikari, A., Fuentes, D., Brown, C. H., & Palinkas, L. A. (2014). A mixed methods approach to network data collection. *Field Methods, 26*(3), 252–268. doi:10.1177/1525822X13518168

Rice, E., Kurzban, S., & Ray, D. (2012). Homeless but connected: The role of heterogeneous social network ties and social networking technology in the mental health outcomes of street-living adolescents. *Community Mental Health Journal, 48*(6), 692–698. doi:10.1007/s10597-011-9462-1

Rice, E., Milburn, N. G., & Monro, W. (2011). Social networking technology, social network composition, and reductions in substance use among homeless adolescents. *Prevention Science, 12*(1), 80–88. doi:10.1007/s11121-010-0191-4

Rice, E., Milburn, N. G., & Rotheram-Borus, M. J. (2007). Pro-social and problematic social network influences on HIV/AIDS risk behaviours among newly homeless youth in Los Angeles. *AIDS Care, 19*(5), 697–704. doi:10.1080/09540120601087038

Rice, E., Monro, W., Barman-Adhikari, A., & Young, S. D. (2010). Internet use, social networking, and HIV/AIDS risk for homeless adolescents. *Journal of Adolescent Health, 47*(6), 610–613. doi:10.1016/j.jadohealth.2010.04.016

Rice, E., Tulbert, E., Cederbaum, J., Barman Adhikari, A., & Milburn, N. G. (2012). Mobilizing homeless youth for HIV prevention: A social network analysis of the acceptability of a face-to-face and online social networking intervention. *Health Education Research, 27*(2), 226–236. doi:10.1093/her/cyr113

Rice, E., Winetrobe, H., & Rhoades, H. (2013). *Hollywood homeless youth point-in-time estimate project: An innovative method for enumerating unaccompanied homeless youth.* Retrieved from http://hhyp.org/wp-content/uploads/2013/02/HHYP_Point-in-Time_Brief_5.pdf

Ringwalt, C. L., Greene, J. M., Robertson, M., & McPheeters, M. (1998). The prevalence of homelessness among adolescents in the United States. *American Journal of Public Health, 88*(9), 1325–1329. doi:10.2105/ajph.88.9.1325

Robertson, M. J., Koegel, P., & Ferguson, L. (1989). Alcohol use and abuse among homeless adolescents in Hollywood. *Contemporary Drug Problems, 16,* 415

Rogers, E. M. (1995). *Diffusion of Innovations* (4th ed.). New York: Free Press

Salomonsen-Sautel, S., Van Leeuwen, J. M., Gilroy, C., Boyle, S., Malberg, D., & Hopfer, C. (2008). Correlates of substance use among homeless youths in eight cities. *The American Journal on Addictions, 17*(3), 224–234. doi:10.1080/10550490802019964

Savin-Williams, R. C. (1994). Verbal and physical abuse as stressors in the lives of lesbian, gay male, and bisexual youths: Associations with school problems, running away, substance abuse, prostitution, and suicide. *Journal of Consulting and Clinical Psychology, 62*(2), 261

Schneider, J. A., Zhou, A. N., & Laumann, E. O. (2015). A new HIV prevention network approach: Sociometric peer change agent selection. *Social Science & Medicine, 125,* 192–202. doi:10.1016/j.socscimed.2013.12.034

Shillington, A. M., Bousman, C. A., & Clapp, J. D. (2011). Characteristics of homeless youth attending two different youth drop-in centers. *Youth & Society, 43*(1), 28–43. doi:10.1177/0044118X09351277

Slesnick, N., Dashora, P., Letcher, A., Erdem, G., & Serovich, J. (2009). A review of services and interventions for runaway and homeless youth: Moving forward *Children and Youth Services Review, 31*(7), 732–742. doi:10.1016/j.childyouth.2009.01.006

Slesnick, N., Feng, X., Guo, X., Brakenhoff, B., Carmona, J., Murnan, A., . . . McRee, A.-L. (2016). A test of outreach and drop-in linkage versus shelter linkage for connecting homeless youth to services. *Prevention Science, 17*(4), 450–460. doi:10.1007/s11121-015-0630-3

Tenner, A. D., Trevithick, L. A., Wagner, V., & Burch, R. (1998). Seattle YouthCare's prevention, intervention, and education program. *Journal of Adolescent Health, 23*(2), 96–106. doi:10.1016/S1054-139X(98)00057-3

The NIMH Collaborative HIV/STD Prevention Trial Group. (2010). Results of the NIMH Collaborative HIV/STD Prevention Trial of a Community Popular Opinion Leader Intervention. *Journal of Acquired Immune Deficiency Syndromes (1999), 54*(2), 204–214. doi:10.1097/QAI.0b013e3181d61def

Thompson, S. J., Bender, K., Ferguson, K. M., & Kim, Y. (2015). Factors associated with substance use disorders among traumatized homeless youth. *Journal of Social Work Practice in the Addictions, 15*(1), 66–89. doi:10.1080/1533256X.2014.996229

Thompson, S. J., Bender, K. A., Lewis, C. M., & Watkins, R. (2008). Runaway and pregnant: risk factors associated with pregnancy in a national sample of runaway/homeless female adolescents. *Journal of Adolescent Health, 43*(2), 125–132. doi:10.1016/j.jadohealth.2007.12.015

Tyler, K. A., & Melander, L. A. (2010). Foster care placement, poor parenting, and negative outcomes among homeless young adults. *Journal of Child and Family Studies, 19*(6), 787–794. doi:10.1007/s10826-010-9370-y

Um, M.-Y., Rice, E., Rhoades, H., Winetrobe, H., & Bracken, N. (2016). Influence of "traveling" youth and substance use behaviors in the social networks of homeless youth. *Network Science, 4*(1), 28–47. doi:10.1017/nws.2015.32

Valente, T. W., & Pumpuang, P. (2007). Identifying opinion leaders to promote behavior change. *Health Education & Behavior, 34*(6), 881–896. doi:10.1177/1090198106297855

Walls, N. E., & Bell, S. (2011). Correlates of engaging in survival sex among homeless youth and young adults. *The Journal of Sex Research, 48*(5), 423–436. doi:10.1080/00224499.2010.501916

Wen, C. K., Hudak, P. L., & Hwang, S. W. (2007). Homeless people's perceptions of welcomeness and unwelcomeness in healthcare encounters. *Journal of General Internal Medicine, 22*(7), 1011–1017. doi:10.1007/s11606-007-0183-7

Whitbeck, L. B., & Hoyt, D. R. (1999). *Nowhere to grow: Homeless and runaway adolescents and their families.* New York: Aldine De Gruyter

Whitbeck, L. B., Hoyt, D. R., & Yoder, K. A. (1999). A risk-amplification model of victimization and depressive symptoms among runaway and homeless adolescents. *American Journal of Community Psychology, 27*(2), 273–296. doi:10.1023/A:1022891802943

Whitbeck, L. B., Johnson, K. D., Hoyt, D. R., & Cauce, A. M. (2004). Mental disorder and comorbidity among runaway and homeless adolescents. *Journal of Adolescent Health, 35*(2), 132–140. doi:10.1016/j.jadohealth.2003.08.011

Winetrobe, H., Rhoades, H., Barman-Adhikari, A., Cederbaum, J., Rice, E., & Milburn, N. (2013). Pregnancy attitudes, contraceptive service utilization, and other factors associated with Los Angeles Homeless Youths' use of effective contraception and withdrawal. *Journal of Pediatric and Adolescent Gynecology, 26*(6), 314–322. doi:10.1016/j.jpag.2013.06.007

Winetrobe, H., Rhoades, H., Rice, E., Milburn, N., & Petering, R. (2017). "I'm not homeless, I'm houseless": Identifying as homeless and associations with service utilization among Los Angeles homeless young people. *Journal of Social Distress and the Homeless, 26*(1), 16–24. doi:10.1080/10530789.2017.1280204

Winetrobe, H., Rice, E., Rhoades, H., & Milburn, N. (2016). Health insurance coverage and healthcare utilization among homeless young adults in Venice, CA. *Journal of Public Health, 38*(1), 147–155. doi:10.1093/pubmed/fdv001

Yadav, A., Marcolino, L. S., Rice, E., Petering, R., Winetrobe, H., Rhoades, H., … Carmichael, H. (2015). Preventing HIV Spread in Homeless Populations Using PSINET. Paper presented at the AAAI, Austin, Texas, January 25–30

Yoshioka-Maxwell, A., & Rice, E. (2017). Exploring the impact of network characteristics on substance use outcomes among homeless former foster youth. *International Journal of Public Health, 62*(3), 371–378. doi:10.1007/s00038-016-0845-5

3

Using Social Networks to Raise HIV Awareness among Homeless Youth

Amulya Yadav, Bryan Wilder, Hau Chan, Albert Jiang, Haifeng Xu, Eric Rice, and Milind Tambe

Introduction

Homelessness has reached a crisis level, with more than 565,000 homeless people in the United States on any given night. Homeless youth (i.e., people below the age of 25) account for almost 34% of the total homeless population [1]. These homeless youth face significant difficulties, having to struggle for basic amenities such as health care, nutritious food, and primary education.

HIV has an extremely high incidence among homeless youth, as they are more likely to engage in high HIV-risk behaviors (e.g., unprotected sexual activity, injection drug use) than other sub-populations. In fact, previous studies show that homeless youth face a 10-times greater risk of HIV infection than do stably housed populations [1].

To help prevent HIV infection among homeless youth, many homeless drop-in centers implement social network–based peer leader intervention programs, where a select number of youth, called peer leaders, are taught strategies for reducing risk of contracting HIV. These intervention programs consist of day-long educational sessions in which these peer leaders are provided with information about HIV prevention measures [2]. These leaders are then encouraged to share these messages with their peers in their social circles, in order to lead all their peers toward safer behaviors and practices.

These peer leader–based intervention programs are motivated by the drop-in centers' limited financial resources, which prevents them from directly assisting the entire homeless youth population. This leads to the question well known in the field of influence maximization, namely how to select "influential" nodes (i.e., homeless youth) to maximize the spread of awareness within a given social network. In the context of homeless drop-in centers, this problem is further complicated by two factors. First, the social network structure is imperfectly known, which makes identifying "influential" nodes challenging [3]. Although some connections (friendships) are known, other connections may be uncertain. This is because homeless youth are a hard-to-reach population, and their social networks are harder to characterize than are networks of stably housed youth [2]. Second, managing homeless youth (some of whom have emotional and behavioral problems) during an intervention, with the homeless drop-in center's limited personnel, is not easy. As a result, the drop-in center officials can only manage small groups composed of three or four youths at one time. Therefore, the drop-in center officials prefer a series of small-sized intervention camps organized sequentially (i.e., one after the other) to maximize the impact of their intervention [4]. In such camps, youth may reveal some additional information about the network, which can be used to inform future interventions.

The drop-in centers need a plan to choose the participants (i.e., peer leaders) of their sequentially organized interventions. This plan must address four key points: (1) it must efficiently deal with uncertainties in the network structure, i.e., uncertainty about existence or absence of some friendships in the network; (2) it needs to take into account new information uncovered during the interventions, which reduces the uncertainty in our understanding of the network; (3) the plan needs to be deviation tolerant, as sometimes homeless youth may choose not to be a peer leader, thereby forcing the drop-in center to modify its plan; (4) our approach should address the challenge of gathering information about social networks of homeless youth, which usually costs thousands of dollars and many months of time [4].

This chapter presents three key contributions in addressing the sequential planning needs of homeless drop-in centers. First, we model the drop-in centers' sequential planning needs by introducing the dynamic influence maximization under uncertainty (or DIME) problem. The sequential selection of intervention participants under network uncertainty in DIME sets it apart from any other previous work on influence maximization, which mostly focuses on single-shot decision problems (i.e., a set of nodes are selected just once, instead of selecting sets of nodes repeatedly) [5–8]. We analyze several novel theoretical aspects of the DIME problem, which illustrates its computational hardness.

Second, we propose a new software agent, HEALER (hierarchical ensembling based agent, which plans for effective reduction in HIV spread), to provide an end-to-end solution to the DIME problem. First, HEALER casts the DIME problem as a partially observable Markov decision process (POMDP) and solves it using HEAL (hierarchical ensembling algorithm for planning), a novel POMDP planner that quickly generates high-quality recommendations (of intervention participants) for homeless drop-in center officials. In this chapter, we discuss the design of HEALER and explain its method of gathering information about the homeless youth social network (at low cost) by interacting with youth via a network construction application. We also give a high-level overview of the HEAL algorithm and refer the reader to Yadav et al. [9] for a more complete understanding.

Third, we introduce the DOSIM algorithm, a novel algorithm for solving the DIME problem when the parameters of the problem are unknown. DOSIM solves a zero-sum game in which nature adversarially chooses the true parameters (e.g., the probability that influence will spread along a given edge).

Lastly, we present experimental simulation results on social networks gathered from homeless youth. We find that both HEALER and DOSIM substantially outperform the heuristic that is currently used in the field.

Related Work

There are three distinct areas of work related to the homeless drop-in center problem that we introduced in the previous section. The primary problem in computational influence maximization is to find optimal "seed sets" of nodes in social networks, which can maximize the spread of information or influence in the social network (according to some a priori known influence model). While there are many algorithms for finding such seed sets [5–8], most of these algorithms assume no uncertainty in the network structure and select a single seed set. In contrast, HEALER selects several seed sets sequentially in our work to select intervention participants for each successive training program, taking into account updates to the network structure revealed in past interventions. The DIME problem also incorporates uncertainty about the network structure and influence status of network nodes (i.e., whether a node is influenced or not). Finally, unlike [5–8], HEALER uses a different diffusion model as we explain later here. Golovin et al. [9] introduced adaptive submodularity and discussed adaptive sequential selection (similar to our problem), and they proved that a Greedy algorithm has a $(1\text{-}1/e)$ approximation guarantee. However, unlike the DIME problem, they assume no uncertainty in the network structure. We show that while the DIME problem can be cast into the adaptive stochastic optimization framework of [10], its influence function is not adaptive submodular (see the "DIME Problem Statement" section) and because of this their Greedy algorithm loses its approximation guarantees. Finally, Lei et al. [11] use multi–armed bandit algorithms to pick influential nodes in social networks when influence probabilities are not known, but their approach requires many iterations to converge, thereby making it unsuitable for a real-world domain like ours.

Next, we discuss literature from social work. The general approach to these interventions is to use peer change agents (PCA) (i.e., peers who bring about change in attitudes) to engage homeless youth in interventions, but most studies do not use network characteristics to choose these PCAs [12]. A notable exception is Valente et al. [13], who proposed selecting intervention participants with highest degree centrality (the most ties to other homeless youth). However, previous studies [14, 15] show that degree centrality performs poorly, as it does not account for potential overlaps in influence of two high-degree centrality nodes.

The final field of related work is planning for reward and cost optimization. We only focus on the literature on Monte-Carlo (MC) sampling based online POMDP solvers, since this approach allows significant scale-up [16]. The POMCP (Partially Observable Monte-Carlo Planning) solver [17] uses Monte-Carlo UCT (upper confidence bound) tree search in online POMDP planning. Also, Somani et al. [18] present the DESPOT (determinized sparse partially observable tree) algorithm, which improves the worst-case performance of POMCP. Our initial experiments with POMCP and DESPOT showed that they run out of memory on even our small-sized networks. A recent paper introduced PSINET-W [14], which is a MC sampling–based online POMDP planner. We have discussed PSINET's shortcomings earlier, and how HEALER remedies them with the use of its heuristics. In particular, HEALER scales up whereas PSINET fails to do so. *HEALER's algorithmic approach also offers significant novelties in comparison with PSINET.*

HEALER's Design

HEALER has a modular design [9], and consists of two major components. First, it has a network construction application for gathering information about social networks. Second, it has an algorithm called HEAL, which solves the DIME problem (introduced later) using heuristics. We first explain HEALER's components individually, and then explain how they are used inside HEALER's design.

Network Construction Application

HEALER gathers information about social ties among homeless youth by interacting with these youth via its network construction application. Once a fixed number of homeless youth register in its network application (which is hosted as a website to ensure ease of access for the youth), HEALER parses contact lists (on Facebook) of all the registered homeless youth and generates the social network that connects these youth. We choose Facebook for gathering information because previous studies [19] show that a large proportion (~80%) of homeless youth are regularly active on Facebook. Specifically, HEALER adds a link between two homeless youth if and only if both youth are (1) friends on Facebook and (2) are registered in its application. Unfortunately, there is *uncertainty* in the generated network, as friendship links between people who are only friends in real life (and have not added each other as friends on Facebook) are not captured by HEALER's network construction application.

Previously, collecting accurate social network data on homeless youth was a technical and financial burden beyond the capacity of most agencies working with these youth [19]. Research staff at homeless drop-in centers conducted tedious face-to-face interviews with homeless youth to infer ties between these youth, a process that costs thousands of dollars and many months of time. HEALER's network construction application enables homeless drop-in centers to quickly generate a first approximation of the homeless youth social network at low cost. The HEAL algorithm (the second component in HEALER) subsequently corrects and improves the social network structure iteratively (as explained later), which is one of the major strengths of this approach. This network construction application has been tested multiple times by our collaborating homeless drop-in centers with positive feedback.

DIME Solver

The DIME Solver then takes the approximate social network (generated by HEALER's network construction application) as input and solves the DIME problem (formally defined later in the paper) using HEAL, the core algorithm running inside HEALER. The HEAL algorithm is an online POMDP solver, i.e., it interleaves planning and execution for each time step (explained later in the paper). The solution of the DIME problem generated by HEAL is provided as a series of recommendations (of intervention participants) to homeless drop-in center officials. Each recommendation would urge the officials to invite a particular set of youth for their intervention camp. For example, in Figure 3.1, HEALER would recommend inviting nodes D and A for the intervention.

HEALER Design

HEALER's design begins with the network construction application constructing an *uncertain* network (as explained above). HEALER has a *sense-reason-act* cycle, where it repeats the following process for T interventions. It *reasons* about different long-term plans to solve the DIME problem, and it *acts* by providing DIME's solution as a recommendation (of intervention participants) to homeless drop-in center officials. The officials may choose to not use HEALER's recommendation in selecting their intervention's participants. After finalizing the selection of participants, the drop-in center officials contact the chosen participants (via phone/email) and conduct the intervention with them. Upon the intervention's completion, HEALER *senses* feedback about the conducted intervention from the officials. This feedback includes new observations about the network, e.g., uncertainties in some links may be resolved as intervention participants are interviewed by the drop-in center officials (explained more later). HEALER uses this feedback to update and improve its future recommendations.

DIME Problem Statement

HEALER represents social networks as directed graphs (consisting of *nodes* and *directed edges*) where each *node* represents a person in the social network and a *directed edge* between two nodes A and B (say) represents that node A *considers* node B as their friend. *HEALER assumes directed-ness of edges, as sometimes homeless drop-in centers assess that the influence in a friendship is very much unidirectional, and so it has to account for uni-directional follower links.* Otherwise friendships are encoded as two unidirectional links. In the following, we provide some background information that helps define a precise problem statement for DIME. After that, we will show some hardness results about this problem statement.

Uncertain Network

The uncertain network is a directed graph $G = (V, E)$ with $|V| = N$ nodes and $|E| = M$ edges. The edges E in an uncertain network are of two distinct types: (1) the set of certain edges (E_c) that consists of friendships we are certain about; and (2) the set of uncertain edges (E_u) that consists of friendships we are uncertain about. Recall that uncertainties about friendships exist because HEALER's network construction application misses out on some links between people who are friends in real life but not on Facebook.

To model the uncertainty about missing edges, every uncertain edge has an existence probability $u(e)$ associated with it, which represents the likelihood of "existence" of that uncertain edge in the real world. For example, if there is an uncertain edge (A, B) (i.e., we are unsure whether node B is node A's friend), then $u(A, B) = 0.75$ implies that B is A's friend with a 0.75 chance. This existence probability allows us to measure the potential value of influencing a given node. For example, if node A is connected to many uncertain edges with low $u(e)$ values, then it is unlikely that node A is highly influential (as most of his supposed friendships may not exist in reality).

In addition, every edge in the network (both certain and uncertain) has a propagation probability $p(e)$ associated with it. A propagation probability of 0.5 on directed edge (A, B) denotes that if node A is influenced (i.e., has information about HIV prevention), it influences node B (i.e., gives information to node B) with a 0.5 probability in each subsequent time step (our full influence model is defined later here). This graph G with all relevant $p(e)$ and $u(e)$ values represents an uncertain network and serves as an input to the DIME problem. Figure 3.1 shows an example of an uncertain network, where the dotted edges represent uncertain edges. We now explain how HEALER generates an uncertain social network.

First, HEALER uses its network construction application to generate a network with no uncertain edges. Next, we use well-known link prediction techniques such as KronEM [20] to infer existence probabilities $u(e)$ for additional friendships that might have been missed by the network construction application. This process gives us an *uncertain network*, which is then used by HEALER to generate recommendations, as we explain next.

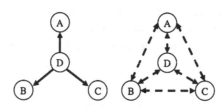

Ground Truth Network   Uncertain Network

Figure 3.1 Illustration of the value of information in the DIME Problem. A, B, C, and D represent nodes, and the edges between them represent friendships. There are two kinds of edges: certain edges (denoted by solid edges as shown in the left figure) and uncertain edges (denoted by dotted edges as shown in the right figure). The propagation and existence probabilities on all the edges is assumed to be fixed.

Given the *uncertain network* as input, HEALER runs for T *rounds* (corresponding to the number of interventions organized by the homeless drop-in center). In each round, HEALER chooses K *nodes* (youth) as intervention participants. These participants are assumed to be influenced after the intervention (i.e., our intervention deterministically influences the participants). Upon influencing the chosen nodes, HEALER "observes" the true state of the *uncertain edges* (friendships) outgoing from the selected nodes. This translates into asking intervention participants about their one-hop social circles, which is within the capabilities of the homeless drop-in center [2].

After each round, influence spreads in the network according to our influence model (explained later here) for L *time steps*, before we begin the next round. This L is the time duration in between two successive intervention camps. *In between rounds, HEALER does not observe the nodes that get influenced during L time steps.* Thus, while HEALER knows the influence model, it does not observe the random samples from the influence model that led to some nodes getting influenced. HEALER only knows that explicitly chosen nodes (our intervention participants in all past rounds) are influenced. Informally then, given an uncertain network $G_0 = (V, E)$ and integers T, K, and L (as defined earlier), HEALER finds an online policy for choosing *exactly K* nodes for T successive rounds (interventions) that maximizes influence spread in the network at the end of T rounds.

Influence Model

Unlike most previous work in influence maximization [5–8], HEALER uses a variation of the independent cascade model [21]. In the standard independent cascade model, all nodes that get influenced at time t get a *single* chance to influence their un-influenced neighbors at time $t + 1$. If they fail to spread influence in this *single* chance, they do not spread influence to their neighbors in future rounds. On the other hand, HEALER's model assumes that nodes get *multiple* chances to influence their un-influenced neighbors. If they succeed in influencing a neighbor at a given time step t', they stop influencing that neighbor for all future time steps. Otherwise, if they fail in step t', they try to influence again with the same propagation probability in the next time step. This variant of independent cascade has been shown to empirically provide a better approximation of the real influence spread than the standard independent cascade model [21, 22]. Further, we assume that nodes that get influenced at a certain time step remain influenced for all future time steps.

We now provide notation for defining HEALER's policy formally. Let $\Delta = \{A \subset V \ s.t. \ |A| = K\}$ denote the set of K sized subsets of V, which represents the set of possible choices that HEALER can make at every time step $t \in [1, T]$. Let $A_i \in \Delta \forall i \in [1, T]$ denote HEALER's choice in the ith time step. Upon making choice A_i, HEALER "observes" uncertain edges adjacent to nodes in A_i, which updates its understanding of the network. Let $G_i \forall i \in [1, T]$ denote the uncertain network resulting from G_{i-1} with *observed* (additional edge) information from A_i. Formally, we define a history $H_i \forall i \in [1, T]$ of length i as a tuple of past choices and observations $H_i = < G_0, A_1, G_1, A_2, \ldots, A_{i-1}, G_i >$. Denote by $Y_i = \{H_k \; s.t. \; k \leq i\}$ the set of all possible histories of length less than or equal to i. Finally, we define an i-step policy $\Pi_i : Y_i \rightarrow \Delta$ as a function that takes in histories of length less than or equal to i and outputs a K node choice for the current time step. We now provide an explicit problem statement for DIME.

Problem Statement
Given as input are an uncertain network $G_0 = (V, E)$ and integers T, K, and L (as defined earlier). Denote by $R(H_T, A_T)$ the *expected total number of influenced nodes at the end of round T*, given the T-length history of previous observations and actions H_T, along with A_T, the action chosen at time T. Let $E_{\{H_T, A_T \sim \Pi_T\}} R(H_T, A_T)$ denote the expectation over the random variables $H_T = < G_0, A_1, G_1, A_2, \ldots, A_{T-1}, G_T >$ and influence of A_T, where A_i are chosen according to $\Pi_T(H_i) \forall i \in [1, T]$, and G_i are drawn according to the distribution over uncertain edges of G_{i-1} that are revealed by A_i. The objective of DIME is to find an optimal T-step policy $\Pi_T^* = \text{argmax}_{\Pi_T} E_{\{H_T, A_T \sim \Pi_T\}} R(H_T, A_T)$.

Next, we show hardness results about the DIME problem. First, we analyze the value of having complete information in DIME. Then, we characterize the computational hardness of DIME.

The Value of Information
We characterize the impact of insufficient information (about the uncertain edges) on the achieved solution value. We show that no algorithm for DIME is able to provide a sufficiently good approximation to the *full-information solution value* (i.e., the best solution achieved with regard to the underlying ground-truth network), even with infinite computational power.

Theorem 1 *Given an uncertain network with n nodes, for any $\epsilon > 0$, there is no algorithm for the DIME problem that can guarantee a $n^{-1+\epsilon}$ approximation to OPT$_{full}$, the full-information solution value.*

Proof: We prove this statement by providing a counterexample in the form of a specific (ground-truth) network for which there can exist no algorithm that can guarantee a $n^{-1+\epsilon}$ approximation to OPT_{full}. Consider an input to the DIME problem, an *uncertain network* with n nodes with $2 \times {}^nC_2$ uncertain edges between the n nodes, i.e., it is a completely connected uncertain network consisting of *only* uncertain edges (an example with $n = 3$ is shown in Figure 3.1). Let $p(e) = 1$ and $u(e) = 0.5$ on all edges in the *uncertain network*, i.e., all edges have the same propagation and existence probability. Let $K = 1$, $L = 1$, and $T = 1$, i.e., we just select a single node in one shot (in a single round). ∎

Further, consider a star graph (as the ground truth network) with n nodes such that propagation probability $p(e) = 1$ on all edges of the star graph (shown in Figure 3.1). Now, any algorithm for the DIME problem would select a single node in the *uncertain network* uniformly at random with equal probability of $1/n$ (as information about all nodes is symmetrical). In expectation, the algorithm will achieve an expected reward $\left\{ \frac{1}{n} \times n \right\} + \left\{ \frac{1}{n} \times 1 + \ldots + \frac{1}{n} \times 1 \right\} = \frac{1}{n} \times n + \frac{n-1}{n} \times 1 = 2 - \frac{1}{n}$. However, given the ground truth network, we get $OPT_{\text{full}} = n$ because we always select the star node. As n goes to infinity, we can at best achieve a n^{-1} approximation to OPT_{full}. Thus, no algorithm can achieve a $n^{-1+\epsilon}$ approximation to OPT_{full} for any $\epsilon > 0$.

Computational Hardness

We now analyze the hardness of computation in the DIME problem in the next two theorems.

Theorem 2 *The DIME problem is NP-Hard.*

Proof: Consider the case where $E_u = \Phi, L = 1, T = 1$, and $p(e) = 1\ \forall e \in E$. This degenerates to the classical influence maximization problem, which is known to be NP-hard. Thus, the DIME problem is also NP-hard. ∎

Some NP-Hard problems exhibit nice properties that enable approximation guarantees for them. Golovin et al. [23] introduced adaptive submodularity, an analog of submodularity for adaptive settings. Intuitively, adaptive submodularity deals with cases in which actions/items are to be picked in multiple stages, and newer information is revealed every time an action is picked. Adaptive submodularity requires that the expected marginal gain of picking an action can only decrease as more actions are picked and more information is revealed. Formally, adaptive submodularity requires that Marginal$(A, \Psi) \leq$ Marginal$(A, \Psi') \forall \Psi \subset \Psi'$, where Marginal$(A, \Psi)$ represents the marginal gain/benefit of picking action A, conditioned on getting information Ψ. This makes the adaptive submodularity framework a natural fit for the DIME problem. Presence of adaptive submodularity ensures that a simply greedy algorithm provides a *(1-1/e)* approximation guarantee with regard to the optimal solution defined on the *uncertain network*. However, as we show next, while DIME can be cast into the adaptive stochastic optimization framework of [23], our influence function is not adaptive submodular, because of which their Greedy algorithm does not have a *(1-1/e)* approximation guarantee.

Theorem 3 *The influence function of DIME is not adaptive submodular.*

Proof: The definition of adaptive submodularity requires that the expected marginal increase of influence by picking an additional node is more when we have less observation. Here the expectation is taken over the random states that are consistent with current observation. We show that this is not the case in DIME problem. Consider a path with three nodes, A, B, and C and two directed edges, $e_1 = (A, B)$ and $e_2 = (B, C)$. Let $p(e_1) = p(e_2) = 1$, i.e., propagation probability is 1; and $u(e_1) = 1$, $u(e_2) = 1 - \epsilon$ for some small enough ϵ to be set. Thus, the only uncertainty comes from incomplete knowledge of the existence of edges. ∎

Let us assume that we pick node A. After picking node A, the expected marginal benefit of picking node C is ϵ. However, after picking node B, if we get information $\Psi = \{(B, C) does\ not\ exist\}$, then the expected marginal benefit of picking node C goes to 1 (up from ϵ). Since the expected marginal benefit of picking node C increased from ϵ to 1 upon receiving more information and picking more actions, this contradicts the definition of adaptive submodularity. This shows that the influence function of DIME is not adaptive submodular.

HEAL: DIME Problem Solver

The above theorems show that DIME is a hard problem, as it is difficult to even obtain any reasonable approximations. HEALER models DIME as a partially observable Markov decision process (POMDP) [24], which is a logical fit for the problem, for two reasons. First, several interventions are conducted sequentially, similar to sequential POMDP actions. Second, there is *partial observability* (similar to POMDPs) due to uncertainties in network structure and influence status of nodes. We now provide a high-level overview of HEALER's POMDP model.

POMDP Model

A *state* in this model includes the influence status of all network nodes (i.e., which nodes are influenced and which nodes are not) and the true state of the uncertain edges (i.e., whether each uncertain edge exists or not in the real world). Thus, there are 2^{N+M} possible POMDP states in a network with N nodes and M uncertain edges. Similarly, an *action* in this model is any possible subset of K network nodes, which can be called for an intervention. Thus, if K nodes are being selected in every intervention on a network with N nodes, there are $^{N}C_{K}$ possible POMDP actions. Finally, an *observation* in this model is based on the assumption that when a set of K nodes (i.e., K distinct homeless youth) are called in for intervention, the drop-in center officials can talk to these nodes (or youth) and resolve the status of the uncertain edges in their local neighborhood. Specifically, the drop-in center official observes the true state of each uncertain edge (i.e., whether it exists in the real world or not) outgoing from the K nodes chosen in that action. The observation of the true state of uncertain edge *(A, B)* leads to resetting of $u(A, B)$ to either 1 or 0 (depending on whether edge *(A, B)* actually exists or not). Thus, when M uncertain edges are outgoing from the K nodes chosen in a POMDP action, there are 2^{M} possible POMDP observations. Finally, the *rewards* in this model keep track of the number of new nodes that get influenced upon taking a POMDP action. Refer to Yadav et al. [9] for the full POMDP model.

HEAL

HEAL is a heuristic-based online POMDP planner for solving the DIME problem. HEAL solves the *original POMDP* using a novel *hierarchical ensembling heuristic*: it creates ensembles of imperfect (and smaller) POMDPs at *two* different layers, in a hierarchical manner (see Figure 3.2). HEAL's *top layer* creates an ensemble of smaller sized *intermediate POMDPs* by subdividing the original *uncertain network* into several smaller sized *partitioned networks* by using graph partitioning techniques [25]. Each of these partitioned networks is then mapped onto a POMDP, and these *intermediate POMDPs* form the *top layer* ensemble of POMDP solvers.

In the bottom layer, each *intermediate POMDP* is solved using TASP (tree aggregation for sequential planning), HEAL's POMDP planner, which subdivides the POMDP into another ensemble of smaller-sized *sampled POMDPs*. Each member of this *bottom layer* ensemble is created by randomly sampling uncertain edges of the partitioned network to get a sampled network having no uncertain edges, and this sampled network is then mapped onto a *sampled POMDP*. Finally, the solutions of POMDPs in both the *bottom* and *top layer* ensembles are aggregated using novel techniques to get the solution for HEAL's original POMDP.

These heuristics enable scale up to real-world sizes (at the expense of sacrificing performance guarantees), as instead of solving one huge problem,

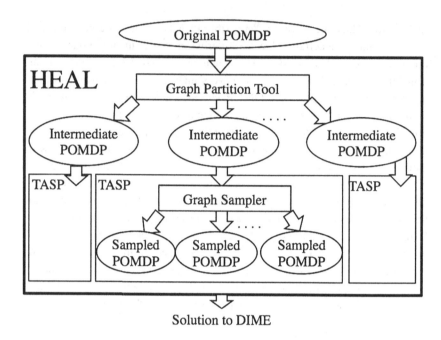

Figure 3.2 Hierarchical decomposition in HEAL (from Yadav et. al. [9]).

HEAL solves several smaller problems. The primary difference between HEAL and PSINET (the previous state-of-the-art) is in the top layer of HEAL, which uses the graph partitioning heuristic. This heuristic divides up the network into different partitions, with each partition corresponding to an intermediate POMDP (Figure 3.2). The partitions are chosen in a way that minimizes the number of cross-edges going across the partitions while ensuring that the partitions have similar sizes. Since these partitions are almost disconnected, we solve each partition separately without accounting for influence going across the partitions. Simulations show that even on smaller settings, HEAL achieves a 100-fold speed-up over PSINET, while providing a 70% improvement in solution quality; and on larger problems, *where PSINET is unable to run at all*, HEAL continues to provide high solution quality.

DOSIM: A New Algorithm for the DIME Problem

DOSIM [26] is a novel algorithm that solves a generalization of the DIME problem. The key motivation behind DOSIM is to be able to select actions (i.e., set of K nodes) for T stages without knowing the exact model parameters (i.e., $p(e)$ and $u(e)$ values for each network edge). HEALER dealt with this issue by assuming a specific $p(e)$ and $u(e)$ value based on suggestions by service providers. DOSIM instead works with interval uncertainty over these model parameters. That is, the exact value of each $u(e)$ and $p(e)$ does not have be exactly supplied; they are just assumed to lie within some interval. This generalizes the model used by HEALER to include higher-order uncertainty over the probabilities in addition to the uncertainty induced by the probabilities themselves. DOSIM chooses an action that is robust to this interval uncertainty. Specifically, it finds a policy that achieves close to optimal value regardless of where the unknown probabilities lie within the interval.

The problem is formalized as a *zero-sum game* between the algorithm, which picks a policy, and an adversary (nature) who chooses the model parameters. A game models a situation where two players must each select an action. Each player receives a payoff depending on the actions that were taken. "Zero sum" indicates that one player's loss is the other's gain. In our situation, we model nature as selecting the model parameters that result in the worst performance for the algorithm. This game formulation represents a key advance over HEALER's POMDP policy (which was constrained to fixed propagation probabilities), as it enables DOSIM to output mixed strategies (distributions) over POMDP policies, which make it robust against worst-case propagation probability values. Moreover, DOSIM receives periodic observations, which are used to update its understanding of its belief state (i.e., probability distribution over different model parameters). However, the number of possible actions for the game is intractably large, because there are an exponential number of policies (each of which specifies an action to take for any possible set of observations).

To resolve this issue, DOSIM uses a *double oracle* approach, illustrated in Figure 3.3. Each of the tables shown is a payoff table, which lists the actions available for each player. Each cell of the table gives the payoff that each player obtains when the corresponding strategies are chosen. Since the game is zero sum, these payoffs always total zero. In a double oracle algorithm, each player starts with only a limited number of arbitrarily chosen strategies available to them. In our case, this means that the algorithm has perhaps one or two policies available, and nature has one or two sets of parameters. Standard techniques from game theory can be used to find the best strategy for each player in such a small game (the best strategies are referred to as an *equilibrium*). Then, DOSIM incrementally adds new strategies to these small starting sets. Specifically, DOSIM has an oracle for each player. The oracle computes that player's best strategy to play in light of the options that the

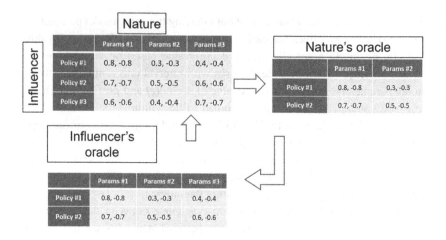

Figure 3.3 Example of the double oracle algorithm.

other player currently has available. This new strategy is then added to the list of those currently under consideration. DOSIM alternates between adding strategies for the two players until neither can benefit from adding any more strategies. At this point, it has reached an equilibrium.

Experimental Results

We compare three algorithms: HEALER, DOSIM, and degree centrality (DC). DC is the current standard practice for influence maximization in this domain, where drop-in center officials recruit the set of youth with the highest degree to serve as peer leaders. In order to compare HEALER and DOSIM, we assume that the problem parameters are known, fixing $u(e) = 0.1$ and $p(e) = 0.6$ for all edges in the network. This was done based on findings in Kelly et. al. [27]. This experiment was run on a 2.33 GHz 12-core Intel machine having 48 GB of RAM, and was averaged over 100 runs. All comparison results are statistically significant under bootstrap-t ($\alpha = 0.05$).

We run the algorithms on two networks, Network A and Network B. Each represents the social network of homeless youth gathered from a different drop-in center in the Los Angeles area. The networks had between 140 and 170 nodes each. Figure 3.4 shows the results for Network A and Figure 3.5 shows the results for Network B. Each figure plots the average influence spread obtained by each algorithm over 100 runs. On the x-axis, we vary the number of seeds K. The number of time steps T is fixed to 5 throughout. We see

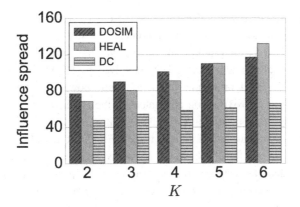

Figure 3.4 Simulated influence spread of each algorithm on Network A.

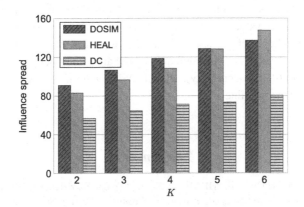

Figure 3.5 Simulated influence spread of each algorithm on Network B.

that both HEALER and DOSIM significantly outperform DC. This holds on both networks and across all values of K. HEALER and DOSIM benefit from considering the global structure of the network. For example, they will (either explicitly or implicitly) avoid placing many seed nodes close together. DC obtains significantly less influence spread because it looks only at the degree of each node in isolation.

Conclusion

In this chapter, we explored design of HEALER and DOSIM, two adaptive software agents that recommend intervention attendees to homeless drop-in center officials. HEALER solves a POMDP on a social network to come up with recommendations for which homeless youth in a social network should be chosen as intervention attendees. We first formally characterized the computational problem (called DIME) solved by HEALER, and showed that it is an NP-Hard problem. Moreover, well-known algorithms such as Greedy lose their approximation guarantees in the DIME problem due to the feedback about network structure received during interventions. We inferred that DIME's computational hardness forces HEALER to rely on heuristic methods for solving DIME. Further, we analyzed these heuristic methods and showed that the primary reason behind the superior performance of HEALER is its graph partitioning heuristic, which works well due to the small-world nature of the real-world networks of homeless youth. We then examined a new algorithm for the problem, DOSIM. DOSIM is motivated by uncertainty about the underlying parameters of the problem. Rather than assuming a fixed value for the parameters, it solves a zero-sum game to determine a policy that is robust to a worst-case set of parameters. We then compared the performance in simulation of both algorithms and of a commonly used heuristic (degree centrality). Both DOSIM and HEALER substantially outperformed the baseline.

References

[1] National HCH Council, "HIV/AIDS among Persons Experiencing Homelessness: Risk Factors, Predictors of Testing, and Promising Testing Strategies." [Online]. Available: www.nhchc.org/wp-content/uploads/2011/09/InFocus_Dec2012.pdf.

[2] E. Rice, E. Tulbert, J. Cederbaum, A. B. Adhikari, N. G. Milburn, "Mobilizing Homeless Youth for HIV Prevention: A Social Network Analysis of the Acceptability of a Face-to-Face and Online Social Networking Intervention," Health Education Research, vol. 27, no. 2, pp. 226–236, 2012.

[3] E. Rice, "The Positive Role of Social Networks and Social Networking Technology in the Condom-using Behaviors of Homeless Young People," Public Health Reports, vol. 125, no. 4, pp. 588–595, 2010.

[4] E. Rice, A. Fulginti, H. Winetrobe, J. Montoya, A. Plant, T. Kordic, "Sexuality and Homelessness in Los Angeles Public Schools," American Journal of Public Health, vol. 102, pp. 200–201, 2012.

[5] C. Borgs, M. Brautbar, J. Chayes, B. Lucier, "Maximizing Social Influence in Nearly Optimal Time," Proc. 25th Annual ACM-SIAM Symposium on Discrete Algorithms (SODA), pp. 946–957, 2014.

[6] Y. Tang, X. Xiao, Y. Shi, "Influence Maximization: Near-Optimal Time Complexity Meets Practical Efficiency," Proc. 2014 ACM SIGMOD International Conference on Management of Data, pp. 75–86, 2014.

[7] D. Kempe, J. Kleinberg, E. Tardos, "Maximizing the Spread of Influence through a Social Network," *Proc. 9th ACM SIGKDD International Conference on Knowledge Discovery and Data Mining*, pp. 137–146, 2003.

[8] J. Leskovec, A. Krause, C. Guestrin, C. Faloutsos, J. VanBriesen, N. Glance, "Cost Effective Outbreak Detection in Networks," *Proc. 13th ACM SIGKDD International Conference on Knowledge Discovery and Data Mining*, pp. 420–429, 2007.

[9] A. Yadav, H. Chan, A.X. Jiang, H. Xu, E. Rice, M. Tambe, "Using Social Networks to Aid Homeless Shelters: Dynamic Influence Maximization under Uncertainty," *Proc. International Conference on Autonomous Agents and Multiagent Systems (AAMAS) 2016*, Singapore, pp. 740–748.

[10] D. Golovin, A. Krause, "Adaptive Submodularity: Theory and Applications in Active Learning and Stochastic Optimization," *Journal of Artificial Intelligence Research*, vol. 42, pp. 427–486, 2011.

[11] S. Lei, S. Maniu, L. Mo, R. Cheng, P. Senellart, "Online Influence Maximization," *Proceedings of the 21th ACM SIGKDD International Conference on Knowledge Discovery and Data Mining*, pp. 645–654, August 2015.

[12] J. Schneider, A. Ning. Zhou, E. O. Laumann, "A New HIV Prevention Network Approach: Sociometric Peer Change Agent Selection," *Social Science & Medicine*, vol. 125, pp. 192–202, 2015.

[13] T. W. Valente, P. Pumpuang, "Identifying Opinion Leaders to Promote Behavior Change," *Health Education and Behavior*, pp. 881–896, 2007.

[14] A. Yadav, L. Marcolino, E. Rice, R. Petering, H. Winetrobe, H. Rhoades, M. Tambe, H. Carmichael, "Preventing HIV Spread in Homeless Populations Using PSINET," *Proc. 27th Conference on Innovative Applications of Artificial Intelligence (IAAI)*, Austin, 2015.

[15] E. Cohen, D. Delling, T. Pajor, R. F. Werneck, "Sketch-Based Influence Maximization and Computation: Scaling up with Guarantees," *Proc. 23rd ACM International Conference on Information and Knowledge Management*, pp. 629–638, 2014.

[16] S. Ross, J. Pineau, S. Paquet, B. Chaib-Draa, "Online Planning Algorithms for POMDPs," *Journal of Artificial Intelligence Research*, pp. 663–704, 2008.

[17] D. Silver, J. Veness, "Monte-Carlo Planning in Large POMDPs," *Proc. Advances in Neural Information Processing Systems (NIPS)*, pp. 2164–2172, 2010.

[18] A. Somani, N. Ye, D. Hsu, W. S. Lee, "DESPOT: Online POMDP Planning with Regularization," *Proc. Advances in Neural Information Processing Systems (NIPS)*, pp. 1772–1780, 2013.

[19] S. D. Young, E. Rice, "Online Social Networking Technologies, HIV Knowledge, and Sexual Risk and Testing Behaviors among Homeless Youth," *AIDS and Behavior*, vol. 15, no. 2, pp. 253–260, 2011.

[20] M. Kim, J. Leskovec, "The Network Completion Problem: Inferring Missing Nodes and Edges in Networks," In *Proc. of the 2011 SIAM International Conference on Data Mining*, Society for Industrial and Applied Mathematics, pp. 47–58, April 2011.

[21] Q. Yan, S. Guo, D. Yang, "Influence Maximizing and Local Influenced Community Detection Based on Multiple Spread Model," *Advanced Data Mining and Applications*, pp. 82–95, 2011.

[22] J. P. Cointet, C. Roth, "How Realistic Should Knowledge Diffusion Models Be?" *Journal of Artificial Societies and Social Simulation*, vol. 10, no. 3, pp. 1–5, 2007.

[23] A. Yadav, B. Wilder, E. Rice, R. Petering, J. Craddock, A. Yoshioka-Maxwell, M. Hemler, L. Onasch-Vera, M. Tambe, D. Woo, "Influence Maximization in the Field: The Arduous Journey from Emerging to Deployed Application," *International Conference on Autonomous Agents and Multiagent Systems (AAMAS) 2017*, Sau Paulo, Brazil, pp. 150–158.

[24] L. P. Kaelbing, M. L. Littman, A. R. Cassandra, "Planning and Acting in Partially Observable Stochastic Domains," *Artificial Intelligence*, Vol. 101, no, 1, pp. 99–134, 1998.

[25] D. LaSalle, G. Karypis, "Multi-Threaded Graph Partitioning," *Proc. 27th IEEE International Symposium on Parallel & Distributed Processing (IPDPS)*, pp. 225–236, 2013.

[26] B. Wilder, A. Yadav, N. Immorlica, E. Rice, M. Tambe, "Uncharted but Not Uninfluenced: Influence Maximization with an Uncertain Network," *Proc. of the 2017 International Conference on Autonomous Agents and Multi-Agent Systems*, International Foundation for Autonomous Agents and Multiagent Systems, pp. 1305–1313, 2017.

[27] J. A. Kelly, D. A. Murphy, K. J. Sikkema, T. L. McAuliffe, R. A. Roffman, L. J. Solomon, R. A. Winett, S. C. Kalichman, "Randomised, Controlled, Community-Level HIV-Prevention Intervention for Sexual-Risk Behaviour among Homosexual Men in US Cities," *The Lancet*, vol. 350, no. 9090. pp. 1500–1505, 1997.

4

Influence Maximization in the Field

The Arduous Journey from Emerging to Deployed Application

Amulya Yadav, Bryan Wilder, Eric Rice, Robin Petering,
Jaih Craddock, Amanda Yoshioka-Maxwell, Mary Hemler,
Laura Onasch-Vera, Milind Tambe, and Darlene Woo

*Center for Artificial Intelligence in Society, University of Southern
California, LA, CA, 90089*

Introduction

The process of building a software agent that can be deployed regularly in the real world to assist underserved communities is very difficult. While significant attention has been paid in the literature to build agents for innovative applications, the topic of transitioning agents from an emerging phase in the lab to a deployed application in the field has not received significant attention [1]. This chapter illustrates the research challenges and complexities of this topic by focusing on agents for a particular health-critical domain, i.e., raising awareness about HIV among homeless youth.

Homeless youth are twenty times more likely to be HIV positive than stably housed youth, due to high-risk behaviors (such as unprotected sex, survival sex, sharing drug needles, etc.) [2, 3]. To reduce rates of HIV infection among youth, many providers of services for homeless youth (henceforth simply "service providers") conduct peer-leader-based social network interventions [4], in which a select group of homeless youth are trained as *peer leaders (PLs)*. This peer-led approach is particularly desirable because service providers have limited resources and homeless youth tend to distrust adults. The training program of these peer leaders includes detailed information about how HIV spreads and what one can do to prevent infection. The PLs are also taught effective ways of communicating this information to their peers [5]. Because of their limited financial and human resources, service providers can only train a small number of these youth and not the entire population. As a result, the selected peer leaders in these intervention trainings are tasked with spreading messages about HIV prevention to their peers in

57

their social circles, thereby encouraging them to move to safer practices. Using these interventions, service providers aim to leverage social network effects to disseminate information about HIV and induce behavior change (increased HIV testing) among more and more people in the social network of homeless youth.

In fact, there are further constraints that service providers face: behavioral struggles of homeless youth means that service providers can only train three or four peer leaders in every intervention. This makes sequential training the most optimal approach, with groups of up to four youth trained one after another. They are trained as peer leaders in the intervention, and are asked *information* about friendships that they observe in the real-world social network. This new information about the social network is then used to improve the selection of the peer leaders for the next intervention. As a result, the peer leaders for these limited interventions need to be chosen strategically so that awareness spread about HIV is maximized in the social network of homeless youth.

The previous chapter discussed HEALER [6] and DOSIM [7], two agents that assist service providers in optimizing their intervention strategies. These agents recommend "good" intervention attendees, i.e., homeless youth who maximize HIV awareness in the real-world social network of youth. In essence, both HEALER and DOSIM reason strategically about the multiagent system of homeless youth to select a sequence of three or four of them at a time to maximize HIV awareness. While HEALER [6] is an adaptive software agent that solves POMDPs to select the best set of peer leaders, DOSIM [7] uses robust optimization techniques to find the correct set of peer leaders, even when the influence probability parameters are not known. Unfortunately, while earlier research [6, 7] published promising simulation results from the lab, neither of these agent-based systems have even been tested so far in the real world. This chapter illustrates that transitioning these agents from the lab into the real world is not straightforward.

Several questions need to be answered before final deployment of these agents. First, do peer leaders actually spread HIV information in a homeless youth social network, and are they able to provide meaningful information about the social network structure during intervention training (as assumed by HEALER and DOSIM)? Second, would agents (which use POMDPs and robust optimization approaches to reason about underlying social networks) outperform standard techniques used by service providers to select peer leaders? If they do not, then a large-scale deployment is unwarranted. Third, which agent out of HEALER or DOSIM performs better in the field? Finally, is the system robust and/or flexible enough to resolve any unforeseen challenges that may arise before deployment?

To answer these questions, it is necessary to conduct real-world pilot tests before deployment of these agents on a large scale. Indeed, the health-critical nature of the domain and complex influence spread models used by social influence maximization agents makes conducting pilot tests even more important to validate their real-world effectiveness. This chapter presents results from three real-world pilot studies involving 173 homeless youth in an American city. *This is an actual test involving word-of-mouth spread of information, and actual changes in youth behavior in the real world as a result.* To the best of our knowledge, these are the first such pilot studies that provide head-to-head comparison of different software agent (with POMDP, robust optimization driven) approaches for social influence maximization, including a comparison with a baseline approach. *Our pilot study results show that HEALER and DOSIM achieve 184% more information spread than Degree Centrality (baseline), and do significantly better at inducing behavior change among homeless youth.* Second, we present analyses of these real-world results, illustrating the strengths and weaknesses of different influence maximization approaches we compare. Specifically, we illustrate how HEALER and DOSIM cleverly exploit the community structure of real-world social networks to outperform Degree Centrality. Third, we present research challenges revealed in conducting these pilot tests, and propose solutions to address them. These challenges dispel any misguided notions about the ease of taking applications from the emerging to the deployed application phase. Finally, the promising results obtained in these pilot studies open the door to future deployment of HEALER and DOSIM by service providers on a regular basis.

Pilot Study Pipeline

Starting in the spring of 2016, we conducted three different pilot studies at two service providers in a large American city over a seven-month period. Each pilot study recruited a unique network of youth. Recall that these pilot studies serve three purposes. First, they help in justifying our assumptions about whether peer leaders actually disseminate HIV information in their social network, and whether they provide meaningful information about the social network structure (i.e., observations) during the intervention training. Second, these pilot studies help in exposing unforeseen challenges that need to be solved convincingly before these agents can be deployed in the field. Third, they provide a head-to-head comparison of two different software agent approaches for social influence maximization, including a comparison with a baseline approach.

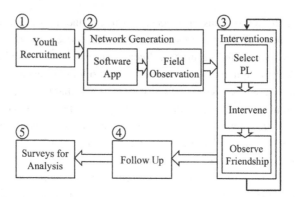

Figure 4.1 Real-world pilot study pipeline

Each of these pilot studies had a different intervention mechanism, i.e., a different way of selecting actions (or a set of K peer leaders). The first and second studies used HEALER and DOSIM (respectively) to select actions, whereas the third study served as the control group, where actions were selected using Degree Centrality (i.e., picking K nodes in order of decreasing degrees). We chose Degree Centrality (DC) as the control group mechanism, because this is the current modus operandi of service providers in conducting these network based interventions [8].

Pilot Study Process The pilot study process consisted of five sequential steps. Figure 4.1 illustrates these five steps.

1. **Recruitment**: First, we recruited homeless youth from a service provider into our study (n = 173 at baseline across the three tests). We provided youth with general information about our study and what was expected of them (i.e., if selected as a peer leader, they would be expected to disseminate information among their peers). The youth took a 20-minute baseline survey, which enabled us to determine their current risk-taking behaviors (e.g., they were asked about the last time they got an HIV test). Every youth was given a 20 USD gift card as compensation for participating in the pilot study. All study procedures were approved by our Institutional Review Board.

2. **Network Generation**: After recruitment, the friendship-based social network that connects these homeless youth was generated. We relied on two information sources to generate this network: (1) online contacts of homeless youth and (2) field observations made by the authors while collecting baseline survey data. To expedite the network generation phase,

online contacts of homeless youth were used (via a software application that the youth were asked to use) to build a first approximation of the real-world social network of homeless youth. This network was then refined using field observations (about additional real-world friendships) made by the authors. All edges inferred in this manner were assumed to be *certain edges*. More information on uncertain edges is provided later.

3. **Interventions**: Next, the generated network was used by the software agents to select actions (i.e., K peer leaders) for T stages. In each stage, an action was selected using the pilot's intervention strategy. The K peer leaders of this chosen action were then trained as peer leaders (i.e., informed about HIV) by pilot study staff during the intervention. These peer leaders also revealed more information (i.e., provide observation) about newer friendships that we did not know about. These friendships were incorporated into the network, so that the agents could select better actions in the next stage of interventions. Every peer leader was given a 60 USD gift card.

   Only four to six peer leaders could be trained at once, and thus peer change agents were enrolled in three subsequent rounds. Training was delivered by three facilitators: Rice, his PhD students with MSWs, or MSW interns. Training was interactive and broken into six hour-long modules on: the mission of peer advocacy, sexual health, HIV prevention, communication skills, leadership skills, and self-care. Peer leaders were asked to focus their communications on their social ties, particularly other youth at the drop-in center, and to promote regular HIV testing.

   The training was designed to be engaging and included a variety of learning activities such as group discussion, games, journaling and reflection, experiential learning, and role-playing. The training minimized lecture-based learning. The small group setting was critical for maintaining a safe and manageable space for youth to learn and reflect. Further, the training was developed from a youth empowerment model. Consistent language was used throughout to reiterate the participants' role as a leader and advocate within their community.

4. **Follow-Up**: The follow-up phase consisted of meetings during which the peer leaders were asked about any difficulties they faced in talking to their friends about HIV. They were given further encouragement to keep spreading HIV awareness among their peers. These follow-up meetings occured on a weekly basis, for a period of seven weeks after Step 3 ended.

5. **Analysis**: For analysis, we conducted in-person surveys. Of the initial 173 youth, 122 (71%) were surveyed a second time, one month after their first survey and after all initial intervention training sessions were completed

(but before the completion of Step 4). Every youth in our study was given a 25 USD gift card to show up for these surveys. During the surveys they were asked if some youth from within the pilot study talked to them about HIV prevention methods after the pilot study began. Their answers helped determine if information about HIV reached them in the social network or not. Thus, these surveys were used to find out the number of youth who became informed about HIV as a result of our interventions. Furthermore, they were asked to take the same survey about HIV risk that they took during recruitment. These post-intervention surveys enabled us to compare HEALER, DOSIM, and DC in terms of information spread (i.e., how successful were the agents in spreading HIV information through the social network) and behavior change (i.e., how successful were the agents in causing homeless youth to test for HIV), the two major metrics that we used in our evaluation section. These two metrics were based on self-reports. First, youth were asked when (if ever) they had been tested for HIV; answer choices included never, in the past month, three to six months ago, and more than six months ago. Second, commmunication was assessed with a series of eight questions about their attitudes toward conversations with peer leaders (if they had such a conversation; if not, they could select "I didn't have a conversation with a Have You Heard Peer Leader about HIV or AIDS." Those who endorsed the non-communication responses were scored as not receiving infromation directly from a peer leader.

We provide these behavior change results in order to quantify the true impact of these social influence maximization agents in the homeless youth domain. In these results, we measured behavior change by asking youth if they have taken an HIV test at baseline and repeating this question during the follow-up surveys. If the youth reported taking an HIV test at one month (after interventions) but not at baseline and that youth also reported getting informed about HIV from a peer leader, we attributed this behavior change to our intervention. This allowed us to measure whether our interventions led to a reduction in risk behaviors.

Uncertain network parameters. While there exist many link prediction techniques [9] to infer *uncertain edges* in social networks, the efficacy of these techniques is untested on homeless youth social networks. Therefore, we took a simpler, less "risky" approach – each edge *not created* during the network generation phase (i.e., Step 2 above) was added to the network as an *uncertain edge*. Thus, after adding these uncertain edges, the social network in each pilot study became a completely connected network, consisting of *certain edges* (inferred from Step 2) and *uncertain edges*. The existence probability on each

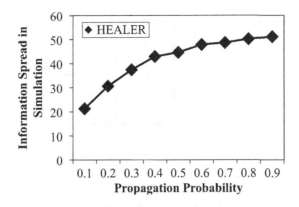

Figure 4.2 Information spread with p_e on HEALER's pilot network

uncertain edge was set to $u = 0.01$. Our approach to adding uncertain edges ensures that no potential friendship is missed in the social network because of our lack of accurate knowledge.

Getting propagation probabilities (p_e) values was also challenging. In the HEALER's pilot, service providers estimated that the true p_e value would be somewhere around 0.5. Since the exact value was unknown, we assumed an interval of [0.4, 0.8] and simulated HEALER's performance with p_e values in this range. Figure 4.2 shows how information spread achieved by HEALER on its pilot study network is relatively stable in simulation for p_e values around 0.5. The y-axis shows the information spread in simulation and the x-axis shows increasing p_e values. This figure shows that information spread achieved by HEALER varied by ~11.6% with p_e in the range [0.4, 0.8]. Since influence spread is relatively stable in this range, we selected $p_e = 0.6$ (the mid-point of [0.4, 0.8]) on all network edges. Later in this chapter we provide ex post justification for why $p_e = 0.6$ was a good choice, at least for this pilot study.

In DOSIM's pilot, we did not have to deal with the issue of assigning accurate p_e values to edges in the network. This is because DOSIM can work with intervals in which the exact p_e is assumed to lie. For the pilot study, we used the same interval of [0.4, 0.8] to run DOSIM. Finally, the control group pilot study did not require finding p_e values, as peer leaders were selected using Degree Centrality, which does not require knowledge of p_e.

Results from the Field

We now provide results from all three pilot studies. In each study, three interventions were conducted (or $T = 3$), i.e., Step 3 of the pilot study process

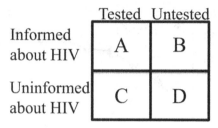

Figure 4.3 Set of surveyed non–peer leaders

(Figure 4.1) was repeated three times. The actions (i.e., set of K peer leaders) were chosen using intervention strategies (policies) provided by HEALER [6], DOSIM [7], and Degree Centrality (DC) in the first, second, and third pilot studies, respectively. Recall that we provide comparison results on two different metrics. First, we provide results on information spread, i.e., how well different software agents were able to spread information about HIV through the social network. Second, even though HEALER and DOSIM do not explicitly model behavior change in their objective function (both maximize the information spread in the network), we provide results on behavior change among homeless youth, i.e., how successful the agents were in inducing behavior change among homeless youth.

Figure 4.3 shows a matrix diagram that explains the results that we collect from the pilot studies. To begin with, we exclude PLs from all our results and focus only on non–peer leaders (non-PLs). This is done because PLs cannot be used to differentiate the information spread (and behavior change) achieved by HEALER, DOSIM, and DC. In terms of information spread, all PLs are informed about HIV directly by study staff in the intervention trainings. In terms of behavior change, the proportion of PLs who change their behavior does not depend on the strategies recommended by HEALER, DOSIM, and DC. Thus, Figure 4.3 shows a matrix diagram of the set of all non-PLs (who were surveyed at the end of one month). This set of non-PLs can be divided into four quadrants based on (1) whether or not they were informed about HIV (by the end of one-month surveys in Step 5 of Figure 4.1) and (2) whether or not they were already tested for HIV at baseline (i.e., during recruitment, they reported that they had been tested for HIV in the last six months).

For information spread results, we report on the percentage of youth in this big rectangle, who were informed about HIV by the end of one month (i.e., boxes A + B as a fraction of the big box). For behavior change results, we exclude youth who were already tested at baseline (as they do not need to

Table 4.1. *Logistic details of different pilot studies*

	HEALER	DOSIM	DC
Youth Recruited	62	56	55
PL Trained	17.7%	17.85%	20%
Retention %	73%	73%	65%
Avg. Observation Size	16	8	15

undergo behavior change because they are already exhibiting desired behavior of testing). Thus, we only report on the percentage of *untested informed youth* (i.e., box B), who now tested for HIV (i.e., changed behavior) by the end of one month (which is a fraction of youth in box B). We do this because we can only attribute conversions (to testers) among youth in box B (Figure 4.3) to strategies recommended by HEALER and DOSIM (or the DC baseline). For example, non-PLs in box D who convert to testers (due to some exogenous reasons) cannot be attributed to HEALER or DOSIM's strategies (as they converted to testers *without* getting HIV information).

Study details. Table 4.1 shows details of the pilot studies. It shows that the three pilots had fairly similar conditions, (1) all three pilots recruited ~60 homeless youth; (2) peer leader training was done on 17–20% of these youth, which is recommended in social sciences literature [4]; and (3) retention rates of youth (i.e., percentage of youth showing up for post-intervention surveys) were fairly similar (~70%) in all three pilots. This figure also shows that peer leaders provided information about 13 uncertain friendships on average in every intervention stage (across all three pilot studies), which validates HEALER and DOSIM's assumption that peer leaders provide *observations* about friendships [6, 7].

Information spread. Figure 4.4 compares the information spread achieved by HEALER, DOSIM, and DC in the pilot studies. The x-axis shows the three different intervention strategies and the y-axis shows the percentage of non-PLs to whom information spread (box A + B as a percentage of total number of non–peer leaders in Figure 4.3). This figure shows that PLs chosen by HEALER and DOSIM are able to spread information among ~70% of the non-PLs in the social network by the end of one month. Surprisingly, PLs chosen by DC were only able to inform ~27% of the non-PLs. This result is surprising, as it means that *HEALER and DOSIM's strategies were able to improve over DC's information spread by over 184%*. We now explain reasons behind this significant improvement in information spread achieved by HEALER and DOSIM over DC.

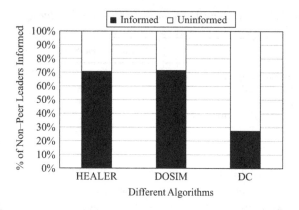

Figure 4.4 Comparison of information spread among non–peer leaders

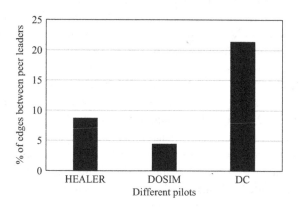

Figure 4.5 Percentage of edges between PLs

Figure 4.5 illustrates a big reason behind DC's poor performance. The x-axis shows different pilots and the y-axis shows what percentage of network edges were *redundant*, i.e., they connected two peer leaders. Such edges are *redundant*, as both its nodes (peer leaders) already have the information. This figure shows that redundant edges accounted for only 8% (and 4%) of the total edges in HEALER and DOSIM pilot studies. On the other hand, 21% of the edges in DC's pilot study were redundant. Thus, DC's strategies pick PLs in a way that creates a lot of redundant edges, whereas HEALER picks PLs that create one-third fewer redundant edges. DOSIM performs best in this regard, by selecting nodes that create the fewest redundant edges (~5 times fewer than DC and half as many as HEALER), and is the key reason behind its good

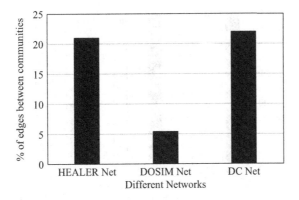

Figure 4.6 Community structure comparison

performance in Figure 4.4. Concomitantly to the presence of redundant edges, HEALER also spreads out its PLs selection across different communities within the homeless youth network, which also aids in information spreading, as discussed later here.

Figure 4.6 shows the community structure of the three pilot studies' social networks. To generate this figure, the three networks were partitioned into communities using METIS [10], an off-the-shelf graph-partitioning tool. We partitioned each network into four different communities (as shown in Figure 4.8) to match the number of PLs (i.e., $K = 4$) chosen in every stage. The x-axis shows the three pilot study networks and the y-axis shows the percentage of edges that go across these four communities. This figure shows that all three networks can be fairly well represented as a set of reasonably disjointed communities, as only 15% of edges (averaged across all three networks) went across the communities. Next, we show how HEALER and DOSIM exploit this community structure by balancing their efforts across these communities simultaneously to achieve greater information spread as compared to DC.

Figure 4.7 illustrates patterns of PL selection (for each stage of intervention) by HEALER, DOSIM, and DC across the four different communities uncovered in Figure 4.6. Recall that each pilot study consisted of three stages of intervention (each with four selected PL). The x-axis shows the three different pilots. The y-axis shows what percentage of communities had a PL chosen from within them. For example, in DC's pilot, the chosen PL covered 50% (i.e., two out of four) communities in the first stage, 75% (i.e., three out of four) communities in the second stage, and so on. This figure shows that HEALER's chosen PLs cover all possible communities (i.e., 100% communities touched)

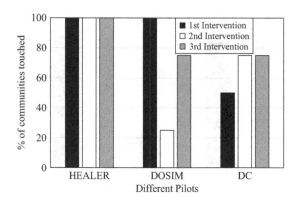

Figure 4.7 Exploiting community structure of real-world networks

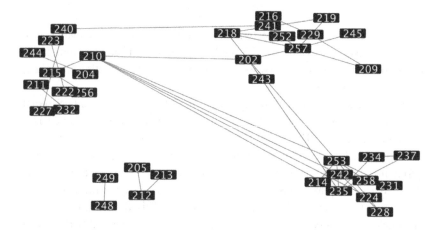

Figure 4.8 Four partitions of DC's pilot network

in the social network in all three stages. On the other hand, DC concentrates its efforts on just a few clusters in the network, leaving approximately 50% communities untouched (on average). Therefore, while HEALER ensures that its chosen PLs covered most real-world communities *in every intervention*, the PLs chosen by DC focused on a single or a few communities in each intervention. This further explains why HEALER is able to achieve greater information spread, as it spreads its efforts across communities, unlike DC. While DOSIM's coverage of communities is similar to DC, it outperforms DC because it generates five times fewer redundant edges than does DC (Figure 4.5).

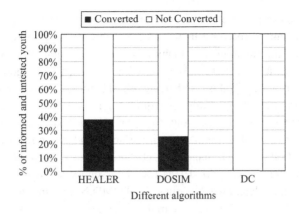

Figure 4.9 Behavior change comparison

Behavior change. Figure 4.9 compares behavior change observed in home-less youth in the three pilot studies. The x-axis shows different intervention strategies, and the y-axis shows the percentage of non-PLs who were untested for HIV at baseline and were informed about HIV during the pilots (i.e., youth in box B in Figure 4.3). This figure shows that PLs chosen by HEALER (and DOSIM) converted 37% (and 25%) of the youth in box B to HIV testers. In contrast, *PLs chosen by DC did not convert any youth in box B to testers.* DC's information spread reached a far smaller fraction of youth (Figure 4.4), and therefore it is unsurprising that DC did not get adequate opportunity to convert anyone of them to testing. This shows that even though HEALER and DOSIM do not explicitly model behavior change in their objective function, the agents' strategies still end up outperforming DC significantly in terms of behavior change.

Challenges Uncovered

This section highlights research and methodological challenges that we uncov-ered while deploying these agent based interventions in the field. While handling these challenges in a principled manner is a subject for future research, we explain some heuristic solutions used to tackle these challenges in the three pilot studies (which may help in addressing the longer-term research challenges).

Research challenges. While conducting interventions, we often encounter an inability to execute actions (i.e., conduct intervention with chosen peer leaders), because a subset of the chosen peer leaders may fail to show up for the intervention (because they may get incarcerated, or find temporary accommodation). Handling this inability to execute actions in a principled manner is a research challenge. Therefore, it is necessary that algorithms and techniques developed for this problem are robust to these errors in execution of intervention strategy. Specifically, we require our algorithms to be able to come up with alternate recommendations for peer leaders, when some homeless youth in their original recommendation are not found. We now explain how HEALER, DOSIM, and DC handle this challenge by using *heuristic solutions*.

Recall that for the first pilot, HEALER's intervention strategies were found by using online planning techniques for POMDPs [6]. Instead of offline computation of the entire policy (strategy), online planning only finds the best POMDP action (i.e., selection of K network nodes) for the current belief state (i.e., probability distribution over state of influence of nodes). Upon reaching a new belief state, online planning again plans for this new belief. This interleaving of planning and execution works to our advantage in this domain, as every time we have a failure that was not anticipated in the POMDP model (i.e., a PL that was chosen in the current POMDP action did not show up), we can recompute a policy quickly by marking these unavailable nodes, so that they are ineligible for future peer leader selection. After recomputing the plan, the new peer leader recommendation is again given to the service providers to conduct the intervention.

For the second pilot study, we augmented DOSIM to account for unavailable nodes by using its computed policy to produce a list of alternates for each peer leader. This alternate list ensures that, unlike HEALER, DOSIM does not require rerunning in the event of a failure. Thus, if a given peer leader does not show up, then study staff work down the list of alternates to find a replacement. DOSIM computes these alternates by maintaining a parameter q_v (for each node v), which gives the probability that node v will show up for the intervention. This q_v parameter enables DOSIM to reason about the inability to execute actions, thereby making DOSIM's policies robust to such failures. To compute the alternate for v, we *condition* on the following event σ_v: node v fails to show up (i.e., set $q_v = 0$), while every other peer leader u shows up with probability q_u. Conditioned on this event σ_v, we find the node that maximizes the *conditional* marginal gain in influence spread, and use it as the alternate for node v. Hence, each alternate is selected in a manner that is robust with respect to possible failures on other peer leader nodes. Finally, in the DC pilot, in case of a failure, the node with the next highest degree is chosen as a peer leader.

Methodological challenges. A methodological challenge was to ensure a fair comparison of the performance of different agents in the field. In the real

Table 4.2. *Similarity of social networks in different pilot studies*

	HEALER	DOSIM	DC
Network Diameter	8	8	7
Network Density	0.079	0.059	0.062
Avg. Clustering Coefficient	0.397	0.195	0.229
Avg. Path Length	3.38	3.15	3.03
Modularity	0.568	0.568	0.602

world, HEALER, DOSIM, and DC could not be tested on the same network, as once we disseminate HIV messages in one network as part of one pilot study, fewer youth are unaware about HIV (or uninfluenced) for the remaining pilots. Therefore, each agent (HEALER, DOSIM, or DC) is tested in a different pilot study with a different social network (possibly with a different structure). Since HEALER's, DOSIM's, and DC's performances are not compared on the same network, it is important to ensure that HEALER and DOSIM's superior performance (observed in Figure 4.4) is not due to differences in network structure or any extraneous factors.

First, we compare several well-known graph metrics for the three distinct pilot study social networks. Table 4.2 shows that most metrics are similar on all three networks, which establishes that the social networks generated in the three pilot studies were structurally similar. This suggests that comparison results would not have been very different had all three algorithms been tested on the same network. Next, we attempt to show that HEALER and DOSIM's superior performance (Figure 4.4) was not due to extraneous factors.

Figure 4.10 compares information spread achieved by PLs in the actual pilot studies with that achieved by the same PLs in simulation. The simulation (averaged over 50 runs) was done with propagation probability set to $p_e = 0.6$ in *our influence model*. The x-axis shows the different pilots and the y-axis shows the percentage of non-PLs informed in the pilot study networks. First, this figure shows that information spread in the simulation closely mirrors pilot study results in the HEALER's and DC's pilots ($\sim$10% difference), whereas it differs greatly in the DOSIM's pilot. This shows that using $p_e = 0.6$ as the propagation probability modeled the real-world process of influence spread in the HEALER's and DC's pilot study network fairly well, whereas it was not a good model for the DOSIM's pilot network. This further suggests that information spread achieved in the real world (at least in HEALER's and DC's pilot studies) was indeed due to the respective strategies used, and

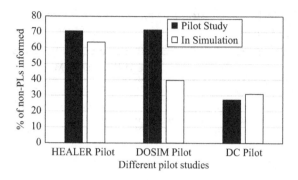

Figure 4.10 Simulation of information spread

not some extraneous factors. In other words, DC's poor performance may not be attributed to some real-world external factors at play, since its poor performance is mimicked in simulation results (which are insulated from real-world external factors) as well. Similarly, HEALER's superior performance may not be attributed to external factors working in its favor, for the same reason.

On the other hand, since DOSIM's performance in the pilot study does not mirror simulation results in Figure 4.10, it suggests the role of some external factors, which were not considered in our models. However, the comparison of simulation results in this figure is statistically significant (p-$value = 9.43E - 12$), which shows that even if DOSIM's performance in the pilot study matched its simulation results, i.e., even if DOSIM achieved only ~ 40% information spread in its pilot study (as opposed to the 70% spread that it actually achieved), it would still outperform DC by ~ 33%.

Having established that DC's poor performance in the field was not due to any external factors, we now show that it also was not tied to some peculiar property/structure of the network used in its pilot study. Figure 4.11 compares information spread achieved by different agents (in simulation over 50 runs) when each agent was run on DC's pilot study network. Again, the simulation was done using $p_e = 0.6$ as propagation probability, which was found to be a reasonable model for real-world influence spread in DC's network (see Figure 4.10). The x-axis in Figure 4.11 shows different algorithms being run on DC's pilot study network (in simulation). The y-axis shows the percentage of non-PLs informed. This figure shows that even on DC's pilot study network, HEALER (and DOSIM) outperform DC in simulation by ~ 53% (and 76%) ($p - value = 9.842E - 31$), thereby establishing that HEALER's and DOSIM's

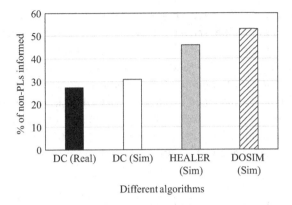

Figure 4.11 Comparison on the DC's network

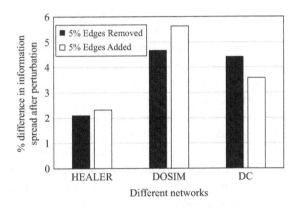

Figure 4.12 Comparison on perturbed networks

improvement over DC was not due to specific properties of the networks in
their pilot studies, i.e., HEALER's and DOSIM's superior performances may
not be attributed to specific properties of networks (in their pilot studies)
working in their favor. In other words, this shows that DC's poor performance
may not be attributed to peculiarities in its network structure working against
it, as otherwise this peculiarity should have affected HEALER's and DOSIM's
performances as well, when they are run on DC's pilot study network (which
does not happen as shown in Figure 4.11).

Figure 4.12 shows information spread achieved by PLs (chosen in the pilot
studies) in simulation (50 runs), averaged across 30 different networks, which
were generated by perturbation of the three pilot study networks. The x-axis

shows the networks that were perturbed. The y-axis shows the percentage difference in information spread achieved on the perturbed networks, in comparison with the unperturbed network. For example, adding 5% edges randomly to HEALER's pilot study network results in only ~2% difference (*p-value* = 1.16E − 08) in information spread (averaged across 30 perturbed networks). These results support the view that HEALER's, DOSIM's, and DC's performances are not due to their pilot study networks being on the knife's edge in terms of specific peculiarities. Thus, HEALER and DOSIM outperform DC on a variety of slightly perturbed networks as well.

Conclusion, Limitations, and Lessons Learned

This chapter illustrates challenges faced in transitioning agents from an emerging phase in the lab to a deployed application in the field. It presents first-of-its-kind results from three real-world pilot studies, involving 173 homeless youth in an American city. Conducting these pilot studies underlined their importance in this transition process: *they are crucial milestones in the arduous journey of an agent from an emerging phase in the lab, to a deployed application in the field*. The pilot studies helped in answering several questions that were raised in the first section of this chapter. First, we learned that peer-leader-based interventions are indeed successful in spreading information about HIV through a homeless youth social network (as seen in Figure 4.4). Moreover, we learned that peer leaders are very adept at providing lots of information about newer friendships in the social network (Table 4.1), which helps software agents refine their future strategies.

   These pilot studies also helped establish the superiority (and hence, their need) of HEALER and DOSIM – we are using complex agents (involving POMDPs and robust optimization), and they outperform DC (the modus operandi of conducting peer-led interventions) by 184% (Table 4.1, Figure 4.9). The pilot studies also helped us gain a deeper understanding of how HEALER and DOSIM beat DC (shown in Figures 4.5–4.7) – by minimizing redundant edges and exploiting community structure of real-world networks. Out of HEALER and DOSIM, the pilot tests do not reveal a significant difference in terms of either information spread or behavior change (Table 4.1, Figure 4.9). Thus, carrying either of them forward would lead to significant improvement over the current state-of-the-art techniques for conducting peer-leader-based interventions. However, DOSIM runs significantly faster than HEALER (~40times), and thus is more beneficial in time-constrained settings [7].

These pilot studies also helped uncover several key challenges (e.g., inability to execute actions, estimating propagation probabilities), which were tackled in the pilot studies using heuristic solutions. However, handling these challenges in a principled manner is a subject for future research. Thus, while these pilot studies opened the door to future deployment of these agents in the field (by providing positive results about the performance of HEALER and DOSIM), they also revealed some challenges that need to be resolved convincingly before these agents can be deployed.

As with any pilot study, some limitations must be acknowledged. The first is that we have a relatively small sample size. While we can demonstrate impressive effect size with these results, we cannot say that these results are statistically significant. Second, we must be cautious about the generalizability of this work. To the extent that homeless populations differ across urban, suburban, and rural settings, this intervention may or may not be effective outside of urban populations of homeless youth. It would also be valuable to include a second control group in which no intervention is delivered to assess the impact of repeated observations of homeless youth with respect to HIV testing and communication. These limitations, however, are typical of many intervention development pilot studies. Despite these limitations, we are very excited and encouraged by these results. Our community partners are likewise excited. At the time of writing this chapter, we have just begun to enroll youth into a large-scale study to establish statistical significance and the efficacy of this intervention model.

Acknowledgments

This research was supported by MURI Grant W911NF-11-1-0332 & NIMH Grant R01-MH093336.

References

[1] M. Jain, B. An, and M. Tambe. An overview of recent application trends at the AAMAS conference: Security, sustainability and safety. *AI Magazine*, 33(3):14, 2012.

[2] N. H. Council. HIV/AIDS among persons experiencing homelessness: Risk factors, predictors of testing, and promising testing strategies. www.nhchc.org/wp-content/uploads/2011/09/InFocus_Dec2012.pdf, Dec. 2012.

[3] CDC. HIV Surveillance Report. www.cdc.gov/hiv/pdf/g-l/hiv_surveillance_report_vol_25.pdf, Mar. 2013.

[4] E. Rice. The positive role of social networks and social networking technology in the condom-using behaviors of homeless young people. *Public Health Reports*, 125(4):588, 2010.

[5] E. Rice, E. Tulbert, J. Cederbaum, A. B. Adhikari, and N. G. Milburn. Mobilizing homeless youth for HIV prevention: A social network analysis of the acceptability of a face-to-face and online social networking intervention. *Health Education Research*, 27(2):226, 2012.

[6] A. Yadav, H. Chan, A. X. Jiang, H. Xu, E. Rice, and M. Tambe. Using social networks to aid homeless shelters: Dynamic influence maximization under uncertainty. In *International Conference on Autonomous Agents and Multiagent Systems (AAMAS)*, 2016.

[7] B. Wilder, A. Yadav, N. Immorlica, E. Rice, and M. Tambe. Uncharted but not uninfluenced: Influence maximization with an uncertain network. In *International Conference on Autonomous Agents and Multiagent Systems (AAMAS)*, 2017.

[8] T. W. Valente. Network interventions. *Science*, 337(6090):49–53, 2012.

[9] M. Kim and J. Leskovec. The network completion problem: Inferring missing nodes and edges in networks. In *Proceedings of the SIAM Conference on Data Mining*. SIAM, 2011.

[10] D. LaSalle and G. Karypis. Multi-threaded graph partitioning. In *Parallel & Distributed Processing (IPDPS), 2013 IEEE 27th International Symposium on Parallel and Distributed Processing*, pages 225–236. IEEE, 2013.

5

Influence Maximization with Unknown Network Structure

Bryan Wilder, Nicole Immorlica, Eric Rice, and Milind Tambe

Introduction

In contexts ranging from health to international development, practitioners have used the social network of their target population to spread information and change behavior. The challenge is to identify the most influential people. While previous work has delivered computationally efficient algorithms for this *influence maximization* problem [1–3], this work assumes that the social network is given explicitly as input. However, in many real-world domains, the network is not initially known and must be gathered via laborious field observations. For example, collecting network data from vulnerable populations such as homeless youth, while crucial for health interventions, requires significant time spent gathering field observations [4]. Social media data are often unavailable when access to technology is limited, for instance in developing countries or with vulnerable populations. Even when such data are available, it often includes many weak links that are not effective at spreading influence [5]. For instance, a person may have hundreds of Facebook friends whom they barely know. In principle, the entire network could be reconstructed via surveys, and then existing influence maximization algorithms applied. However, exhaustive surveys are very labor-intensive and often considered impractical [6]. For influence maximization to be relevant to many real-world problems, it must contend with limited *information* about the network, not just limited *computation*.

The major informational restriction is the number of nodes that may be surveyed to explore the network. Thus, a key question is: *How can we find influential nodes with a small number of queries?* Existing fieldwork uses heuristics, such as sampling some percentage of the nodes and asking them to nominate influencers [6]. We formalize this problem as *exploratory influence maximization* and seek a principled algorithmic solution, i.e., an algorithm that makes a small number of queries and returns a set of seed nodes that are approximately as influential as the globally optimal seed set. To the best of our knowledge, no previous work directly addresses this question from an algorithmic perspective (we survey the closest work in the third section).

Real-world networks often have strong *community* structure, where nodes form tightly connected subgroups that are only weakly connected to the rest of the network [7, 8]. Consequently, influence mostly propagates locally. Community structure has been used to develop computationally efficient influence maximization algorithms [9, 10]. Here, we use it to design a highly information-efficient algorithm. We make three contributions. *First*, we introduce exploratory influence maximization and show that it is intractable for general graphs. *Second*, we present the ARISEN algorithm, which exploits community structure to find influential nodes. *Third*, experiments on both synthetic and real networks verify ARISEN's performance.

Exploratory Influence Maximization

As a motivating example, consider a homeless youth drop-in center that wishes to spread HIV prevention information [4]. It would try to select the most influential peer leaders to spread information, but their social network is not initially known. Constructing the network requires a laborious survey [4]. Our motivation is to mitigate this effort by querying only a few youth. Such queries require much less time than the day-long training peer leaders receive. We now formalize this problem.

Influence maximization: The influence maximization problem [11] starts with a graph $G = (V, E)$, where $|V| = n$ and $|E| = m$. We assume that G is undirected; social links are typically reciprocal [12]. An influencer selects K seed nodes, aiming to maximize the expected size of the resulting influence cascade. We assume that influence propagates according to the independent cascade model (ICM), the most prevalent model in the literature. Initially, all nodes are inactive except for the seeds. When a node activates, it independently activates each of its neighbors with probability q. q is typically assumed to be the same for all edges [1, 11, 13]. Let $f(S)$ denote the expected number of activated nodes with seed set $S \subseteq V$. The objective is to compute $\arg\max_{|S| \leq K} f(S)$.

Local information: The edge set E is not initially known. Instead, the algorithm explores portions of the graph using local operations. We use the popular "Jump-Crawl" model [14], where the algorithm may either jump to a uniformly random node or crawl along an edge from an already surveyed node to one of its neighbors. When visited, a node reveals all of its edges. We say that the *query cost* of an algorithm is the total number of nodes visited using either operation. Our goal is to find influential nodes with a query cost that is much less than n, the total number of nodes.

Stochastic Block Model (SBM): In our formal analysis, we assume that the graph is drawn from the SBM. The SBM originated in sociology [15] and lately has been intensively studied in computer science and statistics (see e.g., [16–18]). In the SBM, the network is partitioned into disjoint communities $C_1 \ldots C_L$. Each within-community edge is present independently with probability p_w and each between-community edge is present independently with probability p_b. Recall that the Erdős-Rényi random graph $\mathcal{G}(n, p)$ is the graph on n nodes where every edge is independently present with probability p. In the SBM, community C_i is internally drawn as $\mathcal{G}(|C_i|, p_w)$ with additional random edges to other communities. While the SBM is a simplified model, our experimental results show that ARISEN also performs well on real-world graphs. ARISEN takes as input the parameters n, p_w, and p_b, but is not given any prior information about the realized draw of the network. It is reasonable to assume that the model parameters are known, since they can be estimated using existing network data from a similar population (in our experiments, we show that this approach works well).

Objective: We compare to the globally optimal solution, i.e, the best performance if the entire network were known. Let $f_E(S)$ give the expected number of nodes influenced by seed set S when the set of realized edges are E. Let $\mathcal{A}(E)$ be the (possibly random) seed set containing our algorithm's selections given edge set E. Let OPT be the expected value of the globally optimal solution that seeds K nodes. We aim for an algorithm that maximizes the value $\mathbb{E}[f_E(\mathcal{A}(E))]/OPT$, where the expectation is over the randomness in the graph, the algorithm's choices, and the ICM.

Related Work

First, Yadav et al. [13] and Wilder et al. [19] studied dynamic influence maximization over a series of rounds. Some edges are "uncertain" and are only present with some probability; the algorithm can gain information about these edges in each round. However, most edges are known in advance. By contrast, our work does not require *any* known edges. Mihara et al. [20] also consider influence maximization over a series of rounds, but in their work the network is initially unknown. In each round, the algorithm makes some queries, selects some seed nodes, and observes all of the nodes that are activated by its chosen seeds. The ability to observe activated nodes makes our problem incomparable with theirs, because activations can reveal a great deal about the network and give the algorithm information that even the global optimizer does not have (their benchmark does not use the activations). Further, activations are unobservable in many domains (e.g., medical ones) for privacy and legal reasons. Carpentier and Valko [21] study a bandit setting where the algorithm does not know the network but observes the number of activations at each round. However, in applications of interest (e.g., HIV prevention) it is more feasible to gather some network data in advance than to conduct many low-reward trial campaigns.

Another line of work concerns local graph algorithms, where a local algorithm only uses the neighborhoods around individual nodes. Borgs, Brautbar, Chayes and Lucier [22] study local algorithms for finding the root node in a preferential attachment graph and for constructing a minimum dominating set. Other work, including Bressen et al. [23] and Borgs et al. [24], aims to find nodes with high PageRank using local queries. These algorithms are not suitable for our problem, since a great deal of previous work has observed that picking high PageRank nodes as seeds can prove highly suboptimal for influence maximization [1, 2, 25]. Essentially, PageRank identifies a set of nodes that are *individually* central, while influence maximization aims to find a set of nodes that are *collectively* best at diffusing information. We also emphasize that our technical approach is entirely distinct from work on PageRank. Lastly, Alon et al. [26] attempt to infer a ground truth from the opinions of agents with an unknown social network, a different task than influence maximization with correspondingly distinct techniques.

The ARISEN Algorithm

We now introduce our main contribution, the ARISEN algorithm (*Approximating with Random walks to Influence a Socially Explored Network*); see Figure 5.1. The idea behind ARISEN (Algorithm 1) is to sample a set of T random nodes $\{v_1 \ldots v_T\}$ from G and explore a small subgraph H_i around each v_i by taking R steps of a random walk (Lines 1–3). R, T and B (explained later) are inputs. Intuitively, T should be greater than K (the number of seeds) so we can be sure of sampling each of the largest K communities. The subgraphs H_i

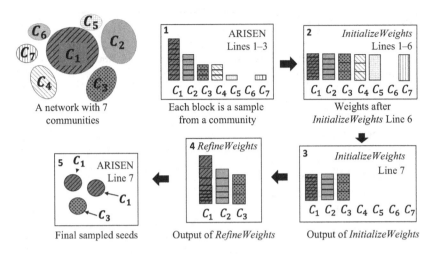

Figure 5.1 Example run of ARISEN with $K = 3$ (explained further in text). Each block is one sample, with current weight proportional to its height (e.g., in Frame 2, C_5 has one sample with very high weight).

Algorithm 1 ARISEN

Require: R, T, B, K, n, p_w, p_b
 1: **for** $i = 1...T$ **do**
 2:     Sample v_i uniformly
          random from G.
 3:     $H_i = R$ nodes on a
          random walk from v_i.
 4: **end for**
 5: $w = $ INITIALIZE WEIGHTS
 6: $w' = $ REFINE WEIGHTS(w)
 7: Sample $u_1...u_K \overset{iid}{\sim} w'$
 8: **return** $u_1...u_K$

---

are used to construct a weight vector w where w_i gives the weight associated with v_i (Lines 5–6). The algorithm then independently samples each seed from $\{v_1 ... v_T\}$ with probability proportional to w (Line 7).

The challenge is to construct weights w that balance two opposing goals. First, we would oftentimes like to disperse the seed nodes throughout the network. For instance, if each community has equal size, we would like to seed K different communities. Second, we would other times like to place

---

Algorithm 2 InitializeWeights

1: **for** $i = 1...T$ **do**
2:     Form H'_i by discarding the first B nodes of H_i and keeping each remaining node v_j w.p. $\frac{1}{d(v_j)}$
3:     $\hat{d} = \frac{1}{R} \sum_{u \in H'_i} d(u)$
4:     $\hat{S}_i = \frac{\hat{d} - p_b n}{p_w - p_b}$
5: **end for**
6: $w_j = \frac{n}{\hat{S}_j T}$.
7: $\tau = \max\{\hat{S}_j | \sum_{\{i | \hat{S}_i \geq \hat{S}_j\}} w_i \geq K\}$
8: For any j with $\hat{S}_j < \tau$, set $w_j = 0$.
9: **return** w, H

Algorithm 3 RefineWeights

1: **for** $i = 1...T$ **do**
2:     $v_i = \arg\max_{v \in H_i} f(v, H_i)$
3:     $w'_i = \frac{n \beta (\hat{S}_i)^2}{T f(s_i, H_i)}$
4: **end for**
5: **sort** w' in increasing order
6: **for** $i = 1...T$ **do**
7:     **while** EstVal$(2w'_i, w_{-i}) >$ EstVal(w') **do**
8:        $w'_i = 2w'_i$
9:     **end while**
10:     $w'_i =$ BinarySearch$(w'_i, 2w'_i)$
11: **end for**
12: **return** w'

---

more seeds in large communities. For instance, if one community has 10,000 nodes and others have only 100 nodes each, we should seed the large community more. ARISEN navigates this trade-off with the following ingredients (Algorithm 2). First, INITIALIZEWEIGHTS uses the random walk around each v_i to estimate the size of the community that v_i lies in (see next page "Initial Weights"). From these estimates it constructs a w that, in expectation, seeds the largest K communities once each. Second, REFINEWEIGHTS (See "Refining the Weights" later in the chapter) tests if using a w' that puts more weight on large communities would increase the expected influence. The main novelty is to carry out these steps using purely local information, since we will not generally be able to tell which of the v_i are in the same community.

We first formalize the objective that ARISEN optimizes, which is a lower bound on its true influence. Let $f(X, C_i)$ denote the influence of seed set X on the subgraph C_i and $g(X) = \sum_{i=1}^{L} f(X, C_i)$, i.e., the influence spread within each community without considering between-community edges. ARISEN aims to optimize $\mathbb{E}[g(X)]$. Note that $f(X, G) \geq g(X)$ always holds. When p_b is low and little influence spreads between communities (which is the case that we study), g is a good proxy for the true influence. We now explain ARISEN in detail, and how it optimizes the surrogate objective g.

Initial weights

In the SBM, each community C_i has expected average degree $d_i = |C_i|p_w + (n - |C_i|)p_b$. Solving for $|C_i|$, we can estimate the size of the community from its average degree (Algorithm 2, Lines 3–4). INITIALIZEWEIGHTS uses the nodes sampled in the random walk (after a burn-in period B) to estimate d_i. Since a random walk is biased toward high degree nodes, we use rejection sampling (Line 2) to obtain an unbiased estimate. In order to choose seed nodes using these estimates, a natural idea would be to choose the K samples with the largest estimated size. However, this fails because large communities are sampled more often and will be seeded many times, which is redundant. For example, in Figure 5.1, placing all of the seeds in C_1 would be suboptimal compared to also seeding C_2. Complicating matters, the estimated sizes are only approximate, which rules out many simple solutions. One solution is to weight each sample *inversely* to its size (Line 6), and then sample seeds with probability proportional to the weights. This evens out the sampling bias toward large communities. Using a weighted sampling scheme gives us a principled way to prioritize samples and facilitates later steps where we tune the weights to improve performance. In the example in Figure 5.1, all communities have total weight of 1 after this inverse weighting (Frame 2).

Next, the weights are truncated so that only the largest K communities receive nonzero weight (Line 7). After this step, the largest K communities have weight 1 and all smaller communities have weight 0 (at least approximately, due to sampling errors). For example, Frame 3 of Figure 5.1 shows that only C_1, C_2 and C_3 have nonzero weight. We draw K seeds; in each draw, each of the top K communities is seeded with probability approximately $\frac{1}{K}$. Thus, the cumulative probability that each is seeded is nearly $1 - (1 - \frac{1}{K})^K \geq 1 - 1/e$.

Refining the weights

The initial weights suffice to obtain the approximation guarantee proved later here and are the best possible for some networks. However, they are overly pessimistic in other cases, such as when some communities are much larger than others. In such cases, it would be better to focus more seed nodes on large communities. We now outline REFINEWEIGHTS, which tunes the weights produced by INITIALIZEWEIGHTS to account for such scenarios. In essence, REFINEWEIGHTS tries to exploit easier cases where some communities are much larger than others by producing new weights w'.

REFINEWEIGHTS (Algorithm 3) starts in Line 2 by defining v_i to be the most influential node in the sampled subgraph H_i (instead of the random starting node). Line 3 then sets w'_i according to v_i's influence instead of the estimated size of its community. Asymptotically, the two weighting schemes are identical, but using influence spread instead of size is more accurate for small networks. Lines 5–11 successively modify each element of w. Starting with the weights corresponding to the largest communities, REFINEWEIGHTS asks whether g would be increased by doubling the w_i under consideration (Line 7). If yes, we set $w_i = 2w_i$ and ask if it can be doubled again. If no, REFINEWEIGHTS performs a binary search between w_i and $2w_i$ to find the best setting (Line 10). Then it moves on to the weight corresponding to the next smallest community. In the example in Figure 5.1, Frame 4 shows that the weights of samples from C_1 and C_2 have been increased. Each change is made only if it improves g, so we have:

Proposition 5.0.1 *Let w the output of INITIALIZEWEIGHTS and w' be the output of REFINEWEIGHTS. Then, $\mathbb{E}_{X \sim w'}[g(X)] \geq \mathbb{E}_{X \sim w}[g(X)]$.*

The key difficulty is determining if each modification increases g. In the ESTVAL procedure, we provide a way to estimate g using only local knowledge: We give the main idea here. Take any seed set X. Note that the influence within each C_i depends only on nodes in $X \cap C_i$, which we write as X_{C_i}. So, g can be rewritten as $g(X) = \sum_{i=1}^{L} \mathbb{E}[f(X_{C_i}, C_i)]$. If we knew X_{C_i}, then we could calculate $\mathbb{E}[f(X_{C_i}, C_i)]$ by simulating draws from the SBM for the unobserved portions of C_i. Concretely, let H_i be the subgraph observed in community C_i, with estimated size $\hat{S}_i$. We simulate the rest of C_i by adding $\hat{S}_i - |H_i|$ new nodes, with edges between them and H_i randomly generated from the SBM. This is sufficient to choose the best seed within H_i, as in Line 2. For Line 7, we need to estimate g. The obstacle is not knowing which of the $v_1 \dots v_T$ lie in the same community (since a node will contribute less influence if there is another seed from the same community). However, we do know (approximately) how

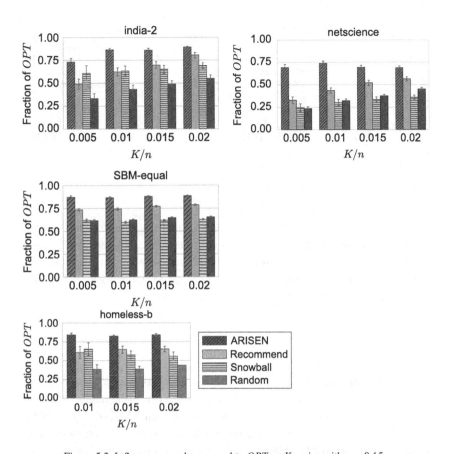

Figure 5.2 Influence spread compared to *OPT* as *K* varies with *q* = 0.15.

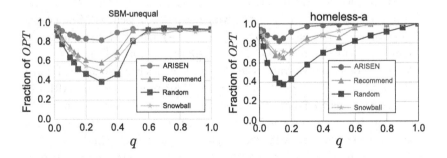

Figure 5.3 Influence compared to *OPT* as *q* varies.

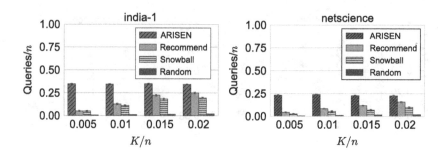

Figure 5.4   Query complexity as K varies.

many other times each community is sampled, and the (approximate) weight that those samples will receive, so g can be estimated by averaging some careful simulations. While runtime is not our focus, we note that via a standard Hoeffding bound (see Kempe et al. [27]), $O(\frac{n^2}{\epsilon^2} \log \frac{1}{\epsilon})$ simulations per EstVal call guarantee multiplicative error ϵ with high probability.

Experiments

We now present experiments on an array of data sets. First, *homeless*: two networks (a and b) gathered from the social network of homeless youth in Los Angeles and used to study HIV prevention with 150–200 nodes each. Second, *india*: three networks of the household-level social contacts of villages in rural India, gathered by Banerjee et al. [28] to study diffusion of information about microfinance programs, with 250–350 nodes each. Third, *netscience*[1]: a collaboration network of network science researchers with 1,461 nodes. Fourth, *SBM*: synthetic SBM graphs with 1,000 nodes each. SBM-equal has 10 communities of equal size ($p_w = \frac{4}{n}$, $p_b = \frac{0.2}{n}$) and SBM-unequal has 10 communities with size ranging from $\frac{1}{3}n$ to $\frac{1}{30}n$ ($p_w = \frac{6}{n}$, $p_b = \frac{0.2}{n}$).

We focus on networks with about 100–1,000 nodes because this is the size of real-world social groups of interest to us. We present results for ARISEN and three benchmarks. First, *random*, which simply selects K nodes uniformly at random. Second, *recommend*, which for each of the K nodes first queries a random node and then seeds their highest-degree friend. Third, *snowball*, which starts from a random node and seeds that node's highest-degree neighbor. It then seeds the highest-degree neighbor of the first seed, and so

---

[1]   www-personal.umich.edu/mejn/netdata/

on. We compare to *recommend* and *snowball* because these are the most common methods used in the field [6]. For each real network, p_w and p_b are estimated from a different network in the same category (for *netscience*, we use another collaboration network, astro-ph[2]). For the SBM data sets, we use another network from the same distribution. We present a cross-section of results across the data sets, but the general trends are the same for all networks.

Our first set of results measures the influence spread of each algorithm against the optimal value. We approximate the optimal value using TIM [3], a state-of-the-art influence maximization algorithm, run on the full network. As in previous work [1], we focus on when K is a small fraction of n. Figure 5.3 shows results as q is varied with $K = 0.01 \cdot n$. Each point gives the fraction of *OPT* achieved for that setting of q. For example, the point at $q = 0.2$ indicates that ARISEN obtained a value of $0.8 \cdot OPT$. Each point averages over 50 runs. We see that ARISEN substantially outperforms all baselines, particularly when q is low. All differences between algorithms are statistically significant (t-test, $p < 10^{-7}$). Previous work [1] has also observed that when q is very high, influence maximization is sufficiently easy that nearly any algorithm performs well. Thus, Figure 5.2 presents results where K is varied with $q = 0.15$ fixed (since low q is when the problem is hard). We see that ARISEN uniformly outperforms the baselines, particularly when K is small. As K becomes larger, the baselines improve (again because the problem becomes easier). However, they are still outperformed by ARISEN.

Figure 5.4 examines each algorithm's query cost. The supplement lists R and T for every data set and value of K; here we just focus on the total number of queries. ARISEN uses more queries than any of the baselines. However, its query cost is uniformly in the range $0.20 \cdot n - 0.35 \cdot n$, a relatively small portion of the network in absolute terms.

References

[1] Wei Chen, Chi Wang, and Yajun Wang. Scalable influence maximization for prevalent viral marketing in large-scale social networks. In *KDD*, pages 1029–1038. ACM, 2010.

[2] Kyomin Jung, Wooram Heo, and Wei Chen. Irie: Scalable and robust influence maximization in social networks. In *ICDM*, pages 918–923. IEEE, 2012.

[3] Youze Tang, Xiaokui Xiao, and Yanchen Shi. Influence maximization: Near-optimal time complexity meets practical efficiency. In *KDD*. ACM, 2014.

[4] Eric Rice, Eve Tulbert, Julie Cederbaum, Anamika Barman Adhikari, and Norweeta G Milburn. Mobilizing homeless youth for HIV prevention. *Health Education Research*, 27(2):226–236, 2012.

[5] Robert M Bond, Christopher J Fariss, Jason J Jones, Adam DI Kramer, Cameron Marlow, Jaime E Settle, and James H Fowler. A 61-million-person experiment in social influence and political mobilization. *Nature*, 489(7415):295–298, 2012.

[6] Thomas W Valente and Patchareeya Pumpuang. Identifying opinion leaders to promote behavior change. *Health Education & Behavior*, 2007.

[7] Michelle Girvan and Mark EJ Newman. Community structure in social and biological networks. *PNAS*, 99(12):7821–7826, 2002.

[8] Jure Leskovec, Kevin J Lang, Anirban Dasgupta, and Michael W Mahoney. Community structure in large networks: Natural cluster sizes and the absence of large well-defined clusters. *Internet Mathematics*, 6(1):29–123, 2009.

[9] Yi-Cheng Chen, Wen-Yuan Zhu, Wen-Chih Peng, Wang-Chien Lee, and Suh-Yin Lee. CIM: community-based influence maximization in social networks. *ACM Transactions on Intelligent Systems and Technology (TIST)*, 5(2):25, 2014.

[10] Yu Wang, Gao Cong, Guojie Song, and Kunqing Xie. Community-based greedy algorithm for mining top-k influential nodes in mobile social networks. In *KDD*, pages 1039–1048. ACM, 2010.

[11] David Kempe, Jon Kleinberg, and Éva Tardos. Maximizing the spread of influence through a social network. In *KDD*, pages 137–146. ACM, 2003.

[12] Tiziano Squartini, Francesco Picciolo, Franco Ruzzenenti, and Diego Garlaschelli. Reciprocity of weighted networks. *Scientific Reports*, 2012.

[13] Amulya Yadav, Hau Chan, Albert Xin Jiang, Haifeng Xu, Eric Rice, and Milind Tambe. Using social networks to aid homeless shelters: Dynamic influence maximization under uncertainty. In *AAMAS*, pages 740–748, 2016.

[14] Michael Brautbar and Michael J Kearns. Local algorithms for finding interesting individuals in large networks. In *Innovations in Theoretical Computer Science*, pages 188–199, 2010.

[15] Stephen E Fienberg and Stanley S Wasserman. Categorical data analysis of single sociometric relations. *Sociological Methodology*, 12:156–192, 1981.

[16] Emmanuel Abbe and Colin Sandon. Community detection in general stochastic block models: Fundamental limits and efficient algorithms for recovery. In *FOCS*, pages 670–688. IEEE, 2015.

[17] Florent Krzakala, Cristopher Moore, Elchanan Mossel, Joe Neeman, Allan Sly, Lenka Zdeborová, and Pan Zhang. Spectral redemption in clustering sparse networks. *PNAS*, 110(52):20935–20940, 2013.

[18] Elchanan Mossel, Joe Neeman, and Allan Sly. Reconstruction and estimation in the planted partition model. *Probability Theory and Related Fields*, 162(3-4): 431–461, 2015.

[19] Bryan Wilder, Amulya Yadav, Nicole Immorlica, Eric Rice, and Milind Tambe. Uncharted but not uninfluenced: Influence maximization with an uncertain network. In *AAMAS*, pages 740–748, 2017.

[20] Shodai Mihara, Sho Tsugawa, and Hiroyuki Ohsaki. Influence maximization problem for unknown social networks. In *ASONAM*, pages 1539–1546. ACM, 2015.

[21] Alexandra Carpentier and Michal Valko. Revealing graph bandits for maximizing local influence. In *International Conference on Artificial Intelligence and Statistics*, pages 10–18, 2016.

[22] Christian Borgs, Michael Brautbar, Jennifer Chayes, Sanjeev Khanna, and Brendan Lucier. The power of local information in social networks. In *WINE*, pages 406–419. Springer, 2012.

[23] Marco Bressan, Enoch Peserico, and Luca Pretto. The power of local information in pagerank. In *WWW*, pages 179–180. ACM, 2013.

[24] Christian Borgs, Michael Brautbar, Jennifer Chayes, and Shang-Hua Teng. Multiscale matrix sampling and sublinear-time pagerank computation. *Internet Mathematics*, 10(1–2):20–48, 2014.

[25] Masahiro Kimura, Kazumi Saito, Ryohei Nakano, and Hiroshi Motoda. Finding influential nodes in a social network from information diffusion data. In *Social Computing and Behavioral Modeling*, pages 1–8. Springer, 2009.

[26] Noga Alon, Michal Feldman, Omer Lev, and Moshe Tennenholtz. How robust is the wisdom of the crowds? In *IJCAI*, pages 2055–2061, 2015.

[27] David Kempe, Jon M Kleinberg, and Éva Tardos. Maximizing the spread of influence through a social network. *Theory of Computing*, 11(4):105–147, 2015.

[28] Abhijit Banerjee, Arun G Chandrasekhar, Esther Duflo, and Matthew O Jackson. Gossip: Identifying central individuals in a social network. Technical report, National Bureau of Economic Research, 2014.

PART II

6

Maximizing the Spread of Sexual Health Information in a Multimodal Communication Network of Young Black Women

Elizabeth Bondi, Jaih Craddock, Rebecca Funke, Chloe LeGendre, and Vivek Tiwari

Introduction

Young Black women (YBW) between the ages of 18 and 25 have higher rates of HIV than any other age or race and ethnicity group of women (Center for Disease Control and Prevention (CDC), 2016). Social networks of YBW might be considered both protective and risky from a public health perspective, as information about sexual behaviors and sexual health may spread within the communication network to the health benefit or detriment of the network's members. However, there is a dearth of literature on the social networks of YBW, particularly regarding how such social networks can be best leveraged to aid in HIV prevention within such networks. With the current HIV/AIDS priority of decreasing incidence of HIV among high-risk groups, examining ways to leverage such networks is essential.

Research has demonstrated that reduction in HIV rates for various populations can be achieved using methodologies from social network theory. Specifically, peer-led interventions have been used to reduce health risk behaviors in high-risk populations (Convey, Dickson-Gomez, Weeks, & Li, 2010; Davey-Rothwell, Tobin,Yang, Sun, & Latkin, 2011; Jennings, Howard, & Perotte, 2014; Mahat, Scoloveno, De Leon, & Frenkel, 2008; McKirnan, Tolou-Shams, & Courtenay-Quirk, 2010; O'Grady, Wilson, & Harman, 2009). Interventions that use peer leaders in network-oriented HIV intervention programs to endorse changes in risk behaviors accelerate behavioral changes by capitalizing on social influence processes (Kelly et al., 1991; Latkin et al., 1996). Diffusion of Innovation is a theoretical framework that posits that people are more likely to adopt new ideas or behaviors if similar people in their network have either already adopted them or have favorable evaluations of these ideas or behaviors (Rogers, 2010). The theory of Diffusion of

Innovation has been used in social network–based interventions to guide the understanding of how information is spread throughout networks.

Ultimately, our goal is to spread sexual health information throughout networks of YBW. Ideally, the information would reach as many individuals in the networks as possible, increasing the likelihood of a reduction of HIV rates within this higher-risk population. To achieve this goal, as with typical peer-led interventions, key members of a social network would be trained to disseminate sexual health information throughout their networks. More specifically, in our approach, the selected individuals would be taught how to effectively communicate about sexual health using one preferred communication platform (for instance, via text messaging).

In this work, we propose that if information about a given social network is known – including the connectivity between individuals, the modes of communication typically employed across each connection, and whether or not the conversations may include topics related to sex or sexual health – we can maximize the spread of information in the network when constrained by limited resources for intervention and training. For example, if we observe some level of communication about sexual health via texting, we might thus consider that this mode of communication might be effective to use for disseminating information pertinent to HIV prevention throughout the network of YBW. Therefore, an effective intervention for information diffusion could perhaps involve training some small subset of the network on how to effectively spread information about sexual health via text messaging specifically.

The communication networks formed by YBW are particularly complex, as such communication is known to be multimodal – composed of a variety of communication methods including in-person conversations, phone calls, and many social media– and mobile phone–based platforms. Communication between YBW and their social network members (SNMs) via social media is becoming normalized due to a rapidly changing social media landscape (Noar & Willoughby, 2012). Black youth and young adults are using social media websites and apps at higher rates than any other American group (Lenhart, 2015; Smith, 2014). Considering that social media is increasingly becoming the mode of communication for many Black young adults, it is essential to understand through what mode (i.e., social media, text message, phone, or in-person) YBW are speaking to their SNMs regarding sexual health, and how these communication networks can be leveraged by social workers to spread information that will benefit the health of the population. Other researchers have examined the possibility of using social network–based peer-led HIV intervention via social media (Young et al., 2014). However, to our knowledge, no HIV intervention studies have considered social networks of YBW, particularly examining the modes of communication used by YBW.

Based on quantitative survey information, we identify four ways that YBW typically communicate with each other about sexual health: in-person (talk), texting (txt), calling on the phone (call), or over social media (soc), including a variety of social media platforms. We present a hypothetical relationship example to demonstrate the potential complexity of a multimodal communication network of YBW, specifically as it relates to sexual health. First, each individual in a social network might currently communicate about sexual health–related topics only with a fraction of the people in her network. Each individual also might only communicate with these people using certain platforms. For instance, take four YBW: individuals denoted as A, B, C, and D. Perhaps A is friends with B, C, and D. Individual A might feel comfortable communicating with B about sexual health via in-person conversation, text message, and social media, but might only talk to C about sexual health via social media. Perhaps, based on the nature of the relationship between A and C and their past interactions, individual A might feel uncomfortable discussing potentially personal or sensitive topics in face-to-face conversation with individual C. Additionally, perhaps A and D do not communicate about sexual health on *any* platform. The quantitative survey we describe and utilize in this work was designed to elucidate such complexities, which are inherent in the multimodal communication networks of YBW, but even further complicated by the inclusion of potentially sensitive or personal subject matter.

By analyzing the spread of sexual health information over a real network of 73 Los Angeles–based YBW for each different communication modality, we propose to select the best mode of communication to utilize for peer-led interventions for YBW (i.e., choosing among in-person, text message, phone call, or social media–based interventions). We also propose that selecting which individuals should be trained as intervention peer leaders varies depending on the communication mode selected for the intervention, which is fundamental to understanding how these network structures should be best used to effectively spread sexual health and HIV prevention information.

In summary, in order to achieve the goal of spreading information to the greatest number of individuals within a given communication network, we propose that one must answer two questions: (1) what mode of communication will be best for a given network, and (2) given this best communication mode, which individuals should be trained as a part of the intervention? To answer these questions, a social worker could employ the approach of Valente and Pumpuang (2007), where individuals are selected based on having high "degree centrality," or the most ties with other individuals in the network.

This approach, however, does not consider that these "popular" individuals may share many connections, and as a result, the network model is not accurate (Yadav et al., 2015; Cohen, Delling, Pajor, & Werneck, 2014). Instead, we propose to analyze one real-world multimodal communication network using tools and techniques developed by computer science researchers. More specifically, we model this information diffusion problem as one of "maximum influence."

One frequent goal of computer scientists is to determine how to most "optimally" perform some given task. For instance, there are numerous situations where a community is faced with a limited budget, and its members or leadership must decide how to best allocate resources. A computer scientist would try to: (1) find out if such an optimal allocation exists; (2) find this optimal allocation; or, alternatively, if this task is impossible or difficult (i.e., the problem-solving approach is too slow to be useful for impactful decision-making), (3) find a "good" way of approximating the optimal solution. This approach can be applied to the HIV prevention domain, where interventionists will have a limited budget to spend on training peer leaders about sexual health but ultimately want the majority of a network to adopt a new behavior to prevent HIV. Thus, interventionists will try to select for training the "k" best people in the network that can spread information to the most network members, where k can be any number of individuals (however many the training budget will allow).

Because maximizing the information spread throughout a network involves "optimizing" for the dissemination of knowledge, this is a tantalizing question for computer scientists. In fact, much research has focused on modeling and optimizing the spread of information throughout social networks. In computer science, the problem of finding the k most influential people in a network is referred to as the "maximum influence problem" (Kempe, Kleinberg, & Tardos, 2003). Note that finding the "k most influential people" implies that there exists no other subset of k people in the network such that if this other group receives the same intervention training, that information will be spread to more network members as compared with the originally selected k individuals. Despite the difficulty of the problem, computer scientists studying network effects have developed computational approaches for solving the maximum influence problem, which we use in this work to propose best practices for peer leader–based network interventions in the presence of multimodal communication.

Using techniques from computer science to optimize the spread of information throughout a network has had proven success in HIV prevention. For example, a heuristic algorithm, HEALER, selects k homeless youth to be trained in HIV prevention. In a real-world deployment of HEALER, they found that using HEALER to select the peer leaders allowed for about 70% of the non–peer leader homeless youth to receive the message about HIV prevention, whereas the method typically used by officials at shelters allowed for 27%. Not only did more individuals learn more about HIV prevention,? nearly 37% of the non–peer leader participants got tested for HIV, whereas no participants got tested when using the typical method (Yadav et al., 2017).

In this chapter, we first describe the survey methodology used to collect the real-world YBW network data set. Then, we describe the mathematical models of the communication network and its information diffusion process. As the maximum influence problem is difficult, we describe some potential simplifying assumptions that we can make to solve the problem efficiently, and we evaluate the efficacy of multimodal and single communication mode intervention trainings under these assumptions. From the results of our simulation experiments using the real-world survey data, we propose a network-based intervention approach where the best communication modality depends on the underlying network structure, and peer leaders are selected depending on the training modality.

Methods

YBW Quantitative Network Survey – Data Collection

As described in the preceding section, we evaluate the spread of information using a real-world quantitative survey data set designed to probe the members of a social network for their communication habits, both generally and in the domain of sexuality and sexual health–related behaviors. The social network structure was developed by surveying 78 YBW aged 18 to 25 and examining sexual health communication at the dyadic level between YBW, though 5 YBW reported no connections with other participants in the study and were not included in analysis. Recruitment was performed using respondent-driven sampling performed from May 2016 to August 2016. Five seeds (initial participants) were recruited from two beauty salons in Los Angeles County. Qualifications for seed participation were age range (18–25 years, inclusive), self-identification as a Black or African American woman, and residence in the Los Angeles County area. During the survey, participants were incentivized to invite at least three other YBW (i.e., friends, family, or acquaintances) via text message to participate in the study, with referred individuals considered eligible based on identical screening requirements. Eligible study participants each answered the same survey and received $25 for completing the study, and an additional $10 for referring at least two other YBW. Informed consent was obtained from all study participants.

Each woman completed both a survey interview and a social network interview. Survey interviews collected demographics, sexual risk behaviors, sexual relationship information, and social media use. Social network interviews asked women to list SNMs to produce a standard egocentric network using an iPad application (Rice, 2010). The social network interview progressed in two stages. First, names and demographic information of all of the participants' network members were collected. Second, questions were asked regarding the types of relationship and communication that participants have with each SNM. The iPad application listed each provided name as an option for each subsequent question, similar to categorical answers of a multiple-choice question. Measures for this study were mode of communication and sex communication. Mode of communication was assessed using two questions: "Who do you talk to [on the phone, via text message, or in person]?" and "Who do you talk with on [Facebook, Instagram, Snapchat, or Twitter]?" These outcomes were binary with 1 equaling a selection and 0 equaling no selection. Sex communication was assessed using the question, "Who do you talk with about sex?" Persons identified as someone the YBW spoke to about sex were coded as 1, and persons not identified were coded as 0.

Mathematically Modeling Information Diffusion in the YBW Network

To examine the spread of information in the real-world network of YBW, we define the abstract model of this network, which enables the application of algorithms used to solve maximum influence problems. The input for a maximum influence problem is a directed graph, $G(N,E,C)$. The set of nodes N is all of the people in the network, where each person is a node. The collection of directed edges, E, includes all edges in the network, where each directed edge is a one-way, person-to-person communication connection. For instance, if nodes u and v communicate, then there may exist at most *two* directed edges connecting them, with these edges denoted $e_{u,v}$ and $e_{v,u}$. In the first edge, labeled $e_{u,v}$, node u communicates to node v, and in the second edge, labeled $e_{v,u}$, node v communicates to node u. Each directed edge will have four associated binary values (txt, talk, call, soc) that denote if the first node communicates *to* the second node about sexual health on each platform. The use of directed edges for the graph G models the directionality of information exchange relating to sexuality and sexual health, which we observed in the real-world network surveyed. As an example, suppose node u provides sexual health information to node v via social media, but node v does not feel comfortable speaking to node u about sexual health using any platform. Stated differently: node v may "receive" information about sexual health from node u, but may or may not "give" any such information to node u. In this example, the binary values associated to the edge $e_{u,v}$ would be (txt = 0, talk = 0, call = 0, soc = 1), and the binary values associated to the $e_{v,u}$ would be (txt = 0, talk = 0, call = 0, soc = 0). In terms of notation, the set of four binary values for each edge is denoted as C.

With the network structure defined, the first natural follow-up question is: How is the extent of the spread of information in a network measured? Traditionally, interventionists must select the k people to be trained *before* implementing the training program, thus the information diffusion process must be accurately modeled and simulated prior to training to provide an expected value of the number of people that will be influenced by the k people selected. Within the domain of maximum influence, there are various developed models that can be used to model the diffusion of information across a network. The two most popular models are the *linear threshold model* and the *independent cascade model* (Kempe et al. 2003). In both models, the initial k people are marked as "active", meaning they have learned or already know the information to be spread throughout the network, and they are willing and able to spread information to their connections. The goal is then to keep track of how many other nodes become active.

In the *linear threshold model*, each node has some threshold for the number of their immediate network connections that must be active in order for them to become active. A node in a linear threshold model becomes active when its node-specific threshold is surpassed. For instance, if a certain number of your friends buy the newest FitBit, then you might also buy the newest FitBit. This threshold is personal, meaning that it varies from individual to individual, and it can potentially be further complicated by unequal "weights" or importance of specific connections. In other words, some friends might influence your Fitbit buying decision more heavily than others, and each friend's influence may vary depending on the subject matter of the particular decision.

In this work, we instead use the *independent cascade model*. With this model, when a node learns some novel information and becomes active, the node attempts to influence each of its neighbors with some *probability* of success. Intuitively, the independent cascade model simulates the uncertainty of information spread that we feel is inherent in our problem due to both the indirect nature of social media exchanges and the highly personal/sensitive domain of sexual health. For instance, suppose YBW A becomes active, meaning that she has learned the new sexual health information helpful for HIV prevention. YBW A can then try to activate all her connections, but this activation may not always be effective. For instance, suppose interventionists choose to do a social media–based training and intervention. After learning about this new sexual health information (or, simply stated, becoming active), YBW A decides to try to spread this message on social media. Perhaps YBW A creates a post on her Facebook wall about this information. Each of her Facebook connections might see this post, read it, and become activated themselves – knowledgeable and also willing to share the message. But each friend also might *not* see, read, or share the information, and there is accordingly some probability associated with both outcomes (each connection of YBW A becomes activated or does not). Using the independent cascade model of information diffusion, we can employ algorithms developed for solving the maximum influence problem to design optimal interventions for multimodal communication networks of YBW.

We also must consider what simplifying assumptions we can make to reduce the computational complexity of the problem, without resulting in an oversimplification that would render the model unrealistic and useless for social workers and interventionists. First, we assume that the network of YBW is *stable*, meaning that new members are not joining or leaving the network and that connections (edges) are neither created nor destroyed over time. In addition, we assume that connections reported from the survey are known to exist with absolute certainty. Both of these assumptions describe "properties" of the network rather than its structure. These simplifying network property assumptions are most likely valid on the whole for our specific population of YBW, but they may not be appropriate for other network populations. For instance, in the work of Yadav et al. (2016), networks of homeless youth were known to be *unstable* owing to the transient nature of such friendships and the geographic mobility of the members of this population.

We also consider other simplifying assumptions about how information spreads across our specific network of surveyed YBW. These assumptions differ from the network stability and edge certainty assumptions mentioned previously because these new assumptions result in the selection of the edge weights to use for the network. In other words, these assumptions may change the *structure* of the network without changing its overall properties. We call these *network structure assumptions*. There are three such sets of assumptions we consider in different experiments. In each experiment, we assume one set of assumptions and then use an algorithm to solve the associated, simplified maximum influence problem. We compare the results obtained when using each set of assumptions to examine how information is spread throughout the network for each set of associated edge weights. Below are the three sets of network structure assumptions, in order of increasingly difficult (as in difficult to determine people to select as peer leader) scenarios:

1. **Any Platform**: We first assume that the mode of communication used to disseminate information is irrelevant. This experiment models the real-world intervention scenario where the k leaders are trained to spread sexual health information via *all* communication platforms (or that training in one platform still spreads information via all communication platforms). We assume that information spreads over the various platforms with equal efficacy. In order to test this assumption, we solve the maximum influence problem using all of the friendship/communication edges, regardless of their binary (txt, talk, call, soc) values. Since we include all possible edges in the network in this experiment, this test yields the "theoretically maximum" amount of activated nodes that we could hope to achieve with an intervention with k selected peer leaders, but we note that this kind of multimodal communication training is not necessarily realistic within the budgetary and time constraints of social work interventions. This test, therefore, is most useful as a comparison. That is, as communication modalities are eliminated from intervention training efforts, we should compare these future results against the network activation achieved using *all* edges or communication modalities.

2. **One Platform Only**: We next assume that we are restricted to training selected peer leaders for the intervention on how to spread information about sexual health using *exactly one* communication platform due to budgetary and time constraints. We assume that information will only be subsequently spread over this single platform, in order to see how we perform should we face a more difficult scenario. Therefore, if an individual in the network is not using that platform, that individual cannot become activated. For instance, if YBW A does not own a phone, we cannot influence her to buy one. We test this scenario by considering the subnetwork for communication type c where we only include the directed edges where the weight corresponding to c is one. We repeat this evaluation for all four communication types in order to select among the most effective communication training modality.

3. **Sex Restricted, One Platform**: Again, we assume that whatever communication method is taught during the intervention is the only communication method that will be used to spread the message. We also assume again that we cannot influence two people to start communicating over some platform if they were not at the time of the network survey. The additional, new assumption we make is if two people are not already

talking about sex on this specific platform, then we cannot influence them to start talking about sex on that platform. For example, perhaps two people are very uncomfortable discussing sex with one another and are unwilling to change their behavior no matter the intervention. These three assumptions together are considered to model a worst-case scenario. We test this by considering the subgraph for each communication class c where we include only the directed edges where the weight for c on an edge is 1 *and* for an edge denoted $e_{u,v}$, where node u is already talking to node v about sex. We note that edge directionality is particularly important here.

Algorithms for Solving the Maximum Influence Problem

With our simplified network structures to evaluate, we now describe algorithms that can be applied to solve the maximum influence problem. As stated earlier, the goal of the maximum influence problem is to find the k most influential people in the network. Using the independent cascade model, we can measure the expected influence of each subset of k people. One strategy for solving the maximum influence problem is that, for each subset of k people, we could use the independent cascade model to determine the expected activated number of people, and then choose the subset that allowed for the most activation. Computer scientists generally refer to this approach as the "brute force" algorithm because every possible solution is considered. Brute force algorithms are rarely used in practice because most real-world problems have a very large number of possible solutions, and it would take too long to evaluate every possible case. For the maximum influence problem, if we were to use this brute force approach, we would have to consider "n choose k" possible solutions where n is the number of people in the network – that is, choosing k people from the set of size n. So, for instance, if the network had 100 people and 20 people were to be selected for the peer-led intervention, then there are 535,983,370,403,809,682,970 (or 5.35×10^{20}) different subsets of 20 that the brute force algorithm would need to evaluate. For comparison, this number of cases is larger than the estimated number of grains of sand on Earth (which is estimated at 7.5×10^{18}). Thus, it is clear that the brute force algorithm is not a practical or possible solution approach for this problem, even when the size of the network is relatively small (about 100 people).

In fact, this "combinatorial" number of solutions is a frequent problem in computer science. It is very often that brute force algorithms cannot evaluate all possible solutions to produce a result during the lifetime of the computer programmer. Maximum influence problems belong to a set of such problems, labeled as *NP-hard*, which is a computer science term that classifies a problem as one where the optimal solution cannot be determined in a reasonable amount of time. When problems are NP-hard, computer scientists design algorithms that can *efficiently* find an *approximation* to the optimal solution. Ideally, the algorithm designers are also able to provide some approximation *guarantees*, meaning that they can mathematically prove how close their solution is to the optimal solution, within some clearly defined margin.

To solve the maximum influence problem, we use two *approximation* algorithms for selecting k nodes for the intervention. In other words, these algorithms are not guaranteed to select the exactly optimal k nodes to maximize information diffusion; however, they will finish in a reasonable amount of time and will yield provably good results. In the maximum influence literature, these algorithms are referred to as the Greedy and HEALER algorithms. The Greedy algorithm provides a (1-1/e) approximation guarantee, meaning the solution generated by the Greedy algorithm will always be approximately $^1/_3$ away from the true optimal solution. Unfortunately, the HEALER algorithm has no proven approximation guarantees.

The Greedy algorithm's approximation guarantees come from the fact that Greedy's influence function is adaptive submodular, whereas HEALER's influence function is not. Submodularity is intuitively the idea of diminishing returns from economics (for example, if trying to allocate grocery stores in a new city, if two are next to one another, people will chose one or the other; you may not get any benefit from the extra grocery store), and adaptive submodularity takes into account observations from the past. Previous work has proven that if an optimization problem is adaptive submodular, then an adaptive Greedy algorithm will provide a near optimal solution (Golovin & Krause, 2011). Though the HEALER algorithm has no proven approximation guarantees, it was shown to outperform the Greedy algorithm in the specific context outlined in Yadav et al. (2016). We utilize both algorithms in our work to see if HEALER will outperform Greedy experimentally in this context as well.

The Greedy algorithm is similar to the brute force approach but uses heuristics to choose nodes for testing (rather than choosing all possible nodes). One heuristic that can be used to choose nodes is "distance centrality," which assumes nodes that are "closest" to one another will most influence each other (Kempe et al., 2003). Another assumption of the Greedy algorithm is that there is no uncertainty in the edge existence in the network. We used a variation on this algorithm for testing, which allows us to account for multiple interventions over time, similarly to the HEALER algorithm.

The HEALER algorithm is quite different from the Greedy and brute force algorithms in that it deals with uncertainty in the social network (Yadav et al., 2016). To do this, HEALER uses a type of model called a Partially Observable Markov Decision Process (POMDP). This model assumes that we cannot tell exactly what is happening in the social network, but we can observe the connections reported in surveys, for example, which makes the network "partially observable." In our work, we assume that we know that edges exist in the surveyed network with absolute certainty, where edge existence probabilities are either 1 or 0. HEALER also allows us to consider the influence of multiple interventions over time, allowing for the restructuring of the network at multiple survey time points. For example, instead of choosing 12 people for a single intervention and modeling how they might influence their peers at one time, we can choose four people for an intervention, wait a month, and then choose another four people for an intervention, where we may also learn new information about the network. While we do not have a data set that allows us to learn new information about the network after each intervention, this could be added in further field studies.

Results and Discussion

To determine the optimal communication method for disseminating sexual health information throughout a network of YBW, both the HEALER and Greedy algorithms were applied to solving the maximum influence problem for the surveyed real-world communication network of YBW, with different edges included based on each of the aforementioned networks' structure assumptions. Each of these assumptions "removes" certain nodes from the network if they do not participate in that method of communication or the network of YBW, so the total number of nodes remaining after such node removal is also presented. Figures 6.1–6.5 show the YBW network diagrams generated using the survey data, where Figure 6.1 represents the full network and Figures 6.2–6.5 represent the network when considering only single communication modes.

For our experiments, we assumed there would be three rounds of interventions, each at a different time point, with four YBW chosen as peer leaders at each stage. For each experiment we report the number of people *indirectly influenced* – the number of people who received sexual health information without being *directly influenced* during an intervention. With 3 interventions

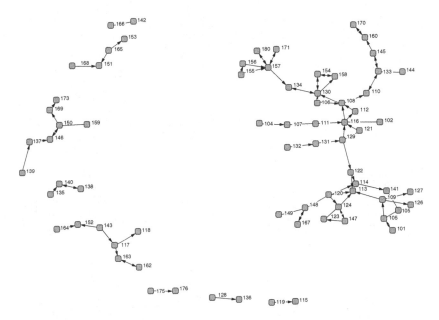

Figure 6.1 *All connections* in the network of 78 YBW, with 5 surveyed nodes excluded who have no direct ties to other study participants. Connections are included regardless of communication mode or discussion topic. As a result, there are 106 total connections (edges) between participants (nodes).

and 4 peer leaders in each intervention, 12 individuals are directly influenced by the peer leader training and therefore excluded from our reported results. We also excluded from our analysis 5 singleton nodes without any self-reported intra-network connections for any communication mode, yielding an analyzed network size 73 instead of 78.

We performed 50 trials for each algorithm using the same parameters and network structure assumptions. We generate results from multiple trials for each algorithm because influence spread is modeled as a random process, wherein a node becomes activated based on the result of a coin flip. In our experiments, we set the probability of activating a node (equivalent to the probability of getting a "heads" result in the coin flip, for example) to be 0.6, as in experiments with HEALER (Yadav et al., 2016). Since influence spread is modeled probabilistically, the experimental results varied from one individual trial to the next, even when using the same algorithm with an identical network structure. Intuitively, the number of indirectly influenced people may change from trial to trial because of the coin flip. Perhaps a less

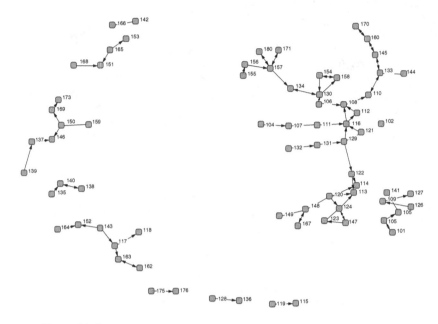

Figure 6.2 *In-person* communication connections in the network, regardless of discussion topic. Note that the large group on the right of the diagram of Figure 6.1 is fractured into three groups and one singleton node when considering only in-person communication. Because we are only considering in-person communication, there are now 83 edges. If we further constrain the network to include connections only if the two participants talk about sex in-person, there are 73 edges.

intuitive result, however, is that the individual nodes selected as peer leaders may also change, since these selections themselves also depend on the coin flip results.

First, in Table 6.1, we report the number of indirectly influenced people for each social network for the Greedy algorithm, considering the average and standard deviation of the 50 trials for each experiment. Next, in Table 6.2 we report the average results for the HEALER algorithm. The total number of nodes in the network is denoted by N in the tables.

As expected, the full network including all communication methods leads to the largest spread of influence for both the Greedy and HEALER algorithms, since this network includes the most nodes and edges. This result shows that, ideally, interventions should train peer leaders to spread information using multiple modes of communication. When this is not possible due to resource or time constraints, our simulation results using both algorithms show that texting-based interventions would yield the most information diffusion for our

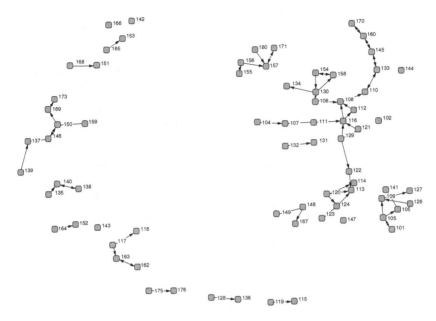

Figure 6.3 *Phone* communication connections, regardless of discussion topic. Note that the large group on the right of the diagram of Figure 6.1 is fractured into five groups and three single nodes when considering only phone communication. There are 74 edges when only phone communications are considered, with only 68 edges when considering only phone communications about sex.

surveyed network of YBW. In particular, there is only a very slight difference in the spread of information when using only texting as compared with using all modes of communication. This is a promising result in favor of text message–based interventions for networks of YBW, since simpler single communication mode interventions would likely require less time and resources from social workers and interventionists.

While our results suggest that text messaging is the best single mode of communication for information diffusion, we note that the study subjects were referred to participate via text messages from their peers. As a result of this recruitment methodology, we advise the reader to consider that this particular network may be biased toward text messaging as an overall preferred mode of communication.

Our results also show that peer leader training designed to encourage the discussion of sexual health among connections that do not typically discuss sex would also be modestly beneficial, although texting still results in the largest spread of information among networks where edges are removed if they do not already discuss sexual health.

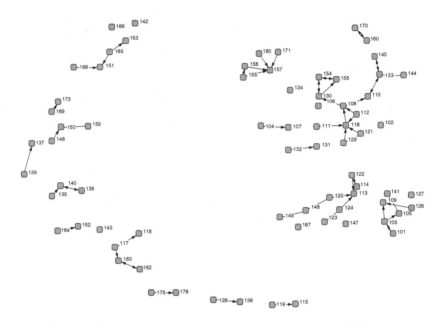

Figure 6.4 *Social media* communication connections, regardless of discussion topic or social media platform. Note that the large group on the right of the diagram of Figure 6.1 is fractured into seven groups and six single nodes when considering only social media communication. There are 67 edges when only social media communications are considered, with only 59 edges when considering only social media communications about sex.

Additionally, the Greedy algorithm performs better than the HEALER algorithm in our experiments. This is likely because HEALER is best used when new information is gathered between intervention rounds, and when there is uncertainty in the network. This was not the case in our survey data set, where data was collected only at one point in time, and connections were certain. However, we still include the results for HEALER in our discussion, because a future data set could be collected for a population that would utilize HEALER's full potential for approximating maximum influence under a dynamic and potentially uncertain network structure. For future studies seeking to employ HEALER, Greedy should still be used for comparison so that the best results can be achieved.

In Figure 6.6, we show the most commonly selected peer leader nodes from among the 50 trials for the Greedy algorithm. We show the results for texting-based interventions in Figure 6.6a, and the result for in-person conversation-based interventions in Figure 6.6b. Comparing the nodes selected by the Greedy algorithm in Figure 6.6 with those selected using the HEALER algorithm in Figure 6.7, we see that the Greedy algorithm more frequently

Table 6.1. *Greedy algorithm for maximum influence: Average number of indirectly influenced people*

	All Connections	Only Those Who Discuss Sex Already
All Communication Methods	33.412 ± 0.420 (N = 73)	
All Social Media	21.690 ± 0.277 (N = 64)	20.007 ± 0.259 (N = 60)
In Person	25.579 ± 0.340 (N = 72)	24.177 ± 0.381 (N = 65)
Phone	25.852 ± 0.276 (N = 67)	24.624 ± 0.171 (N = 67)
Texting	29.888 ± 0.512 (N = 72)	28.697 ± 0.507 (N = 64)

Note: n = 50 trials for each condition using the Greedy algorithm to choose peer leaders for interventions.

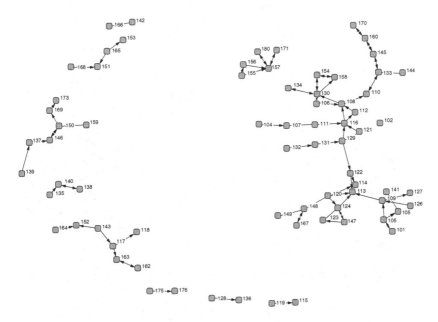

Figure 6.5 *Text messaging* communication connections, regardless of discussion topic. Note that the large group on the right of the diagram of Figure 6.1 is fractured into just two groups and one single node when considering only social media communication. Of all the communication methodologies, text messaging leaves the greatest number of links of the diagram of Figure 6.1 intact. There are 95 edges when only text message communications are considered, with 81 edges when considering only text message communications about sex.

Table 6.2. *HEALER algorithm for maximum influence: Average number of indirectly influenced people*

	All Connections	Only Those Who Discuss Sex Already
All Communication Methods	25.250 ± 1.739 (N = 73)	
All Social Media	17.105 ± 1.560 (N = 64)	15.024 ± 1.272 (N = 60)
In Person	19.910 ± 1.493 (N = 72)	19.182 ± 1.361 (N = 65)
Phone	19.270 ± 1.327 (N = 67)	19.248 ± 1.227 (N = 67)
Texting	23.057 ± 1.872 (N = 72)	22.047 ± 1.679 (N = 64)

Notes: n = 50 trials for each condition using the HEALER algorithm to choose peer leaders for interventions.

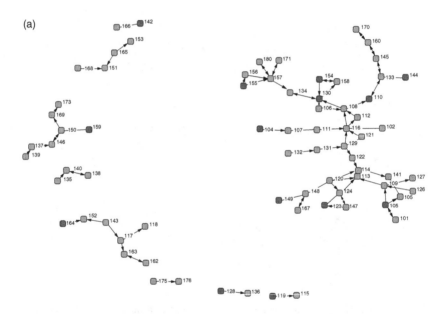

Figure 6.6 Dark gray nodes identify the 12 most commonly selected peer leader nodes among the 50 trials of the Greedy algorithm for (a) texting based interventions and (b) in-person interventions. Here we assume that nodes can be influenced regardless of whether or not sex is already discussed. Note that the 12 nodes do not appear as the selected peer leaders during one trial, but rather are the most commonly selected nodes across trials.

(b)

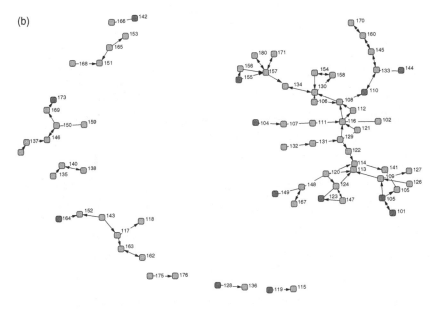

Figure 6.6 (*cont.*)

selects individuals from many different cliques. For example, Greedy selects nodes 128 and 119 (Figure 6.6a), while HEALER does not (Figure 6.7a), which might explain its greater influence spread as compared with HEALER for our data set.

In Figure 6.7, we show the most commonly selected peer leader nodes from among the 50 trials for the HEALER algorithm. We show the results for texting-based interventions in Figure 6.7a, and the results for in-person conversation-based interventions in Figure 6.7b.

The most striking difference between Figures 6.7a and 6.7b is that some nodes are selected from among the medium-sized groups to the left-hand side of the network diagram for the texting intervention, most likely because the large clique on the right-hand side of the diagram can be influenced by fewer selected peer leaders owing to the larger number of edges in the texting communication network. In contrast, for the in-person communication network, all but one of the most frequently selected nodes originate from the large right-hand clique. This example demonstrates how the communication modality may directly impact the selection of peer leaders in a network for intervention training.

In Figure 6.8, we show the result of one iteration of the Greedy algorithm in selecting individuals for the time series interventions using the edges from all

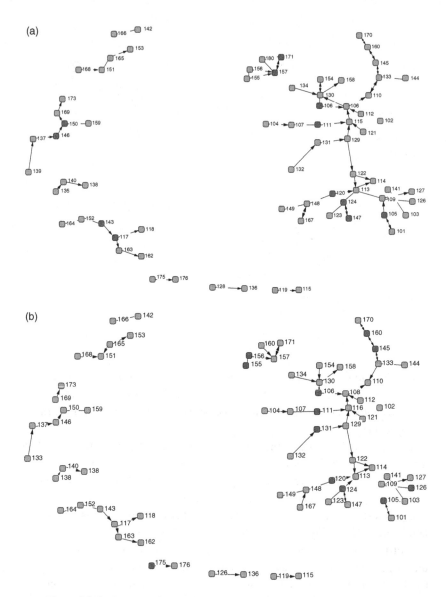

Figure 6.7 Dark gray nodes identify the 12 most commonly selected peer leader nodes among the 50 trials of the HEALER algorithm for (a) texting based interventions and (b) in-person interventions. Here we assume that nodes can be influenced regardless of whether or not sex is already discussed. Note that the 12 nodes do not appear as the selected peer leaders during one trial, but rather are the most commonly selected nodes across trials.

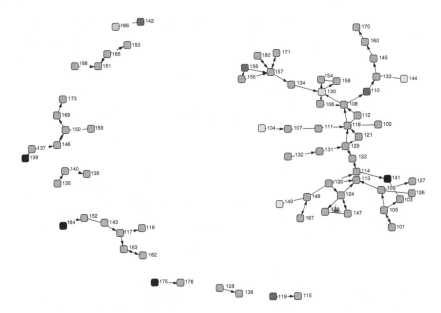

Figure 6.8 Dark gray nodes identify the selected peer leaders in the first time series intervention of the Greedy algorithm, including all possible edges in the network. Light gray nodes identify the selected peer leaders in the second time series intervention, and black nodes identify the selected peer leaders in the third (final) intervention. This is a result from one specific trial.

communication modes regardless of whether or not sex is discussed. Similarly, in Figure 6.9, we also show a result of one iteration of the HEALER algorithm in selecting individuals for the time series interventions. The dark gray nodes are selected for the first intervention, the light gray nodes are selected for the second intervention, and the black nodes are selected for the third intervention. Note that in some cases, counterintuitive nodes can be selected (for example, node 173). These cases typically have a slightly smaller reward than the example provided in Figure 6.9, though they sometimes can have a higher reward than the example provided in Figure 6.9. These variations are due to the randomness in influence spread. Also note that the order of the nodes chosen in each round in our case is irrelevant, as there is no additional information after each round. We include multiple rounds in these experiments, since future work could provide additional information after each round.

Conclusions and Future Work

In this work, we used real-world survey data from a social network of YBW in combination with computational approaches for solving the *maximum*

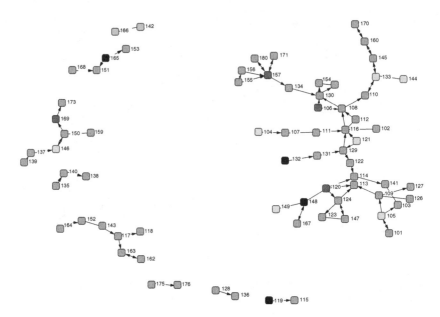

Figure 6.9 Dark gray nodes identify the selected peer leaders in the first time series intervention of the HEALER algorithm, including all possible edges in the network. Light gray nodes identify the selected peer leaders in the second time series intervention, and black nodes identify the selected peer leaders in the third (final) intervention. This is a result from one specific trial.

influence problem. We demonstrated that in the communication modality of a peer leader, social network–based intervention program for HIV reduction can impact the extent of information spread and the best individuals to select for training. We also compared the results of two known approximation algorithms for solving the maximum influence problem. We considered several different network structures, each of which allowed us to evaluate information diffusion when making different simplifying assumptions about intra-network communication. The results of our experiments show that while a multimodal communication intervention training program would likely result in the greatest spread of information, a texting-based intervention would yield similar results for our surveyed network of YBW in the case of limited training resources. Cost and benefit analysis could further be used to determine which of the solutions (i.e., text-based or multimodal communication) would be most advantageous for interventionists depending on the time and resources needed for development, training, and implementation, and the overall reach of the intervention and changes in behavioral outcomes.

Currently, many social network–based interventions are designed with limited consideration on the best mode of dissemination for effective and efficient diffusion of information and behavioral changes within targeted social networks. We propose that for future peer-led intervention studies, knowledge of the communication modalities and their prevalence within the target network is critical to maximize the diffusion of information. Since our experiments considered one specific network of YBW in the Los Angeles area, with a data set collected specifically to understand communication among the network members on the subject of sex and sexual health, the conclusion of texting as the best intervention platform is specific to this network. However, we hope that our results convince intervention researchers who are designing future peer-led and/or social network–based intervention studies to consider the effects of multimodal communication in their intervention designs and dissemination protocols. With knowledge of the network structure and the communication mode for each edge of the network, computer-based simulations of social network–based interventions can be completed at virtually no cost to assist in determining the best mode of dissemination (e.g., in-person, social media, text, or a multimodal variation).

Within the computer science domain, our experiments considered a simplified network that did *not* exhibit highly complex behaviors or properties. In the most general case, a network could be unstable, that is, with members joining and leaving the network and connections being formed and destroyed over time. Or, perhaps individuals could also influence other network members to use new platforms for communication, which we assumed in our experiments was not possible. One could also assume that information is spread over each communication platform with some specific probability of success, which could vary from connection to connection, from individual to individual, or as a function of the communication modality. Additionally, perhaps the peer leaders trained to spread information using a single communication mode (and the subsequently activated individuals in the network) might also disseminate information using communication modes *other* than the one originally selected for training. In other words, perhaps information could be modeled as moving "across platforms," rather than being restricted to flow over one channel. Furthermore, we could also consider the uncertainty on the probability of influence on neighboring network members, which we simply assumed was 0.6 for all edges in this work. These complex network properties and modes of information diffusion increase the computational difficulty of the maximum influence problem, rendering it significantly more difficult to model mathematically. However, the inclusion of these network behaviors or properties would be of interest to consider in future work, where novel algorithms would likely need to be designed to address these complex network properties.

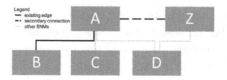

Figure 6.10 Say individual A is a YBW who has been recruited and qualified to participate in the study. Suppose individual A then listed SNMs B, C, and D as her connections, but only individuals B and C were YBW eligible to participate in the study. Perhaps A encouraged B and C to participate in the study, but only B followed up and was enrolled. With our existing network analysis, the only possible edges to be included in the network would be links between individuals A and B (denoted by a solid black line), because C and D are not themselves study participants (linked only by dotted gray lines). Now suppose that another study participant, individual Z, also listed D as a top connection, but did not list individual A. In other words, suppose that individuals A and Z do not know each other but have one friend (D) in common. This type of connection, called a "secondary" connection (denoted by a dashed black line), can be important for modeling information diffusion throughout real-world networks. In this example, if information flows from A to D and then from D to Z, then individual A could influence Z, even though these two nodes are not directly connected by an edge.

The social network survey methodology allowed for study participants to list all of their top network connections – the people with whom they most frequently communicated. This often included parents, significant others, and friends, many of whom were not themselves surveyed panelists. For example, see Figure 6.10. Since our analysis included only study participants, we are most likely missing some secondary and tertiary connections involving non-participants. Such added connections would lead to more information diffusion throughout the network. Hence, our results should be considered as a conservative estimate of indirect influence, and future work should endeavor to include connections to individuals who are not study participants for a more accurate model.

In summary, we found that a texting-based intervention would yield similar results to a multimodal intervention for our surveyed network of YBW in the case of limited training resources. To expand on this result in the future, we suggest examining social networks longitudinally to account for structural changes in networks of YBW and considering more complex networks with characteristics such as instability and communication spread via modalities other than those used for training, using a full network for analysis, including secondary and tertiary connections, and taking multimodal communication into account in recruitment and study design. These next steps will allow us to define more accurate models of the possible influence we can spread in a real YBW network.

References

Social Work Sources

Centers for Disease Control and Prevention. (2016). *HIV Surveillance Report, 2015*; vol. 27. Retrieved December 15, 2016, from National Centers for HIV/AIDS, Viral Hepatitis, STD, and TB Prevention: www.cdc.gov/hiv/library/reports/hiv-surveillance.html

Convey, M. R., Dickson-Gomez, J., Weeks, M. R., & Li, J. (2010). Altruism and peer-led HIV prevention targeting heroin and cocaine users. *Qualitative Health Research, 20*(11), 1546–1557.

Davey-Rothwell, M. A., Tobin, K., Yang, C., Sun, C. J., & Latkin, C. A. (2011). Results of a randomized controlled trial of a peer mentor HIV/STI prevention intervention for women over an 18 month follow-up. *AIDS and Behavior, 15*(8), 1654–1663.

Jennings, J. M., Howard, S., & Perotte, C. L. (2014). Effects of a school-based sexuality education program on peer educators: The Teen PEP model. *Health Education Research, 29*(2), 319–329.

Kelly, J. A., St. Lawrence, J. S., Diaz, Y. E., Stevenson, L. Y., Hauth, A. C., Brasfield, T. L., ...& Andrew, M. E. (1991). HIV risk behavior reduction following intervention with key opinion leaders of population: An experimental analysis. *American Journal of Public Health, 81*(2), 168–171.

Lenhart, A., & Center, P. R (2015). Teens, social media & technology overview 2015. *Pew Research Center, 9*. Retrieved October 13, 2016, from Internet, Science & Tech: Report: www.pewinternet.org/2015/04/09/teens-social-media-technology-2015/

Mahat, G., Scoloveno, M. A., De Leon, T., & Frenkel, J. (2008). Preliminary evidence of an adolescent HIV/AIDS peer education program. *Journal of Pediatric Nursing, 23*(5), 358–363.

McKirnan, D. J., Tolou-Shams, M., & Courtenay-Quirk, C. (2010). The Treatment Advocacy Program: A randomized controlled trial of a peer-led safer sex intervention for HIV-infected men who have sex with men. *Journal of Consulting and Clinical Psychology, 78*(6), 952.

Noar, S. M., & Willoughby, J. F. (2012). eHealth interventions for HIV prevention. *AIDS Care, 24*(8), 945–952.

O'Grady, M. A., Wilson, K., & Harman, J. J. (2009). Preliminary findings from a brief, peer-led safer sex intervention for college students living in residence halls. *The Journal of Primary Prevention, 30*(6), 716.

Rice, E. (2010). The positive role of social networks and social networking technology in the condom-using behaviors of homeless young people. *Public Health Reports, 125*(4), 588–595.

Schneider, J. A., Zhou, A. N., & Laumann, E. O. (2015). A new HIV prevention network approach: sociometric peer change agent selection. *Social Science & Medicine, 125*, 192–202.

Smith, A. (2014). *African Americans and technology use: A demographic portrait.* Washington, DC: Pew Research Center. Retrieved from Pew Research Center: http://www.pewinternet.org/2014/01/06/african-americans-and-technology-use/

Rogers, E. M. (2010). *Diffusion of innovations.* New York: Simon and Schuster.

Young, S. D., Rivers, C., & Lewis, B. (2014). Methods of using real-time social media technologies for detection and remote monitoring of HIV outcomes. *Preventive Medicine, 63,* 112–115.

Valente, T. W., & Pumpuang, P. (2007). Identifying opinion leaders to promote behavior change. *Health Education & Behavior, 34*(6), 881–896.

Artificial Intelligence Sources

Borgs, C., Brautbar, M., Chayes, J., & Lucier, B. (2014, January). Maximizing social influence in nearly optimal time. In *Proceedings of the Twenty-Fifth Annual ACM-SIAM Symposium on Discrete Algorithms* (pp. 946–957). Society for Industrial and Applied Mathematics.

Cohen, E., Delling, D., Pajor, T., & Werneck, R. F. (2014, November). Sketch-based influence maximization and computation: Scaling up with guarantees. In *Proceedings of the 23rd ACM International Conference on Conference on Information and Knowledge Management* (pp. 629–638). ACM.

Golovin, D., & Krause, A. (2011). Adaptive submodularity: Theory and applications in active learning and stochastic optimization. *Journal of Artificial Intelligence Research, 42,* 427–486.

Kempe, D., Kleinberg, J., & Tardos, É. (2003, August). Maximizing the spread of influence through a social network. In *Proceedings of the Ninth ACM SIGKDD International Conference on Knowledge Discovery and Data Mining* (pp. 137–146). ACM.

Tang, Y., Xiao, X., & Shi, Y. (2014, June). Influence maximization: Near-optimal time complexity meets practical efficiency. In *Proceedings of the 2014 ACM SIGMOD International Conference on Management of Data* (pp. 75–86). ACM.

Yadav, A., Chan, H., Xin Jiang, A., Xu, H., Rice, E., & Tambe, M. (2016, May). Using social networks to aid homeless shelters: Dynamic influence maximization under uncertainty. In *Proceedings of the 2016 International Conference on Autonomous Agents & Multiagent Systems* (pp. 740–748). International Foundation for Autonomous Agents and Multiagent Systems.

Yadav, A., Soriano Marcolino, L., Rice, E., Petering, R., Winetrobe, H., Rhoades, H., ... & Carmichael, H. (2015). *Preventing HIV spread in homeless populations using PSINET: emerging application case study.* IAAI.

Yadav, A., Wilder, B., Rice, E., Petering, R., Craddock, J., Yoshioka-Maxwell, A., Hemler, M., Onasch-Vera, L., Tambe, M., Woo, D. (2017). *Influence maximization in the field: The arduous journey from emerging to deployed application.* AAMAS.

7

Minimizing Violence in Homeless Youth

Ajitesh Srivastava, Robin Petering, and Michail Misyrlis

Introduction

There are an estimated 1.6–2.8 million youths experiencing homelessness in the United States [1]. Although violence in the United States has steadily decreased during the past decade, homeless youth (HY) remain disproportionately susceptible to violent victimization and perpetration [2]. These youths experience all types of violence at higher rates than their housed counterparts [3–5].

Interpersonal violence is defined as the intentional use of physical force or power between two or more individuals resulting in injury, death, or psychological harm [6]. This is typically the result of many contributing factors including childhood experiences of trauma such as physical abuse or neglect [7]. Many youths cite escaping a violent family environment as a reason for becoming homeless [8–12]. This experience and exposure to violence may contribute a propensity toward violence during adolescence or young adulthood as the youth may reenact violent behaviors learned from previous perpetrators of abuse [13]. Subsistence survival strategies, including delinquent activities such as stealing, burglary, prostitution, and dealing drugs to obtain money, food, or shelter [14–16], and exposure to perpetrators while living on the streets increase likelihood of experiencing violence [8–10]. A street-entrenched life increases exposure to violence, and many youths utilize physical aggression to guarantee safety from future victimization [17–19]. Further, interpersonal violence occurs within a dyadic space, but it is also contagious in a social network, diffusing across social space. A young person's risk of engaging in violence increases as the proportion of violent peers in his or her network increases [3].

119

The consequences of violence for homeless youth are severe. The proximal consequence of physical injury is a primary health concern for HY [20–22], who do not proactively seek health services [21]. Minor, treatable injuries can often escalate into more severe health problems [20, 23, 24]. Violence can also lead to nonphysical ailments as posttraumatic stress disorder [25–27], depression [28, 29], and externalizing behavior (i.e., delinquency and aggression; [27]. Interpersonal violence also limits a youths ability to successfully exit homelessness by increasing the risk of of interaction with law enforcement, arrest, and imprisonment [30–33], which can limit employment and housing opportunities. Violence can also result in the temporary or permanent termination of services at agencies designed to support and assist HY in meeting needs or securing housing.

Reducing violence in the lives of homeless youth is imperative and will contribute to a young person's ability to safely and successfully exit the streets and lead a long and productive life in society. However, public health and social interventions to reduce violence within adolescent and young adult populations are difficult [34], because, again, this phenomenon is complex, with many intrinsic and extrinsic contributing factors.

Additionally, violence perpetuates violence and diffuses through a network like a contagious disease [35]. Motivated by this contagious nature, a diffusion model is ideal for modeling the spread of violence. Doing so can lead to optimal intervention strategies under certain assumptions. To the best of our knowledge, intervention strategies to reduce violence using diffusion models have received very little attention in the literature [36, 37]. Violence is modeled based on susceptibility and infectiousness in [36]. In [37], the idea of opposing forces – "provocation" and "repression" – is used to model violence as two diffusion processes. This is more accurate as it captures the nonprogressive nature of violence, where an individual may switch between being "violent" and "nonviolent." However, it is a macroscopic approach, which disregards the network structure. We propose the Uncertain Voter Model (UVM), which is an extension of the Voter Model [38]. In the Voter Model, individuals are influenced by a randomly selected neighbor.[1] UVM allows for some uncertainty in the knowledge of the neighborhood that may arise from an individual being influenced by someone they did not explicitly state as their "friends" during the survey to create the network. Our model also allows for uncertainty in number of time-steps for which the model needs to be run to

---

[1] We use the terms "neighbor" and "neighborhood" to refer to the links of a given individual in the network and not their physical neighborhood

estimate the expected spread of violence. Specifically, our contributions are as follows:

- We propose the Uncertain Voter Model for spread of violence, which can capture its nonprogressive nature and take into account the uncertainty in a neighborhood as well as uncertainty in the time period over which the model is run.
- We formally define the Violence Minimization problem where the task is to perform intervention with a finite resource, i.e., change the state of k individuals so that total expected number of violent individuals is minimized.
- We show that the Uncertain Voter Model can be reduced to the classic voter model, and thus a Greedy algorithm forms the optimal solution to Violence Minimization.
- We perform experiments on a real-life network of HY and find the nodes to be selected for intervention.

Data Collection

A sample of 481 HY aged 18 to 25 years accessing services from two day-service drop-in centers for HY in Hollywood and Santa Monica, CA, were approached for study inclusion in October 2011 and February 2012. The research team approached all youths who entered the service agencies during the data collection period and invited them to participate in the study. The selected agencies provided weekday services to eligible HY, including basic needs, medical and mental health services, case management, and referrals and connections to other programs such as housing services. Each youth signed a voluntary consent form, and a consistent pair of research staff members was responsible for all recruitment to prevent youths from completing the survey multiple times during each data collection period per site. The overall response rate was 80.1%; 19.9% of HY approached declined to participate, 6.2% did not complete the full survey, and 2.6% completed the surveys at both sites three months apart. Four participants were excluded because they were younger than 18 to limit the sample to late adolescence and early adulthood. The final sample consisted of 366 participants. The institutional review board of University of Southern California approved all procedures and waived parental consent for minors without parents or guardians. All participants received $20 in cash or gift cards as compensation for their time.

The study consisted of two parts: a computerized self-administered survey and a social network interview. The computerized survey included an audio-assisted version for participants with low literacy and was available in English or Spanish. The computerized survey included approximately 200 questions and took an average of 1 hour to complete. The social network interview was interactive, conducted by a trained research staff member. Social network interviews took between 15 and 30 minutes to complete, depending on each participant's personal network size. For the social network interview, each participant was asked to name anyone they interacted with in person, on the phone, or through the internet in the previous month, prompted by interviewers stating, "These might be friends; family; people you hang out with/chill with/kick it with/ have conversations with; people you party with – use drugs or alcohol; boyfriend/girlfriend; people you are having sex with; baby mama/baby daddy; case worker; people from school; people from work; old friends from home; people you talk to (on the phone, by email); people from where you are staying (squatting with); people you see at this agency; other people you know from the street." Details describing the social network data collection can be read in [3].

Dependent Variable

The variable of interest is violent behavior. Violent behavior was assessed by recent participation in a physical fight. Participants were asked: "During the past 12 months, how many times were you in a physical fight?" Eight ordinal responses ranged from "zero times" to "over 12 times." Due to the skew of the original variable, responses were dichotomized similar to previous literature on youth violence [5, 39] to distinguish between participants who had been in no physical fights and participants who had been in at least one physical fight during the previous year. This question was adopted from the Youth Risk Behavior Survey [40] and did not distinguish between victims and perpetrators of violence.

Model

To model the spread of violence, we model the network of homeless youth as a graph $G(V, E)$ where every individual is a node that can exist in one of two states: violent or nonviolent. We have chosen to model violence as a nonprogressive diffusion process, i.e, a node may switch its state, unlike the progressive diffusion where once a node is violent, it cannot become nonviolent again. Next, we provide a background on the Voter Model [38] on which our model is based.

Voter Model

In the Voter Model [38], at every time step a node u picks an incoming neighbor v at random with a probability $p(v, u)$. The incoming probabilities are normalized such that $\sum_v p(v, u) = 1$. Let $x_{u,t}$ represent the probability of node u being violent at time t. According to the model,

$$x_{u,t} = \sum_v p_{v,u} x_{v,t-1} . \tag{7.1}$$

Let $\mathbf{x_t}$ represent the state of all the nodes at time t, with ith element representing the probability that $v_i \in V$ is violent at time t. Suppose matrix M represents the transpose of the adjacency matrix of the weighted network, i.e., $M_{u,v} = p(v, u)$. Then

$$\mathbf{x_t} = M\mathbf{x_{t-1}}. \tag{7.2}$$

It follows that

$$\mathbf{x_t} = M^t\mathbf{x_0}. \tag{7.3}$$

Here $\mathbf{x_0}$ is the initial state of nodes, which is assumed to be known. Now we wish to select k nodes out of those who are violent at $t = 0$ and turn them into nonviolent so that the expected number of nodes that are violent at time t is minimized. Define I_X for $X \subseteq V$ as the vector in which the i-th element is 1 if $v_i \in X$. Then the expected number of violent nodes at time t is given by

$$\sum_i P(v_i \text{ is violent at time}) = \sum_i x_{i,t} = I_V^T \mathbf{x_t} \tag{7.4}$$

Formally we define the problem of Violence Minimization as follows.

Problem Definition (Violence Minimization)   Given a weighted graph $G(V, E)$, an initial set of violent nodes S, a time frame t, and an integer k, find $T \subseteq S$ such that $|T| = k$, turning the nodes in T into nonviolent minimizes the expected number of violent nodes after time t, i.e., $I_V^T \mathbf{x_t}$ under voter model.

Uncertain Voter Model

A network formed through a survey may have missing edges due to the uncertainty in a person's ability to recall all "friends" they might be influenced by. To capture this aspect, we propose the Uncertain Voter Model, where we assume that any node not directly connected to the node of interest may also influence it. In this model, two mutually exclusive events happen: (1) with probability θ a node randomly selects one incoming neighbor and adopts its state; (2) with probability $(1-\theta)$ it selects a random node that is not its neighbor in the network and adopts its state. Mathematically,

$$x_{u,t} = \theta \sum_{\{v|p(v,u)>0\}} p_{v,u} x_{v,t-1} + (1-\theta) \sum_{\{v|p(v,u)=0\}} \frac{1}{|\{v|p_{v,u}=0\}|} x_{v,t-1} \qquad (7.5)$$

If n is the total number of nodes and d_u is the number of incoming neighbors of u, then $|\{v|p_{v,u}=0\}| = n - d_u$. Suppose we define,

$$q_\theta(v,u) = \begin{cases} \theta p_{v,u} & \text{if } p_{v,u} > 0 \\ \frac{1-\theta}{n-d_u} & \text{if } p_{v,u} = 0. \end{cases}$$

Now, Equation (7.5) can be rewritten as

$$x_{u,t} = \sum_v q(v,u) x_{v,t-1} \text{ or } \mathbf{x_t} = Q_\theta \mathbf{x_{t-1}} \qquad (7.6)$$

where $[Q_\theta]_{u,v} = q_\theta(u,v)$, which reduces to the Voter Model (Equation 7.1), where the transpose of the adjacency matrix is Q_θ.

Greedy Minimization

Let $\mathbf{x_0'}$ be the vector formed by turning some k nodes nonviolent, resulting in the vector of probabilities $\mathbf{x_t'}$ at time t. Now, minimizing $I_V^T \mathbf{x_t'}$ is equivalent to maximizing $I_V^T(\mathbf{x_t} - \mathbf{x_t'}) = I_V^T Q_\theta^t(\mathbf{x_0} - \mathbf{x_0'})$, i.e., the problem reduces to maximizing

$$I_V^T \Delta \mathbf{x_t} = I_V^T Q_\theta^t \Delta \mathbf{x_0} = \sum_{\{u|\Delta x_0(u)=1\}} I_V^T Q_\theta^t I_u \qquad (7.7)$$

which can be optimized using Greedy strategy [38] as presented in Algorithm 1.

The most expensive step of the algorithm is the computation of Q_θ^t that can be computed in $O(|V|^{2.3} \log t)$.

Algorithm 1 Greedy algorithm to minimize violence

---

function MINVIOLENCE(G, S, θ, k, t)
    Compute Q_θ^t for G
    $\forall u \in S$ compute $\sigma(u) = I_V Q_\theta^t I_u$
    Sort $\{\sigma(u)\}$ in descending order and return top k.
end function

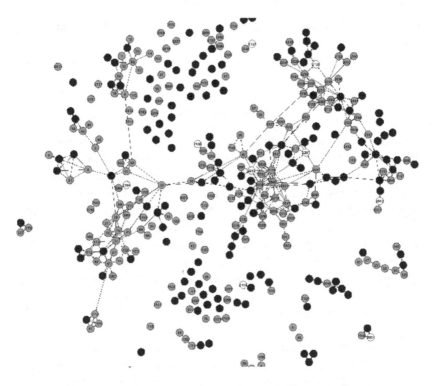

Figure 7.1 Visualization of the homeless youth network. The grey nodes represent the violent nodes and the green ones represent the nonviolent ones. The black nodes have an unknown state.

Uncertainty in Time

The Uncertain Voter Model requires t as a parameter that is unknown in real life. While we may have a certain time period (days or weeks) over which we want the intervention to work, finding a relation between that time period and the parameter t is nontrivial, as it depends on how often the individuals interact. To capture this uncertainty, we assume that time t takes a value τ with probability $P(t = \tau)$. Now, we wish to minimize $\mathbb{E}(I_V \mathbf{x_t})$ where the expectation is taken over t. Therefore,

$$\mathbb{E}(I_V^T \mathbf{x_t'}) = \sum_{\tau} P(t = \tau) I_V^T Q_\theta^\tau \mathbf{x_0'}$$

$$= I_V^T \left(\sum_{\tau} P(t = \tau) Q_\theta^\tau \right) \mathbf{x_0'}. \tag{7.8}$$

Notice from Equation (7.8) that a Greedy solution like Algorithm 1 still applies.

Experiments

We construct the network obtained by the surveyed data, which consists of 369 nodes and 558 directed edges. Due to the lack of the knowledge of edge-weights, we assume that all incoming links for a node are equally weighted. We assume that the surveyed data is the current snapshot of the diffusion process ($\mathbf{x}_0'$). Out of the 369 nodes, 55.01% are "violent" ($x_{u,0} = 1$) and 42.55% are "nonviolent" ($x_{u,0} = 0$). Data on the rest of 2.44% are missing and are assumed to be equally likely to be of either state ($x_{u,0} = 0.5$). Based on this "initial state," we run Greedy Minimization for the Uncertain Voter Model. The t parameter, for the sake of simplicity, was assumed to be uniformly distributed between 1 to 10. The range was selected, keeping in mind that homeless youth networks are dynamic, and so in practice, the intervention should be performed in "waves," making the the selection process short-term.

We experimented with different values for parameter $\theta = 1, 0.9, 0.8, 0.7, 0.6$ and 0.5, i.e., increasing edge uncertainty. We refrain from using lower values of θ as it would represent very low confidence in the collected data, i.e, it would mean that a node is more likely to be influenced by one of the other nodes it is not connected to. Table 7.1 presents the top 10 nodes (in terms of PID assigned in the survey) chosen for intervention. Note that there are many nodes such as PIDs 35, 47, 2007, 4, and 2156 that consistently appear in the top 10. Some of these nodes are shown in Figure 7.2. It is nontrivial to find them, as they are a mix of high-degree and low-degree nodes. We also varied the value of $t = 2, 4, 6, 8, 10$, and 12. The value of θ was set to 0.75 because it

Table 7.1. *Top 10 seeds for various values of θ output by Greedy Minimization*

θ					Selected Seeds						$\mathbb{E}(I_V^T \mathbf{x}_t')$
1	35	2156	47	13	4	2115	2007	51	38	2086	160.9487
0.9	35	47	2156	4	13	2007	2115	51	38	2086	119.8357
0.8	35	47	2007	4	2156	2115	51	13	2086	38	117.3772
0.7	47	35	2007	4	51	2115	2156	2086	13	38	116.6939
0.6	47	2007	35	4	51	2115	2086	2038	2156	38	117.9434
0.5	47	2007	35	4	51	2086	2115	2038	38	2110	121.4455

Table 7.2. *Top 10 seeds for various values of t output by Greedy Minimization*

t				Selected Seeds							$\mathbb{E}(I_V^T \mathbf{x}_t')$
2	47	2007	2038	51	2086	2115	4	35	2110	38	147.2344
4	47	2007	35	4	51	2115	2086	2038	2110	38	138.0431
6	47	35	2007	4	51	2115	2156	2086	2110	13	130.1730
8	47	35	2007	4	2115	51	2156	13	2086	2110	123.1098
10	47	35	2007	4	2156	2115	51	13	2086	38	116.7971
12	47	35	2007	4	2156	2115	51	13	2086	38	111.0703

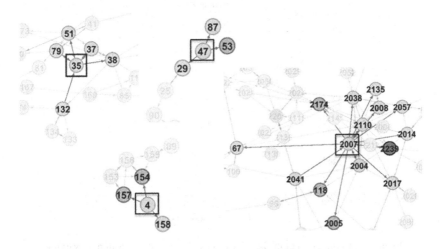

Figure 7.2 Visualization of some PIDs consistently selected by the Greedy Algorithm for various parameters.

can be shown that it is equivalent to assuming that θ is randomly picked from the interval $[0.5, 1]$.

We have shown that the Greedy Algorithm described in Algorithm 1 is optimal. However, to compare how much better it is from a different choice of intervention strategy, we compare it against the following baselines:

- Degree: We define the degree of a node based on the weighted graph as $d_v = \sum_u p_{v,u}$. Then we select top k nodes.
- Betweenness Centrality: Top k nodes are selected based on the betweenness centrality in the graph.

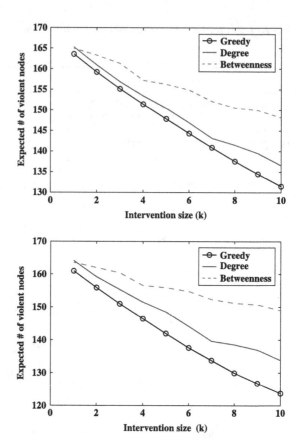

Figure 7.3 Comparison of the baseline against the Greedy Algorithm for varying intervention sizes under the Uncertain Voter Model.

Figure 7.3 shows the comparison for expected number of nodes that are violent after time $t = 5$ and $t = 10$. The value of θ was set to 1 to generate these plots. Other values for parameters t and θ show similar trends and, hence, have been omitted. We observe that the Greedy Algorithm significantly outperforms both baselines.

Demographics of Chosen Individuals. Finally, to study the demographics of the individuals who are selected for intervention using Greedy Algorithm, we performed the selection by setting $\theta = 0.75$ (which is equivalent to averaging for all $\theta \in [0.5, 1]$), and for $t = 5$. Individuals were selected until the expected violence was reduced to 25%. This resulted in the selection of 38 individuals. The demographics of the selected individuals are presented in

Table 7.3. *Demographics of selected top 38 nodes*

	Top Violent Nodes		Remaining Sample		
	n	%	n	%	
Total	38	10.38	328	89.62	
Male	27	71.05	233	71.04	
Age	21.54	2.01	21.05	1.64	
Time Homeless[1]	4.75	2.89	3.65	2.83	*
White	16	42.11	117	35.67	
Latino	4	10.53	50	15.25	
Black	11	28.95	97	29.66	
Mixed	7	18.42	48	14.68	
LGBTQ	14	36.84	75	23.29	
site	19	50.00	183	55.79	
Child Abuse	14	36.84	130	39.63	
Fight	38	100.00	167	51.23	***
Injury from Fight	16	42.11	61	18.83	***
highboth	10	26.32	54	16.46	
highaware	6	15.79	59	17.99	
highcontrol	6	15.79	53	16.16	
dersboth	24.30	7.67	24.31	7.27	
Degree[1]	4.76	3.64	1.90	1.89	***
% Violent network[1]	0.70	0.33	0.42	0.41	***
Core	17	44.74	51	15.55	***

[1]Indicates Mean and standard deviation
*$p < 0.05$, ***$p < 0.001$

Table 7.3. The basic demographics match the larger sample where there is no indication of selection biases based on race, gender, or sexual orientation. The selected nodes represent approximately 10% of the network. Those selected have been homeless on average for longer than the remaining sample (4.75 years versus 3.65, $p < 0.05$). They are also more likely to have experienced severe violence resulting in injury ($p < 0.001$). They have an average of 4.76 connections in the HY social network, which is significantly more than the remaining sample average (1.90 connections, $p < 0.001$). Additionally, they had a greater proportion of their network who were violent (0.70 versus 0.42, $p < 0.001$) and are more likely to be in the core of the homeless youth network ($p < 0.001$).

Discussion

We have proposed the Uncertain Voter Model in which, with probability θ, a node selects one of its neighbors and with $1 - \theta$ it selects one of the remaining nodes and adopts its state. We have shown that a Greedy Algorithm is the optimal intervention strategy to minimize violence under this model. The model captures uncertainty in time by assuming that the time over which intervention is to be performed has a probability distribution over a certain range. We show in our experiments that for sensible choice of these parameters, the top individuals selected for intervention roughly remain the same. However, for more accurate learning of the parameters, more data is necessary. Moreover, with more data, a more complex model can be learned that more accurately models the dynamics of violence diffusion by accounting for personal characteristics. These extensions of our model are discussed in the following.

Multiple Waves

We have performed all our experiments on one snapshot (wave) of data. Having multiple waves of data may help obtain a more accurate modeling. Suppose the two snapshots generate the vector of states $\mathbf{x_0}$ and $\mathbf{x_r}$. Then, according to UVM, $\exists\, \theta, r$, such that

$$\mathbf{x_r} = Q_\theta^r \mathbf{x_0} \qquad (7.9)$$

We can learn these parameters using maximum likelihood, i.e., $\arg\max_\theta P(\mathbf{x_0}, \mathbf{x_r}|G, \theta)$. More generally, given a sequence of observations: $< \mathbf{x_{i1}}, \mathbf{x_{i2}}, \mathbf{x_{i3}}, \cdots >$,

$$\theta = \arg\max_\theta P(< \mathbf{x_{i1}}, \mathbf{x_{i2}}, \mathbf{x_{i3}}, \cdots > |G, \theta). \qquad (7.10)$$

We performed a similar analysis to the single snapshot that was available $\mathbf{x_0}$, assuming that it is a steady state, i.e., $\mathbf{x_0} = Q_\theta \mathbf{x_0}$. Maximum likelihood resulted in $\theta = 1$. However, this is under a steady state assumption that might not hold. Therefore, more snapshots are necessary for a more accurate modeling. Multiple snapshots would also enable the analysis of how quickly the diffusion process takes place. This would aid in understanding a mapping between time parameter of the model and time elapsed in real life. Another advantage of multiple snapshots would be to understand and take into account the evolution of the network itself, i.e., rate of addition and removal of nodes and links.

We also suggest that the intervention should be performed over short periods of time and the effects should be observed. This new wave would help in retraining the model and finding more accurate nodes for intervention in the next iteration.

Utilizing Other Variables

We have only taken into account the state of the individuals (violent or nonviolent), which came from whether they had been involved in a fight over the past 12 months. Many more features for individual nodes are available from the collected data. One feature of particular interest is Difficulty in Emotion Regulation (DERS) [41]. Intuitively, an individual with high DERS is likely to have a higher propensity for violence. Suppose $\alpha(u)$ is the probability that a node u, given its DERS score, would prefer to be violent. Mathematically,

$$x_{u,t} = \frac{\alpha(u) \sum_j q_\theta(v, u) x_{v,t-1}}{\alpha(u) \sum_j q_\theta(v, u) x_{v,t-1} + (1 - \alpha(u)) \sum_j q_\theta(v, u)(1 - x_{v,t-1})}. \quad (7.11)$$

Assuming steady state for the available snapshot, we attempted to learn a monotonic function $\alpha()$ using maximum likelihood. Inclusion of this function made the error worse. In other words, $\alpha(u) = 0.5, \forall u$ produced the minimum error, which reduces this model to our Uncertain Voter Model. One reason could be the fact that DERS scores and the state of violence/nonviolence has a high correlation, and thus inclusion of DERS does not improve the results. Again, having more snapshots may provide a more accurate learning framework, and $\alpha(.)$ might play an important role. Moreover, we have observed from the data that some nodes have been involved in violence more frequently than others. With more snapshots we also wish to incorporate this information into our model and form a more accurate representation of violence diffusion that can take into account more information that is available in the collected data.

Implications from Social Work Perspective

There are many implications for social work practice. Reducing violence within homeless youth populations is imperative, as there are many consequences. Even minimal incidents, such as those that do not result in an injury, can severely impact a young person's life. For example, verbally aggressive conflict with another youth or a service provider can result in interruption of supportive services, which impacts a youth's ability to exit homelessness. Additionally, violence perpetuates violence. A minimal reduction in violence could have a global impact on the lives of young people. The use of artificial intelligence and advanced analytics augments social work research and practice to maximize efforts that may already be in place or provide a better understanding of real-world behavioral dynamics. What is unique about the approach presented in this chapter is that artificial intelligence is being used to determine how to disrupt the spread of violence within the network. The violence minimization algorithm presented takes into consideration the contagious nature of violence as well of the dynamic state of being violent. Violence is different than other public health behaviors in that it is learned and can be unlearned and then relearned. This property of violence requires a different diffusion approach than prevention approaches that hinge on information dissemination.

Future directions for applying this approach would be to use the violence minimization algorithim to identify the key individuals in a network that could be targeted for specific behavior change related to violence. Imagine inviting key network nodes to particpate in a program to enhace intrinsic skills when confronted with conflict, reducing impulsitivty and increased emotional regulation. Such an intervention would attempt to eliminate violent nodes in the larger network structure and therefore disrupt the spread of violence. Implementing such an intervention will undoubtedly be challenging, as it selects a group of individuals that are confirmed to be violent. It will be necessary to think creatively, inclusively, and trauma-informed when designing the specific intervention strategy to reduce intrinsic violent behaviors in these individuals. However, as noted before, peer-based violence interventions are being implemented with success. Despite the potential challenges, deploying and testing an intervention program that utilizes this modeling technique should be a priority given that violence-specific interventions for homeless youth are currently lacking [34]. Future directions for this study will be to explore the transmission of violence within a social network of homeless youth using more precise metrics and watch changes overtime, without intervention, to refine the algorithm modeling. Following that, developing and piloting an intervention that incorporates the algorithim would be necessary. Regardless, results from this chapter are extremely promising for reducing violence in homeless youth populations as well as other groups that are at high risk of experiencing violence.

References

[1] M. J. Terry, G. Bedi, and N. D. Patel. Healthcare needs of homeless youth in the United States. *Journal of Pediatric Sciences*, 2(1):e17–e28, 2010.

[2] Department of Justice Office of Victims of Crime. *2013 National Crime Victims' Rights Week Resource Guide: Section 6. Statistical Overviews*, 2013.

[3] R. Petering, E. Rice, H. Rhoades, and H. Winetrobe. The social networks of homeless youth experiencing intimate partner violence. *Journal of Interpersonal Violence*, 29(12):2172–2191, 2014.

[4] J. A. Heerde, S. A. Hemphill, and K. E. Scholes-Balog. "Fighting" for survival: A systematic review of physically violent behavior perpetrated and experienced by homeless young people. *Aggression and Violent Behavior*, 19(1):50–66, 2014.

[5] D. K. Eaton, L. Kann, S. Kinchen, S. Shanklin, K. H. Flint, J. Hawkins, W. A. Harris, R. Lowry, T. McManus, D. Chyen, et al. Youth risk behavior surveillance – United States, 2011. *Morbidity and Mortality Weekly Report. Surveillance Summaries (Washington, DC: 2002)*, 61(4):1–162, 2012.

[6] E. G. Krug, J. A. Mercy, L. L. Dahlberg, and A. B. Zwi. The World Report on Violence and Health. *The Lancet*, 360(9339): 1083–1088, 2002.

[7] S. M. Wolfe, P. A. Toro, and P. A. McCaskill. A comparison of homeless and matched housed adolescents on family environment variables. *Journal of Research on Adolescence*, 9(1):53–66, 1999.

[8] N. G. Milburn, M. J. Rotheram-Borus, E. Rice, S. Mallet, and D. Rosenthal. Cross-national variations in behavioral profiles among homeless youth. *American Journal of Community Psychology*, 37(1–2):63, 2006.

[9] M. J. Robertson and P. A. Toro. Homeless youth: Research, intervention, and policy. In *Practical Lessons: The 1998 National Symposium on Homelessness Research*. Washington, DC: US Department of Housing and Urban Development and US Department of Health and Human Services, 1999.

[10] L. B. Whitbeck and D. R. Hoyt. *Nowhere to Grow: Homeless and Runaway Adolescents and Their Families*. Transaction Publishers, 1999.

[11] L. B. Whitbeck, D. R. Hoyt, and K. A. Ackley. Abusive family backgrounds and later victimization among runaway and homeless adolescents. *Journal of Research on Adolescence*, 7(4):375–392, 1997.

[12] M. R. Zide and A. L. Cherry. A typology of runaway youths: An empirically based definition. *Child and Adolescent Social Work Journal*, 9(2):155–168, 1992.

[13] T. I. Herrenkohl, C. Sousa, E. A. Tajima, R. C. Herrenkohl, and C. A. Moylan. Intersection of child abuse and children's exposure to domestic violence. *Trauma, Violence, & Abuse*, 9(2): 84–99, 2008.

[14] S. W. Baron. Street youth, gender, financial strain, and crime: Exploring broidy and agnew's extension to general strain theory. *Deviant Behavior*, 28(3):273–302, 2007.

[15] D. M. Crawford, L. B. Whitbeck, and D. R. Hoyt. Propensity for violence among homeless and runaway adolescents: An event history analysis. *Crime & Delinquency*, 57(6):950–968, 2011.

[16] P. A. Toro, A. Dworsky, and P. J. Fowler. Homeless youth in the united states: Recent research findings and intervention approaches. In *National Symposium on Homelessness Research*, 2007.

[17] S. W. Baron. Street youth violence and victimization. *Trauma, Violence, & Abuse*, 4(1):22–44, 2003.

[18] S. W. Baron, L. W. Kennedy, and D. R. Forde. Male street youths' conflict: The role of background, subcultural, and situational factors. *Justice Quarterly*, 18(4):759–789, 2001.

[19] S. Gaetz. Safe streets for whom? Homeless youth, social exclusion, and criminal victimization. *Canadian Journal of Criminology and Criminal Justice*, 46(4):423–456, 2004.

[20] J. Ensign and J. Gittelsohn. Health and access to care: Perspectives of homeless youth in Baltimore City, USA. *Social Science & Medicine*, 47(12):2087–2099, 1998.

[21] J. Ensign and A. Panke. Barriers and bridges to care: Voices of homeless female adolescent youth in seattle, washington, usa. *Journal of Advanced Nursing*, 37(2):166–172, 2002.

[22] M. L. Forst, J. Harry, and P. A. Goddard. A health-profile comparison of delinquent and homeless youths. *Journal of Health Care for the Poor and Underserved*, 4(4):386–400, 1993.

[23] S. W. Hwang. Homelessness and health. *Canadian Medical Association Journal*, 164(2):229–233, 2001.

[24] J. Vanderleest. Medically uninsured and the homeless. In *The Care of the Uninsured in America*, pages 153–160. Springer, 2010.

[25] K. Bender, S. Thompson, K. Ferguson, and L. Langenderfer. Substance use predictors of victimization profiles among homeless youth: A latent class analysis. *Journal of Adolescence*, 37(2):155–164, 2014.

[26] K. M. Fitzpatrick and J. P. Boldizar. The prevalence and consequences of exposure to violence among African-American youth. *Journal of the American Academy of Child & Adolescent Psychiatry*, 32(2):424–430, 1993.

[27] S. Overstreet and S. Braun. Exposure to community violence and post-traumatic stress symptoms: Mediating factors. *American Journal of Orthopsychiatry*, 70(2):263, 2000.

[28] R. D. Latzman and R. R. Swisher. The interactive relationship among adolescent violence, street violence, and depression. *Journal of Community Psychology*, 33(3):355–371, 2005.

[29] J. J. Mazza and S. Overstreet. Children and adolescents exposed to community violence: A mental health perspective for school psychologists. *School Psychology Review*, 29(1):86, 2000.

[30] X. Chen, L. Thrane, L. B. Whitbeck, and K. Johnson. Mental disorders, comorbidity, and postrunaway arrests among homeless and runaway adolescents. *Journal of Research on Adolescence*, 16(3):379–402, 2006.

[31] B. W. Miles and S. K. Okamoto. The social construction of deviant behavior in homeless and runaway youth: Implications for practice. *Child and Adolescent Social Work Journal*, 25(5):425, 2008.

[32] M. Schwartz, H. K. Sorensen, S. Ammerman, and E. Bard. Exploring the relationship between homelessness and delinquency: A snapshot of a group of homeless youth in San Jose, California. *Child and Adolescent Social Work Journal*, 25(4):255, 2008.

[33] J. R. Yoder, K. Bender, S. J. Thompson, K. M. Ferguson, and B. Haffejee. Explaining homeless youths' criminal justice interactions: Childhood trauma or surviving life on the streets? *Community Mental Health Journal*, 50(2):135–144, 2014.

[34] R. Petering, S. Wenzel, and H. Winetrobe. Systematic review of current intimate partner violence prevention programs and applicability to homeless youth. *Journal of the Society for Social Work and Research*, 5(1):107–135, 2014.

[35] J. Fagan, D. L. Wilkinson, and G. Davies. Social contagion of violence. *The Cambridge Handbook of Violent Behavior*, Daniel Flannery, A. Vazsonyi, I. Waldman, eds., Cambridge University Press, 2007; Columbia Public Law Research Paper No. 06-126. Available at SSRN: https://ssrn.com/abstract=935104

[36] D. J. Myers. The diffusion of collective violence: Infectiousness, susceptibility, and mass media networks 1. *American Journal of Sociology*, 106(1):173–208, 2000.

[37] D. J. Myers and P. E. Oliver. The opposing forces diffusion model: The initiation and repression of collective violence. *Dynamics of Asymmetric Conflict*, 1(2):164–189, 2008.

[38] E. Even-Dar and A. Shapira. A note on maximizing the spread of influence in social networks. In *International Workshop on Web and Internet Economics*, pages 281–286. Springer, 2007.

[39] J. Duong and C. Bradshaw. Associations between bullying and engaging in aggressive and suicidal behaviors among sexual minority youth: the moderating role of connectedness. *The Journal of School Health*, 84(10): 635–645, 2014.

[40] Centers for Disease Control and Prevention: 2011 State and Local Youth Risk Behavior Survey. Available: http://www.cdc.gov/healthyyouth/yrbs/pdf/questionnaire/2011_hs_questionnaire.pdf.2011. Accessed August 11, 2011

[41] K. L. Gratz and L. Roemer. Multidimensional assessment of emotion regulation and dysregulation: Development, factor structure, and initial validation of the Difficulties in Emotion Regulation Scale. *Journal of Psychopathology and Behavioral Assessment*, 26(1): 41–54, 2004.

8

Artificial Intelligence for Improving Access to Sexual Health Necessities for Youth Experiencing Homelessness

Aida Rahmattalabi, Laura Onasch-Vera, Orlando Roybal,
Kien Nguyen, Luan Tran, Robin Petering,
Professor Eric Rice, and Professor Milind Tambe

Introduction

Homelessness and HIV Risk

Homelessness has been an issue in the United States for several decades and is continuing to grow. In 2013, the U.S. Department of Education and the U.S. Census found that there were approximately 1.6 million youth who were experiencing homelessness. More than 500,000 of those youth were homeless in California (Bassuk, DeCandia, Beach, and Berman, 2014). Homeless youth are at a greater risk of being infected with HIV because they are more likely to engage in risky behaviors such as inconsistent use of condoms, multiple sexual partners, and engaging in survival sex (Barman Adhikari, Begun, Rice, Yoshioka Maxwell, and Perez-Portillo, 2016).

When looking at homeless youth who access drop-in centers in Los Angeles, one in ten were HIV positive, compared to 0.3% rate of their housed counterparts. Additionally, about 40% of these youth do not know their status because they do not participate in regular testing, meaning it is very likely that the number of infected youth is substantially higher. Due to these findings a group of social workers are working to create a "Smart Kiosk" to address this public health epidemic.

Our Innovation: "Smart Kiosks"

The "Smart Kiosks" would allow youth to take their sexual health into their own hands. These kiosks provide free rapid HIV tests, condoms, and feminine hygiene products. Feminine hygiene products were included because the team discovered that one out three people experiencing homelessness in California are women and thus wanted to tailor their innovation to that increasing population (Evans, 2016).

The locations of the "Smart Kiosks" are very important in providing youth experiencing homelessness with the power to access these services in their own terms. For this purpose, our first step was to locate an area or city where youth experiencing homelessness frequented. We were able to narrow down our search to Venice, California. Our goal is to identify a specific location that is safe and accessible for youth experiencing homelessness. Due to limited funding and that these kiosks are stationary, it is important we find the best location before actual deployment. This problem led to the collaboration with AI.

We model the problem of identifying the "Smart Kiosks" locations as a variant of the well-known *k-center* problem. Given a metric space d, the *k-center* problem finds, among n locations, the best k locations to place facilities that are as close as possible to the rest of the points.

Our problem is also very similar to the *k-center* problem except that we are faced with several other requirements. First, an important constraint is that not all places in the area are eligible for placing the kiosks. The only eligible places are those that are city-owned, with access to utility. Secondly, the population distribution is a key factor in deciding the right places for the kiosks. A good estimation of the this distribution will help find locations that are accessible to larger population. Therefore, we will leverage data on where these youth are most likely to reside and we will estimate the distribution and density of homeless youth in the area. Finally, we would like to consider other existing centers that provide the same resources to these youth. This is particularly important because it is undesirable to place a kiosk near an existing service provider, which results in that kiosk not being utilized and not reaching the youth who might need these resources the most.

Problem Definition

In the following sections, we will first give a concrete description of the problem, then we discuss the required parameters, and how we use existing data to estimate these parameters. Next, we present the algorithm to solve the problem. Finally, we will conclude with experiments and results.

Weighted *K-Center* Problem

The *k-center* problem is a well-studied problem within operations research and computer science, which has different variants (Dyer and Frieze, 1985;

Kariv and Hakimi, 1979; Hochbaum and Shmoys, 1985; Plesnik, 1987). Also known as facility location problem, the problem in general is how one should select locations for new facilities or centers – "Smart Kiosks" in this work – to minimize a measure of distance to those locations, under some specific constraints.

A variant of this problem, which is particularly relevant to this work, is the weighted *k-center*, where the weights are used to represent the homeless youth population estimate, used as a proxy to measure demand. In this problem, the youth experiencing homelessness are not spread evenly in the area, and as a result, different sectors have different demands. Clearly, highly populated areas have higher weights as compared to sparsely populated areas.

Given a network $G(V, E, \omega)$, where V is the set of points, E is the set of weighted edges (a measure of cost between nodes) that form a complete metric space d, and ω is the set of all the nodes' weights, the weighted *k-center* problem is defined as selecting a subset S of the nodes in the graph, $S \subset V$, to minimize the maximum distance from all kiosks or shelters to the population of the homeless youth. The weights ω are the population density at each location.

In order to formalize all the above assumptions, let V' be the set of all eligible points to place these "Smart Kiosks." Also, let V'' be the set of existing centers and kiosks. The objective of the optimization problem can be formulated as:

$$\underset{K=(V' \cup V''), \ |V'|=k}{Minimize} \ \underset{v \in V}{Max} \ \underset{r \in K}{Min} \ [\omega(v) * d(v, r)] \qquad (8.1)$$

where $d(v, r) \in E$ is the cost associated with traveling from node v to node r. This objective summarizes as: For an arbitrary point with population density $\omega(v)$, $\underset{r \in K}{Min} \ [w(v) * d(v, r)]$ yields the kiosk r with minimum weighted distance from point v. Then for all points in V, the maximum distance to the closest kiosk will be minimized in order to find the best set of K kiosks.

Datasets

We use a dataset containing information of 118 youth experiencing homelessness in Venice, California. The data set includes survey data that asks the participants to indicate where they slept last night, where they spend time with friends, and their favorite locations. The dataset was collected in 2012. We also use a dataset containing information of existing services, including their locations and the type of services they provide, e.g., HIV testing, needle exchange, mental health service, drop-in center. The regions in Venice that are eligible to put kiosks are also collected.

Homeless Youth Geographic Data

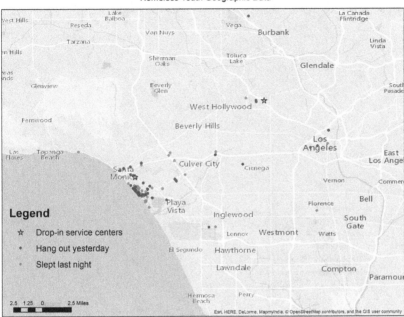

Figure 8.1a Homeless youth geographic data, Venice area

Figure 8.1a shows the reported locations for where the youth spent last night and where they usually spend time with friends. Figures 8.1b and 8.1c show the locations by type. As seen in the figures, Venice beach region is an attractive place for this population, which confirms the necessity and potential for installing the "Smart Kiosks."

Area Division

As our target area, we only consider Venice in Los Angeles, CA, as shown in Figure 8.2a. This area is about 3 square miles with a fairly large population of homeless youth. This area is divided into a grid with cells of size 100 m × 100 m, as shown in Figure 8.2b. Further discussion will be based on this grid.

Model Parameters

We modeled this problem using the notion of points, distances, and weights. In this section, we explain in more details how to collect such data and what we mean by abstract points.

Homeless Youth Sleeping Locations

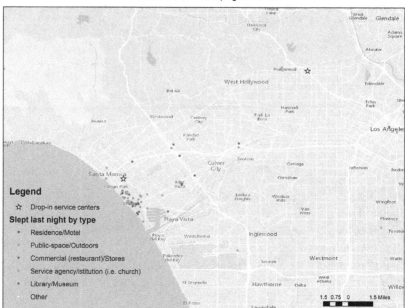

Figure 8.1b Homeless youth sleeping locations, Venice area

Points V

As discussed before, points in V can be the centers of the $100\,\text{m} \times 100\,\text{m}$ cells in the grid of Venice area. The eligible cells to install the kiosks can only be the cells that are owned by the city and have accessibility to utility. Therefore, we need to specify such cells beforehand. Also, note that the optimization is performed to maximize access for the entire region, and this restriction only applies to the candidate cells to place the kiosks.

Existing Centers V''

We are also interested in finding solutions that work best in the presence of other competing centers. If we fail to do so, chances are the proposed solutions is near an existing center and therefore will not be utilized as anticipated, which is indeed a waste of resources. In this problem, we assume there is a set of nodes that contain existing centers (denoted by V''), and $|V''| = m$ is the number of exiting centers.

Homeless Youth Hang Out Locations

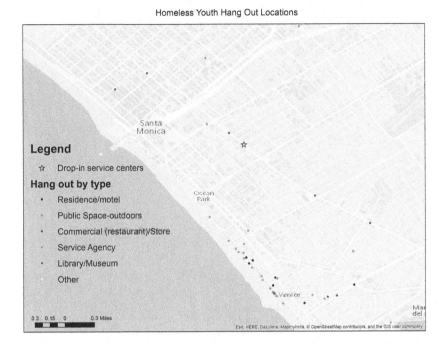

Figure 8.1c Homeless youth hangout locations, Venice area

Distances $d(v, r)$

For d, the distance between pairs of points in V, Euclidean distance, Manhattan distance, or walking distance can be used. While Euclidean distance and Manhattan distance can be calculated based on coordinates of the points, calculating walking distance is more challenging. Thus, external online services, e.g., Google Distance API, must be used to achieve this. In this work, we primarily use the Manhattan distance as it is provides a good proxy to the actual traveling distance. Given two points with (x, y) coordinates as $p_1 = (x_1, y_1)$ and $p_2 = (x_2, y_2)$, Manhattan distance (denoted by d) is calculated by:

$$d(p_1, p_2) = |x_1 - x_2| + |y_1 - y2|. \tag{8.2}$$

Weights $W(v)$

The point's weights, or the normalized population density of homeless youth residing in each cell, can be determined from existing survey data. This part is explained in more detail in the "Population Estimation" subsection.

Figure 8.2a Target area: Venice, Los Angeles, CA

Proposed Approach

The *k-center* problem is shown to be NP-hard, and therefore it is hard to find the optimal solution for equation 8.1, and approximation algorithms are often used to find near-optimal solutions.

Approximation algorithms for the basic *k-center* problem are well studied in Hochbaum and Shmoys (1985), Gonzalez (1985), and Plesnik (1987). These schemes present a natural approximation factor of 2. (This means that the

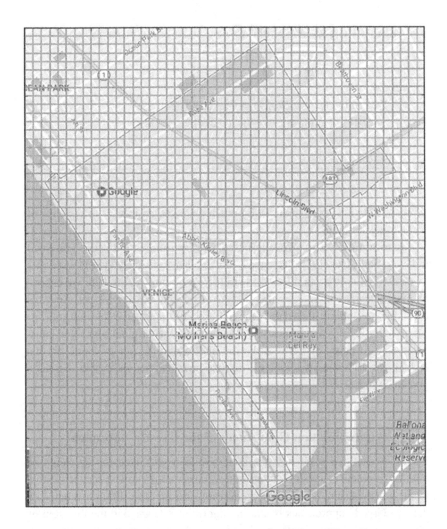

Figure 8.2b   Venice area, divided into a grid of 100m × 100m cells

solution of the approximate algorithm cannot perform worse than 2 times the value of the optimal solution.) Several approximation algorithms are known for the interesting generalizations of the basic *k-center* problem, including ones that add costs or weights (Hochbaum and Shmoys, 1986; Plesnik, 1987). From the literature, the weighted *k-center* problems in Dyer and Frieze (1985) and Plesnik (1987) are closest to the present work, as they consider weights on points in their models. In particular, we develop an algorithm similar to the one proposed in Dyer and Frieze (1985), who present a greedy-based approach

---

Algorithm 8.1 Greedy Algorithm for weighted *k-center* problem

1: $i \leftarrow 1$
2: Set $D(v) = \min\{\omega(v) * d(v, v_j)\}, \quad \forall v \in V \quad \forall j \in M$
3: **repeat**
4:     Determine v_{i+1} by $D(v_{i+1}) = \max_{v \in V} D(v)$
5:     Set $D(v) = \min\{\omega(v) * d(v, v_{i+1}), D(v)\}, \quad \forall v \in V$
6:     $i = i + 1$
7: **until** $(i < K)$

---

shown to provide approximate solutions no worse than $\min(3, 1+\alpha)$ factor of the optimal solution.

Algorithm 8.1 is also a Greedy-based approach similar to the one presented in Dyer and Frieze (1985). However, unlike Dyer and Frieze (1985) that starts by selecting the first point (kiosk) with the maximum weight, here we choose the one with maximum weighted distance from the existing kiosks. And this procedure is continued until the desired number of points are selected.

As a result, the approximation guarantee of the original algorithm must be studied to make sure it is still valid and extends to our problem. To this end, in the following section, we discuss how we can show that the same guarantee holds.

Approximation Guarantees of the Greedy Approach

In this section, we prove how the approximation guarantee for the weighted *k-center* problem can also be extended for the *k-center* variant proposed in this work, which assumes m centers are already chosen. The difference between the two Greedy approaches is that in Algorithm 8.1, we skip the first step of selecting the first node with maximum weight. However, we can still show that the same approximation guarantee holds, and to do so we simply assume that the already chosen nodes (existing centers) have very high weight values. This is a legit assumption, since these nodes are already chosen, and it will not affect the final solution to the problem. In fact, if we run the original Greedy algorithm on the new problem, with modified weights of the nodes associated with the existing centers and assuming no existing centers, the algorithm chooses those centers as the first m centers, and from that point on, it will select the additional points that are in fact the solutions to our problem. Therefore, we showed that the solution of Algorithm 8.1 for weighted *k-center* with existing centers is the same as the solution of the algorithm in Dyer and

Frieze (1985) for the basic weighted *k-center* problem. Based on the argument made, we see that the Greedy approach provides the same approximation of $\min\{3, 1 + \alpha\}$, where α is the maximum ratio of weights between the points in V. Based on the assumption made, α also takes a high value, and therefore, factor of 3 is the approximation guarantee for the weighted *k-center* problem with existing centers.

Population Estimation

Since the objective is to provide a better access to these kiosks, it is important to factor in the distribution of homeless youth in the area. Therefore, estimating the number of homeless youth in a given cell is a crucial part of this research. This problem is considered as density estimation problem (Silverman, 1986).

Let z be a discrete random variable, where $z = (X, Y)$ indicates that a person resides at cell (X, Y). More formally, the probability mass function Rao (2009):

$$f_z(x, y) = Pr(z = (x, y))$$

gives the probability that a person is at cell (x, y). Density estimation is the process of estimating the function f_z, given the observed data of homeless youth locations.

In this study, we consider three different density estimations: *histogram based distribution estimation, mixture of Gaussian estimation*, and finally we compare with a *uniform distribution estimation* that assumes the population is uniformly distributed over the area. In other words, in *uniform distribution estimation*, cells in the region have the same probability of a homeless youth being present,

$$f_z(x, y) = \frac{1}{N},$$

with N being the total number of cells. In this approach, the estimated number of homeless youth in each cell is the same and it leads the optimization to only consider the distances between cells and kiosks. This estimation approach can be used for the regions that have homeless youth distributed approximately uniformly over cells. In the second approach, *histogram based distribution estimation*, the counts of homeless youth in cells are used to estimate the density function $f_z(x, y)$. Let $count_1, count_2, \ldots, count_N$ denote the number of homeless youth in cells $(x^1, y^1), (x^2, y^2) \ldots, (x^N, y^N)$, respectively. The probability that a person stays at cell $x^i, y^i, 1 \le i \le N$ is:

$$f_z(x^i, y^i) = \frac{count_i}{\sum_{i=1}^{N} count_i}.$$

This approach is better than uniform distribution estimation when all the counts are collected. But in reality, there is a lot of missing data. Figure 8.3a shows the counts of homeless youth over cells. As we can see in this figure, there are areas that have high number of homeless youth and also a lot of missing data. In this approach, for cell x^i, y^i in which the count of number of homeless youth is missing, we assume that count is 0 and therefore $f_z(x^i, y^i) = 0$. However, imputing the missing data is one critical problem. There are a lot of studies on this problem: temporal prediction (Shi et al., 2016), which exploits the temporal relationship of value at one location at multiple times; spatial interpolation (Lam, 1983), which exploits the relation between the values at nearby locations; and others. With the *mixture of Gaussian estimation* approach, we try to estimate the missing information by spatial interpolation of the observed data. We assume the distribution of homeless

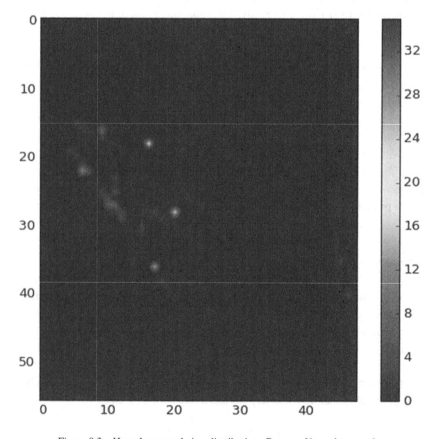

Figure 8.3a Homeless population distribution: Counts of homeless youth

youth is a mixture of Gaussian so that the homeless youth are distributed smoothly over cells. The probability that a person is present in the cell x^i, y^i is a linear combination of q two dimensional Gaussian distribution density functions,

$$f_z(x^i, y^i) = \sum_{i=1}^{q} w_i \frac{exp(\frac{1}{2}(x - \mu)^T \sum^{-1}(x - \mu))}{\sqrt{(2\pi)^2|\sum|}},$$

with $\sum_i^q w_i = 1$ where x is a two-dimensional real-valued column vector representing the coordinate of a cell, $|\sum|$ is the determinant of the covariance matrix $\sum$, μ is the vector mean, and w_i is the coefficient determining the weight of component i. With only one Gaussian distribution, the mean value gets the highest probability. Therefore, we choose the q cells with highest counts to be the means of the k components. Figure 8.3b shows the heat map of estimated

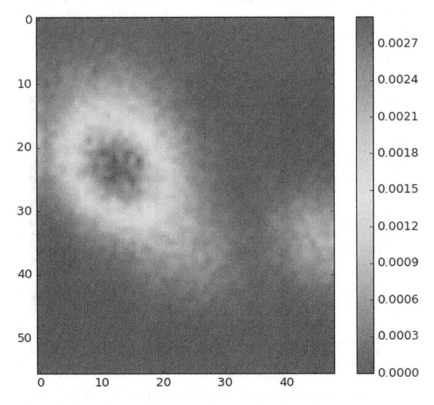

Figure 8.3b Homeless population distribution: Estimated mixture of Gaussian distributions

homeless youth distribution with $q = 50$. The means of the Gaussians are locations with the top 50 counts of youth and the covariance matrix is equal to: $\Sigma = \begin{bmatrix} 30 & 5 \\ 5 & 30 \end{bmatrix}$. The weights for the components are set proportionally to the number of homeless youth at the center of each component. As we can see in this figure, the missing data is imputed smoothly over the entire area.

Results

To demonstrate the effectiveness of our algorithm, we compare it with a baseline algorithm. The baseline algorithm selects nodes consecutively in the most populated cells. Figure 8.4 compares the maximum weighted distance to centers for three different population distributions and the case of installing two new centers ($K = 2$). As indicated, the Greedy algorithm outperforms the baseline in all three cases with a maximum improvement of 40%. Also, Figure 8.5 shows the output of the Greedy algorithm on the map of the Venice area. In the discussion section, we explain how these suggested spots are reasonable.

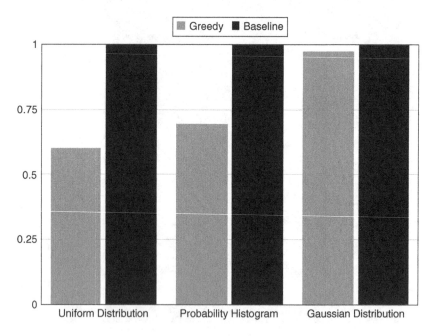

Figure 8.4 Normalized maximum distance to centers for different population distributions for the case of selecting two centers. In all three cases, the Greedy algorithm outperforms the baseline algorithm.

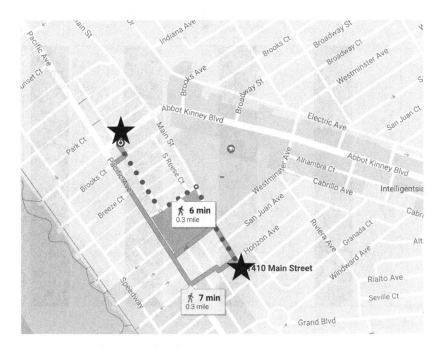

Figure 8.5 The two candidate locations for placing kiosks under Gaussian population distribution assumption.

In another experiment, we looked at how the algorithm scales with the number of centers. Figures 8.6–8.8 indicate the results for the three population distribution models when the number of centers is increased from $K = 1$ to $K = 5$. As seen, the Greedy algorithm still performs significantly better than the baseline. Interestingly, with Gaussian distribution model, as we increase the number of centers, the marginal improvement from the Greedy algorithm also increases. This indicates that with more information about the population, it is increasingly more difficult to perform well, and more careful optimization is required.

Discussion and Conclusions

In this study, we specifically focused on placing Smart Kiosks in the Venice area in Los Angeles, CA. We viewed this problem as an optimization task where we aimed to minimize the maximum traveling distance to the Smart Kiosks. This problem is very important to our target population, as it can

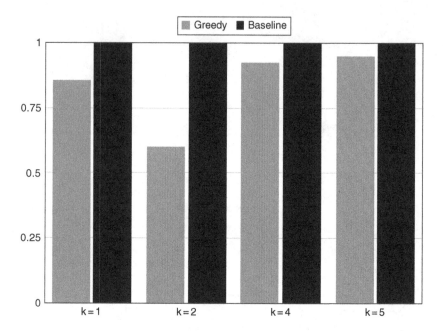

Figure 8.6 Normalized maximum distance to centers for uniform distribution for different number of centers.

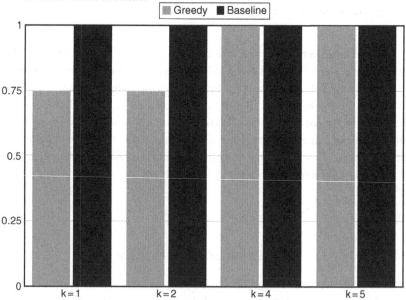

Figure 8.7 Normalized maximum distance to centers for probability histogram distribution for different number of centers.

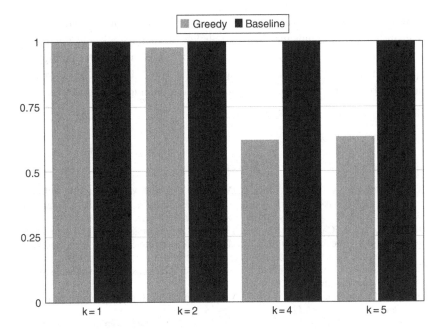

Figure 8.8 Normalized maximum distance to centers for Gaussian distribution for
different number of centers.

greatly impact the usability of the kiosks for such a transient and vulnerable
group. We formulated this problem using a weighted variant of the well-known
k-center problem and we used a Greedy-based approach to choose the kiosk
locations. We compared the results of the Greedy algorithm to a baseline
algorithm, and we observed that the Greedy approach outperforms the baseline
(up to 40% improvement). As an example, in the case of placing two new
kiosks, the Greedy algorithm suggested locations that are in central areas of
Venice. One is a location on the Main Street, a central street in Venice located
in an area that would capture foot traffic of the youth who go between seeking
services more inland and going back to the Venice Beach Boardwalk and skate
park. By examining the proposed locations, we can observe that the algorithm
has not only identified areas that are viable through using data, but it is also
selecting areas that are meaningful and understandable when learning more
about the patterns of youth experiencing homelessness. Therefore, by the help
of artificial intelligence, we were able to provide places to deploy these kiosks
that not only make it more accessible to the youth but also have the potential
to reach and serve a greater number of youth experiencing homelessness.
Through this partnership between computer science and social work we have

shown that complex social problems can be addressed with innovative ideas that are created through the dual knowledge of social work and computer science. There will need to be further work to assess if such technology is appropriate and if it would have an impact on the HIV/AIDS epidemic. We are hopeful to see this innovation continue with the continued support of social work and computer science experts.

References

Barman Adhikari A., Begun S., Rice E., Yoshioka Maxwell A., and Perez-Portillo A. 2016. Sociometric network structure and its association with methamphetamine use norms among homeless youth. *Social Science Research*, **58**, 292–308.

Bassuk E. L., DeCandia C. J., Beach C. A., and Berman F. 2014. America's youngest outcasts: A report card on child homelessness. The National Center on Family Homelessness at American Institutes for Research. https://www.air.org/sites/default/files/downloads/report/Americas-Youngest-Outcasts-Child-Homelessness-Nov2014.pdf.

Dyer, M. E, and Frieze, A. M. 1985. A simple heuristic for the p-centre problem. *Operations Research Letters*, **3**(6), 285–288.

Evans, Erica. 2016. L. A. County will try to house 100 homeless youths in 100 days. *Los Angeles Times*, July 26.

Gonzalez, T. F. 1985. Clustering to minimize the maximum intercluster distance. *Theoretical Computer Science*, **38**, 293–306.

Hochbaum, D. S., and Shmoys, D. B. 1985. A best possible heuristic for the k-center problem. *Mathematics of Operations Research*, **10**(2), 180–184.

Hochbaum, D. S., and Shmoys, D. B. 1986. A unified approach to approximation algorithms for bottleneck problems. *Journal of the ACM (JACM)*, **33**(3), 533–550.

Kariv, O., and Hakimi, S. L. 1979. An algorithmic approach to network location problems. I: The p-centers. *SIAM Journal on Applied Mathematics*, **37**(3), 513–538.

Lam, N. S.-N. 1983. Spatial interpolation methods: A review. *The American Cartographer*, **10**(2), 129–150.

Plesnik, J. 1987. A heuristic for the p-center problems in graphs. *Discrete Applied Mathematics*, **17**(3), 263–268.

Rao, S. S. 2009. *Engineering Optimization: Theory and Practice, 4th ed.* Hoboken, NJ: John Wiley and Sons.

Shi, W., Zhu, Y., Yu, P. S., Huang, T., Wang, C., Mao, Y., and Chen, Y. 2016. Temporal dynamic matrix factorization for missing data prediction in large scale coevolving time series. *IEEE Access*, **4**, 6719–6732.

Silverman, B. W. 1986. *Density Estimation for Statistics and Data Analysis*. London: Chapman & Hall.

9

Know-Stress

Predictive Modeling of Stress among Diabetes Patients
under Varying Conditions

Subhasree Sengupta, Kexin Yu, and Behnam Zahiri

Introduction

Around 422 million people worldwide had diabetes mellitus in 2014 (World Health Organization, 2016). The global diabetes prevalence rate has increased from 4.7% in 1980 to 8.5% now (World Health Organization, 2016). Type 2 diabetes (T2D) diminishes patients' quality of life. Diabetes patients are more likely to suffer from visual and hearing impairments, overweight issues, osteoarthritis, stroke, and possess two- to threefold increased risk of physical disability than people not suffering from diabetes (Gregg et al., 2000; Kirkman et al., 2012; Schwartz et al., 2002; Volpato et al., 2002; Volpato, Leveille, Blaum, Fried, & Guralnik, 2005).

T2D has been widely recognized as a chronic disease caused by unhealthy lifestyle. However, in recent years, psychological factors were brought to researchers' attention because physical factors could not fully explain the development and progression of T2D. Compared to nondiabetic individuals, diabetes patients experience chronic allostatic load, which manifests as impaired post-stress recovery and blunted stress reactivity (Carvalho et al., 2015; Steptoe et al., 2014).

The prevalence of diabetes is higher among low-income groups and ethnic minorities (Lanting, Joung, Mackenbach, Lamberts, & Bootsma, 2005). Former research presents the trend that stress level increases as the socioeconomic status decreases (Orpana, Lemyre, & Kelly, 2007). Occupational and financial stressors, frequently experienced by low-income groups, have been shown to be significantly associated with the development and progression of T2D (Morikawa et al., 2005). Social stressors – for example, social rejection – have also been indicated to be correlated with physiologic stress response (Slavich, O'Donovan, Epel, & Kemeny, 2010). Considerable amount of empirical evidence implies the importance of delivering stress relief intervention for low-income T2D patients.

In existing studies, social scientists employ statistical analyses to identify the association between stress and the development of T2D on a group level (Kelly & Ismail, 2015). Machine learning algorithms to make prediction of stress levels in individual cases becomes possible.

The purpose of this chapter is to predict stress levels of low-income T2D patients using machine learning–based classification techniques, aspiring to build models that can be utilized to help identify vulnerable individuals and thus provide timely interventions.

Data Description

A Brief Background of the Data Set Used

This project employs secondary data from the Diabetes–Depression Care-management Adoption Trial (DCAT). The purpose of the DCAT program was to reduce health disparities of low-income population by optimizing depression screening, treatment, follow-up, outcomes, and cost saving using technology (Wu et al., 2014). In collaboration with Los Angeles County Department of Health Services (DHS) Ambulatory Care Network (ACN), DCAT intervention was implemented from 2010 to 2013 among 1,400 low-income diabetes patients in Los Angeles County (Wu et al., 2014). The participants were predominantly Hispanic/Latino Immigrants (89%). The DCAT program collected baseline and 6-, 12-, and 18-month follow-up data (Wu et al., 2014). This current study analyzes **only** the baseline data.

Description of Variables Presented in the Dataset

The DCAT baseline data was collected through surveys, interviews, and medical records. Interviews provide socio-demographic information (e.g., age, gender, ethnicity) as well as self-reported health information. Depression symptoms are assessed with Patient Health Questionnaire-9 (PHQ-9) and Symptom Checklist-20 (SCL-20). Dysthymia is measured using two standard questions from Diagnostic and Statistical Manual of Mental Disorders (DSM)-IV. Functional impairment was measured using Sheehan Disability Scale. Medical Outcomes Study Short-Form Health Survey (MOS SF-12), and Physical and Mental component summaries (PCS, MCS) were used to assess Health-related quality of life. Pain impact was measured using SF-12. Anxiety was measured with Brief Symptom Inventory (BSI). Diabetes distress is measured

Table 9.1. *Description of the variables in the data set*

Variables Category	Measurement Scales Used/Description of the Variables
Social demographics	Age, gender, marital status, racial/ethnic group, birthplace, time living in the United States, language, and education
Depression	PHQ-9, SCL-20
Dysthymia	Two standard question from DSM-IV
Functional impairment	Sheehan Disability Scale
Health-related quality of life	Medical outcome study short-form health survey (MOS SF-12), physical and mental component summaries (PCS, MCS)
Chronic pain	Pain present most of the items for 6 months or longer
Pain impact	Short Form-12
Anxiety	Brief symptom inventory (BSI)
Patient satisfaction with diabetes care and emotional care	A 5-point Likert scale from "very dissatisfied" to "very satisfied."
Diabetes symptoms	Whitty 9-item questionnaire
Diabetes distress	Diabetes distress scale
Body Mass Index	Self-reported weight and height
Medical history	Including hospitalization, clinic and emergency department visits, pharmacy pick-up, and International Statistical Classification of Diseases and Related Health Problems (ICD)-9 codes for diagnostic diseases, as well as the lab results of glycated hemoglobin (A1C), micro-albumin, and a lipid panel during the same period.
Health service utilization	Previous outpatient (medical and mental health), inpatient, and emergency room service utilization.
Administrative cost	Using data from DHS outpatient and pharmacy billing records, electronic emergency room and hospitalization billing cost, and mental health care use data from medical records.

using a two-item diabetes distress scale. Diabetes symptoms are assessed using Whitty-9 item questionnaire. The DCAT research team also acquired medical record data that included medical history, health service utilization, and administrative costs. All these variables were used as predictors of stress in our data set. Table 9.1 presents a summary of these predictor variables.

Socioeconomic stress is the outcome this project aims to predict, which is measured with 12 items that describe a list of stressful life issues, including work problems, unemployment problems, financial problems, marital conflicts, family conflict, parenting concerns, caregiving problems, cultural conflicts, legal problems, immigration problems, serious illness or loss of a close person, and community violence concerns. The participants give answers using a scale from 0 to 10, which represents stress level ranging from "no stress at all" to "the most stress you can imagine." In subsequent sections we provide a description of how to convert the 12-item measurement into a single variable using a technique called factor analysis.

Aim of Our Analysis

We address three fundamental objectives in our analysis:

1. Predicted variable creation: As mentioned, our desired outcome variable is expressed as a combination of 12 separate outcome variables. We present an empirical process of aggregating these into a single outcome variable.
2. Determining optimal cutoff: We want to predict if the stress level of the patient falls into the high stress level category or into the low stress level category. Thus, since we have only two possible categories, we want our stress predictor variable to be a binary variable ('1' – high stress and '0' – low stress). However, after the initial aggregation process as mentioned in (1), the final aggregated variable is a continuous variable whereas we needed a categorical variable. Thus, we also present a mechanism creating this binary classification scheme from our aggregated predictor variable by determining the most optimal "cutoff score," i.e. for any value above the cutoff we will consider the level of the associated patient to fall into the high stress category, and vice versa for any value below the cutoff.
3. Feature selection: Our data set has a large number of predictor variables, so collecting this information might need a lot of time and effort; furthermore, it may not always be possible to have all this information. Hence the most important goal for us was to identify a small subset of predictor variables without affecting the overall performance of the model as compared to the case when all the predictor variables are present. To achieve this, we experiment with different data sets formed by grouping our predictor variables into four categories. Then we create a dataset for each of these four categories having predictor variables pertaining to only that category to predict socioeconomic stress. We also conduct a feature selection experiment using a machine learning algorithm called Extremely Randomized Trees (Geurts, Ernst, & Wehenkel, 2006), which we will briefly explain in subsequent sections.

More Detailed Description of the Aims of the Project

Predicted Variable Creation

In the data set, there are 12 indicators of socioeconomic stress. Since we want a single indicator variable for stress, we create a single variable for indicating stress level using the following aggregation technique. First, we conduct factor analysis (Thompson, 2004) to find latent factors in the 12 variables. We found that there was only a single dominant latent factor and hence we could aggregate these 12 variables into a single variable. Using this knowledge, we know that a single variable is sufficient to represent the combined effect of these 12 variables. We compute the single variable as the sum of the 12 stress variables to create the single continuous variable, which we shall refer to as "stress_sum." Thus, we use the "stress_sum" value to express the combined effect of the 12 different stress indicator variables.

Determining Optimal Cutoff

As mentioned earlier, we aim to be able to distinguish high–stressed patients from low–stressed patients. Thus, we want to create a binary classification scheme to divide our continuous "stress_sum" variable into the two required categories. The way we achieve this is by creating several cutoff values. All the individuals whose stress level was below the cutoff value were assigned to the low–stress category, and the values above were assigned to the high–stress category.

To find the optimal cutoff, we want to determine the cutoff value that performs best among our experimental models. To choose the cutoff values, we first sort the "stress_sum" value in ascending order for all records. Next, we choose the values at 20th percentile, 25th percentile, 33rd percentile, and finally 50th percentile from the aforementioned ordering. The corresponding values were 15, 19, 25, and 39, respectively. We did not choose cutoff values beyond this point, as doing so would lead to severe class imbalance (the proportion of low-stress patients would significantly outnumber the proportion of high-stress patients) thus affecting the prediction ability of our machine learning models.

Feature Selection and Various Data Sets

To choose the ideal set of features (predictor variables), we started by selecting different subsets of the entire data set.

1. Cleansed data set: One major drawback of our data set is that there are several missing values and so the first data set we made was by removing all these missing values. In total we had 130 features and 1,340 patient records in this cleansed data set. We removed about 35% of the data. This data set acts as the baseline against which we compare the performances of the data sets described below.

2. Data sets based on categories of predictor variables: There can be several ways in which the features or predictor variables can be divided into categories. However, we divided the data set into four major categories, namely demographic, biological (health-related variables like weight, other ailments, etc.), psychological, and social variables. The intuition behind this classification of predictor variables is the fact that sometimes, due to financial or time constraints, it might not be feasible to run the entire study to collect all the information we had in our data set. Hence, if we can have access to only some categories of information, can we still get a model with comparable performance to model using the data set in (1)?

3. We used a machine learning model called extremely randomized trees, which is a tree-based ensemble method for learning the Top 25 features. We chose 25 as per consultation with domain experts. The goal was to compare the predictor variables selected here using this method with those in the data sets in (2) and to get an intuitive reason behind the features selected by the machine learning model.

Experimental Setup

For each of the data sets mentioned on the preceding list, we randomly divide the data into 70% for training and 30% for testing. Training implies the we use 70% of the data in each data set to learn the machine learning models and then evaluate the learned models using the test data sets. The metrics used for evaluation are as described in the metrics section that follows.

Models of Classification

Our problem is a classification task (Caruana & Niculescu-Mizil, 2006): i.e., using the machine learning algorithms described in this section, we want to classify each patient in the data sets into either the high-stress or the low-stress category.

An important term used in the context of classification is decision boundary – i.e., a separation point. The idea of the decision boundary is basically that it serves as a threshold such that any value above the threshold is classified as "True" (or high stress in our application) and anything below is classified as "False" (or low stress in our application). This separation can be expressed as a line or hyperplane in case of linear decision boundaries, but often a line cannot serve as an efficient separator. So, depending on the distribution of the data, we might need to revert to nonlinear separators.

Given this, we use three widely used machine learning models of classification. Their popularity stems from several reasons, such as efficient software that enables the model to scale very well with the increasing size of the data set; interpretability – ease of understanding what the model is accomplishing; etc.

Very briefly, the mathematical intuition behind classification is expressed as follows:

1. Let us assume we have a vector <P> of predictors, where $P = <p_1, p_2, \ldots>$.
2. We want to learn a function f(w,p), a weighted combination of P, such that the error between the computed functional value and the true value in the training data set is minimized.
3. Then we test and evaluate this computed function using the test data set.

Neural Networks: Neural networks have recently gained widespread popularity in health care, as reported in Lisboa & Taktak (2006). Neural networks have demonstrated to be very useful for classification, since they can approximate both linear and nonlinear decision boundaries very well, making the neural networks very powerful and efficient. Further, with the growing size of data sets, neural network–based classification can be very effective, and on this basis has gained tremendous popularity as a standard image classification/speech recognition tool.

The inspiration behind this method is the neural architecture found in the human brain. Like the human brain, the different layers act as multiple layers of processing or functional transformations (also called hidden layers) on the initial input before the final output layer is reached.

Briefly the working of a neural network can be explained as follows:

1. Each layer consists of a set of neurons that serve the input for that layer.
2. We then take a weighted combination of the inputs coming through these neurons.
3. Some form of activation function is applied.
4. Now we take the output of (3) to become inputs of the next layer, and this follows until the output layer.

5. Finally, the output obtained from the final layer is compared against the actual output; the error is computed and the weights all the way back to the input layer are adjusted. This process is also called back propagation.
6. This entire process can be repeated many times to better train the model – each full cycle (steps 1–5 are called an epoch.)

The neural network model we use has the following characteristics:

1. Neurons in the input layer equal the number of predictor variables.
2. Two hidden layers, with 20 neurons per hidden layer.
3. Two neurons in the output layer, since we have two classes.
4. We use the "Relu" activation function for connecting the input layer to the first hidden layer and for connecting the first hidden layer to the second one.
5. The final connection from the second hidden layer to the output layer will use a SoftMax activation function, since this is a multi-class classification case.

We use the keras wrapper for implementing the architecture of the neural network with Tensor flow as the backend for training the weights.

Decision Tree

Using a decision tree–based aid has gained a lot of importance in mining of health care data (Koh & Tan, 2011). The ease of interpretability of this method makes it a popular choice among machine learning methods. For a concrete understanding of how a decision tree is constructed, please refer to Quinlan (1987).

Aside from adding validity to the results obtained by the neural network, another purpose of the decision tree method is to get an idea about which predictor variables significantly affect the predictive capability of the learned model, thereby giving us an intuition into which features we necessarily need to keep when selecting the top 25 features from the dataset.

Logistic Regression

Logistic regression is the common technique used in a multi-class classification used when the outcome variable is categorical (binary in this application). Thus, this technique will serve more as a baseline or benchmark for us to compare with the machine learning classifiers as described earlier.

Feature Selection

The top 25 features were selected by a machine learning model called extremely randomized trees (Geurts, Ernst, & Wehenkel, 2006). It is a tree-based ensemble method. An ensemble is a collection of many decision trees. Besides accuracy, the main strength of the resulting algorithm is computational efficiency. This technique gives us the importance value for each feature (predictor) in obtaining the output. We then sort the features by this value in descending order and select the top 25 features.

Metrics of Evaluation

Some important terminology:

1. True positives (TP): Those patients in the test set who had "high" stress and were predicted to have high stress.
2. False positives (FP): Those patients in the test set who had "low" stress and were predicted to have high stress.
3. True negatives (TN): Those patients in the test set who had "low" stress and were predicted to have low stress.
4. False negatives (FN): Those patients in the test set who had "high" stress and were predicted to have low stress.

The metrics used are:

1. Accuracy: $(\Sigma\ TP + \Sigma TN)/(\Sigma\ TP + \Sigma TN + \Sigma FN + \Sigma FP)$
2. Recall: $\Sigma\ TP/(\Sigma\ TP + \Sigma\ FN)$ {Over all the actual "high" samples how many "high" samples did the model correctly "recall"}
3. Precision: $\Sigma TP/(\Sigma\ TP + \Sigma\ FP)$ {Over all the "high" samples the model identifid how many were actually "high"}
4. Confusion matrix A matrix representation of TP, FP, TN, FN. This tabular representation provides more of a visual aid to understand the effectiveness of our models. For example, here we find that the rate of true

Table 9.2. *A sample confusion matrix*

	Predicted Low	Predicted High
Actual Low	189 (TN)	10 (FP)
Actual High	5 (FN)	198 (TP)

positives and true negatives is high, which means we have learned a very
good model.
5. AUC: Area under the ROC (Receiver Operating Characteristic).
   AUC value gives the area under the curve (where the x-axis is the false
   positive rate and the y-axis is the true positive rate), and since we want to
   increase the true positive rate, we want a higher AUC value. That indicates
   that the larger the area under the plotted curve, the better our model's
   performance will be.

Experimental Results and Discussion

A total of 84 different models were experimented on. Here we present and
discuss the results obtained from the neural network experiments. We also
discuss the results from performing feature selection as described in the
previous section. The results and trends obtained from the decision tree and
logistic regression are very close numerically to the results of the neural

Table 9.3. *Results for the cleansed data set*

	Accuracy	Precision	Recall	Confusion Matrix		AUC
Cutoff = 15	0.72	0.718	0.67	171	49	0.791
				61	125	
Cutoff = 19	0.736	0.713	0.8	135	66	0.813
				41	164	
Cutoff = 25	0.682	0.607	0.842	122	100	0.792
				29	155	
Cutoff = 39	0.73	0.7318	0.682	166	48	0.801
				61	131	

Table 9.4. *Results for data set with only demographic info*

	Accuracy	Precision	Recall	Confusion Matrix		AUC
Cutoff = 15	0.685	0.708	0.6108	160	51	0.764
				79	124	
Cutoff = 19	0.714	0.583	0.608	209	62	0.774
				56	87	
Cutoff = 25	0.705	0.458	0.541	232	71	0.699
				51	60	
Cutoff = 39	0.874	0.5	0.08	358	4	0.77
				48	4	

network experiments, which means they reflect the same trends and hence have not been explicitly presented here.

An important observation here is that we find with increasing the cutoff value there is a significant drop in the recall score obtained. This can further

Table 9.5. *Results for data set with only biological info*

	Accuracy	Precision	Recall	Confusion Matrix		AUC
Cutoff = 15	0.504	0.486	0.974	20	204	0.704
				5	193	
Cutoff = 19	0.644	0.53	0.631	168	89	0.708
				56	87	
Cutoff = 25	0.734	0.566	0.146	293	13	0.679
				99	17	
Cutoff = 39	0.817	0.222	0.255	333	42	0.701
				35	12	

Table 9.6. *Results for data set with demographic and biological info*

	Accuracy	Precision	Recall	Confusion Matrix		AUC
Cutoff = 15	0.725	0.774	0.587	189	34	0.777
				82	117	
Cutoff = 19	0.741	0.72	0.471	241	28	0.794
				81	72	
Cutoff = 25	0.748	0.459	0.583	260	66	0.786
				40	56	
Cutoff = 39	0.843	0.345	0.387	337	36	0.794
				30	19	

Table 9.7. *Results for data set with demographic, biological and psychological info*

	Accuracy	Precision	Recall	Confusion Matrix		AUC
Cutoff = 15	0.73	0.69	0.74	164	63	0.79
				51	144	
Cutoff = 19	0.71	0.76	0.35	248	17	0.81
				102	55	
Cutoff = 25	0.77	0.73	0.395	280	18	0.779
				75	49	
Cutoff = 39	0.88	0.4	0.127	336	9	0.78
				41	6	

Table 9.8. *Results for data set with demographic, biological, and psychological and social info*

	Accuracy	Precision	Recall	Confusion Matrix		AUC
Cutoff = 15	0.72	0.74	0.59	191	39	0.79
				51	144	
Cutoff = 19	0.73	0.76	0.37	253	18	0.81
				95	56	
Cutoff = 25	0.78	0.62	0.41	287	27	0.80
				64	44	
Cutoff = 39	0.89	0.66	0.04	375	1	0.85
				44	2	

Table 9.9. *Results for feature selection*

	Accuracy	Precision	Recall	Confusion Matrix		AUC
Cutoff = 15	0.73	0.67	0.89	112	89	0.815
				22	183	
Cutoff = 19	0.7	0.77	0.51	186	28	0.76
				94	98	
Cutoff = 25	0.73	0.74	0.67	166	45	0.81
				63	132	
Cutoff = 39	0.75	0.7	0.83	144	69	0.84
				32	161	

be observed from the confusion matrix; the number of false negatives is significantly higher as compared to the number of true positives. The chief cause of this is class balance, i.e., there are many more data points labeled as "low stress" than "high stress." This trend can also be seen in many of the results presented below.

Discussion on the Results

Optimal Cutoff Range

From the results presented in the previous section it appears that pretty much all the different cutoffs give a reasonably good model performance when the cleansed data set is used. When the experiments are performed on the demographic or biological data sets, or combinations of these, we find that choosing a higher cutoff value (>20) severely affects the recall score of the model and the true positive rate drastically falls, which is not a desirable outcome. Overall, taking all the metrics into consideration, based on the results, a cutoff score of 15 seems to be perform best. **In terms of a range for the cutoff value, the range of 15–19 performs best.**

Model Stability

One significant observation about the experiments described earlier in the chapter is that when the data set is manually partitioned into the demographic, biological, psychological, and social data sets, experimenting on these or a combination of these data sets severely affects model performance. For example, in the combined demographic, biological, psychological, and social data set we find that at the cutoff of 39 the recall score drops to 0.04 and the ratio of FP:TP is 22:1, which is not desired at all. This is a bit counterintuitive, as based on our feature selection results where most of the selected features are psychological, we would presume that the model would perform better. A probable reason for this can be that some form of over-fitting is taking place. We also find that, rather than experimenting with only demographic or biological data, using a combination of both reflects improvements in model performance, but adding psychological and social variables does not boost the performance – in fact, quite the opposite.

Feature Selection

We perform feature selection using a machine learning model called extremely randomized trees. Using this we can identify the top 25 features in the data set. The selected features are a mixture of biological, psychological, and some demographic features. Interestingly, we find that the features located at the top two levels of the decision tree as applied to the demographic and biological data sets also appear in the features selected by the machine learning algorithm for feature selection. This helps interpret the machine learning–based feature selection method.

We find that there is not as much fluctuation in model performance as we have seen when trying the data sets with distinct categories created manually (demographic, biological, psychological, and social). Thus, using this machine learning approach would be better/more stable than the manual category–based data-partitioning method we have presented.

Briefly explaining the features selected using this method: in terms of demographic features, we had some items such as age and gender; in terms of biological features, we had onset age of diabetes, BMI, and measures of any form of disability; in terms of psychological features, we had measures of depression and anxiety; and for social factors, we had some measures related to economic status.

We also understand that using only demographic or only biological or only psychological or only social features may not be enough to build a powerful and efficient classification model. However, the machine learning–based feature learning experiment provides a guide on how to select these features.

Conclusion

We present a rigorous machine learning-based analysis with varying data sets. We present results based on three popular classification models (neural networks, decision trees, logistic regression). We address the challenge of transforming our continuous predicted outcome variable in a categorical variable with two categories (high versus low). To achieve this, we experiment with several "cutoff scores" to divide the values into the two categories. We present a comparison of various cutoffs used on these different data sets and find an optimal cutoff range to be used. We reason that the optimal cutoff should be in the range of 15–19 based on the experiments and across all data sets. We also conduct feature selection to select top 25 features in the data set in view of situations where gathering all the extended list of variables in the given data set might be infeasible and present the results. The selected features are predominantly psychological variables, some biological variables, and a few demographic variables. We further validate this feature selection process by comparing it with results obtained from manual splits of the data based on demographics, biological, social, and psychological categories. In conclusion, our extensive analysis provides important insights and a foundation of using computational tools from artificial intelligence to answer challenging social work questions.

Future Work

There are several ways to extend upon the analysis techniques presented in this chapter. An interesting direction of further exploration will be to add in the layer of time series analysis to the current investigation. This can be achieved by gathering data at different time periods and then predicting stress using that information along with historical observations. Further, the process of feature selection can be used for each data set representing the four categories as previously mentioned. In that regard, more categories of the predictor variables can be explored than those we have used. Also, more sophisticated machine learning techniques can be used to answer the question about tackling missing data.

References

Caruana, R., & Niculescu-Mizil, A. (2006, June). An empirical comparison of supervised learning algorithms. In *Proceedings of the 23rd International Conference on Machine Learning* (pp. 161–168). Association for Computing Machinery.

Carvalho, L. A., Urbanova, L., Hamer, M., Hackett, R. A., Lazzarino, A. I., & Steptoe, A. (2015). Blunted glucocorticoid and mineralocorticoid sensitivity to stress in people with diabetes. *Psychoneuroendocrinology, 51*, 209–218. https://doi.org/10.1016/j.psyneuen.2014.09.023

Geurts, P., Ernst, D., & Wehenkel, L. (2006). Extremely randomized trees. *Machine Learning, 63*(1), 3–42.

Gregg, E. W., Beckles, G. L., Williamson, D. F., Leveille, S. G., Langlois, J. A., Engelgau, M. M., & Narayan, K. M. (2000). Diabetes and physical disability among older US adults. *Diabetes Care, 23*(9), 1272–1277.

Kelly, S. J., & Ismail, M. (2015). Stress and type 2 diabetes: A review of how stress contributes to the development of type 2 diabetes. *Annual Review of Public Health, 36*, 441–462. https://doi.org/10.1146/annurev-publhealth-031914-122921.

Kirkman, M. S., Briscoe, V. J., Clark, N., Florez, H., Haas, L. B., Halter, J. B., . . . Swift, C. S. (2012). Diabetes in older adults. *Diabetes Care, 35*(12), 2650–2664. https://doi.org/10.2337/dc12-1801.

Koh, H. C., & Tan, G. (2011). Data mining applications in healthcare. *Journal of Healthcare Information Management, 19*(2), 65.

Lanting, L. C., Joung, I. M. A., Mackenbach, J. P., Lamberts, S. W. J., & Bootsma, A. H. (2005). Ethnic differences in mortality, end-stage complications, and quality of care among diabetic patients. *Diabetes Care, 28*(9), 2280–2288. https://doi.org/10.2337/diacare.28.9.2280.

Lisboa, P. J., & Taktak, A. F. (2006). The use of artificial neural networks in decision support in cancer: A systematic review. *Neural Networks, 19*(4), 408–415.

Morikawa, Y., Nakagawa, H., Miura, K., Soyama, Y., Ishizaki, M., Kido, T., . . . Nogawa, K. (2005). Shift work and the risk of diabetes mellitus among Japanese male factory workers. *Scandinavian Journal of Work, Environment & Health, 31*(3), 179–183.

Orpana, H. M., Lemyre, L., & Kelly, S. (2007). Do stressors explain the association between income and declines in self-rated health? A longitudinal analysis of the National Population Health Survey. *International Journal of Behavioral Medicine, 14*(1), 40–47.

Quinlan, J. R. (1987). Simplifying decision trees. *International Journal of Man-Machine Studies, 27*(3): 221. https://doi.org/10.1016/S0020-7373(87)80053-6.

Schwartz, A. V., Hillier, T. A., Sellmeyer, D. E., Resnick, H. E., Gregg, E., Ensrud, K. E., ... Cummings, S. R. (2002). Older women with diabetes have a higher risk of falls. *Diabetes Care, 25*(10), 1749–1754.

Slavich, G. M., O'Donovan, A., Epel, E. S., & Kemeny, M. E. (2010). Black sheep get the blues: A psychobiological model of social rejection and depression. *Neuroscience & Biobehavioral Reviews, 35*(1), 39–45.

Steptoe, A., Hackett, R. A., Lazzarino, A. I., Bostock, S., La Marca, R., Carvalho, L. A., & Hamer, M. (2014). Disruption of multisystem responses to stress in type 2 diabetes: Investigating the dynamics of allostatic load. *PNAS Proceedings of the National Academy of Sciences of the United States of America, 111*(44), 15693–15698. https://doi.org/http://dx.doi.org.libproxy1.usc.edu/10.1073/pnas.1410401111

Thompson, B. (2004). *Exploratory and confirmatory factor analysis: Understanding concepts and applications.* Washington, DC: American Psychological Association.

Volpato, S., Blaum, C., Resnick, H., Ferrucci, L., Fried, L. P., & Guralnik, J. M. (2002). Comorbidities and impairments explaining the association between diabetes and lower extremity disability. *Diabetes Care, 25*(4), 678–683. https://doi.org/10.2337/diacare.25.4.678

Volpato, S., Leveille, S. G., Blaum, C., Fried, L. P., & Guralnik, J. M. (2005). Risk factors for falls in older disabled women with diabetes: The women's health and aging study. *The Journals of Gerontology Series A: Biological Sciences and Medical Sciences, 60*(12), 1539–1545.

World Health Organization Global report on diabetes. (2016). Retrieved January 21, 2017 from http://www.who.int/diabetes/global-report/en/.

Wu, S., Ell, K., Gross-Schulman, S. G., Sklaroff, L. M., Katon, W. J., Nezu, A. M., ... Guterman, J. J. (2014). Technology-facilitated depression care management among predominantly Latino diabetes patients within a public safety net care system: Comparative effectiveness trial design. *Contemporary Clinical Trials, 37*(2), 342–354.

10

A Multidisciplinary Study on the Relationship between Foster Care Attributes and Posttraumatic Stress Disorder Symptoms on Foster Youth

Amanda Yoshioka-Maxwell[1], Shahrzad Gholami, Emily Sheng,
Mary Hemler, Tanachat Nilanon, and Ali Jalal-Kamali

Introduction

Nearly 2 million unaccompanied youth aged 13–24 years experience homelessness in the United States each year (National Alliance to End Homelessness, 2012). Almost 40% of these youth have spent time in foster care (Dworsky et al., 2012). Homeless former foster youth are a vulnerable population receiving relatively little attention in the scientific literature, compared to both homeless youth and youth with foster care experiences. However, 30% of all homeless adults report a foster care history, compared to 4% of the general public (Courtney, Piliavin, Grogan-Kaylor, & Nesmith, 2001; Reilly, 2003; Roman & Wolfe, 1995), and research has shown that between 11% and 36% of the foster youth population experience homelessness (Dworsky et al., 2012).

Among both homeless youth and former foster youth, rates of trauma experiences and PTSD symptomatology are significantly higher than those of the general public (Hudson & Nandy, 2012). Studies have indicated that trauma experiences common among homeless youth and former foster youth impact the development of PTSD symptoms, and that experiences in the child welfare system can exacerbate the impact of trauma on youths' mental health (Bruskas, 2008; Pecora, White, Jackson, & Wiggins, 2009; Stewart et al., 2004). In examination of issues such as homelessness, foster care, and PTSD, social sciences have historically utilized statistical modeling, such as regression models, to examine the relationship between these variables. Statistically significant models have been produced as a result, indicating associations between foster care experiences, homelessness experiences, and PTSD symptoms. And while these models have produced valuable information for intervention and treatment

---

[1] Amanda Yoshioka-Maxwell and Shahrzad Gholami are joint first authors.

programs aimed at treating PTSD symptoms, statistical modeling assumes that cause-and-effect relationships remain unchanged, and it is based on the collection of limited data, making it difficult to extrapolate findings more generally. Additionally, for predicting outcomes such as PTSD symptoms, statistical models may not be the most effective modeling strategy based on the types of data largely accessible in social sciences (Lette et al., 1994). Toward this end, modeling based on the use of artificial intelligence (AI) through machine learning may be effectively used to predict outcomes that typical regression models cannot. Given the limited use of AI in many social sciences, and given the need to continue to explore the impact of foster care experiences on PTSD symptoms among homeless former foster youth, this analysis seeks to explore how effectively a number of AI modeling techniques can predict PTSD symptoms, compared to more traditional statistical models.

Literature Review

PTSD Symptoms among Youth with Homelessness and Foster Care Histories

As children and youth are placed into foster care primarily as a result of substantiated physical abuse, sexual abuse, or neglect, youth with child welfare experience are often at elevated risk for symptoms associated with trauma exposure (Badeau & Gesiriech, 2004). In a study assessing alumni of the foster care system, 30% of respondents met lifetime diagnostic criteria for PTSD, while only 7.6% of a general population sample with comparable demographics met such criteria (Pecora et al., 2009). Similar disparities have been found in other studies, with two studies on adolescents aged 17–18 years preparing to exit the child welfare system reporting PTSD lifetime prevalences of 14% and 16% among participants (Keller, Salazar, & Courtney, 2010; McMillen et al., 2005). In contrast, research has demonstrated that the lifetime prevalence of PTSD among 17- and 18-year-olds in the general population is approximately 7% (Merikangas et al., 2010). In addition, a study involving a large sample of lower-income adults in an urban setting aged 19–23 years reported a lifetime prevalence of 7%; transition-age youth with foster care history therefore appear to experience lifetime prevalence rates approximately twice that of same-age peers in the general population (Breslau et al., 2004).

Research has indicated that youth exiting foster care are at substantially greater risk for homelessness than their peers without foster care history

(Dworsky, Napolitano, & Courtney, 2013), and homeless adults have nearly eight times the likelihood of having foster care history than the housed general public (Reilly, 2003). It has been suggested that many youths leave home to escape abuse; a recent study demonstrated that up to 85% of homeless youth may have experienced either physical or sexual abuse prior to becoming homeless, with 42% of these youth having reported experiencing both (Keeshan & Campbell, 2011). However, while many of these youth leave home to escape abuse, experiencing homelessness puts them at higher risk for victimization, with evidence demonstrating that homeless youth experience disproportionately high rates of robbery, assault, and sexual assault (Thrane, Hoyt, Whitbeck, & Yoder, 2006). The increased rates of victimization that homeless youth experience are associated with significantly higher rates of PTSD, even among the youth who witnessed an assault but did not experience one (Bender, Ferguson, Thompson, & Langenderfer, 2014).

Although the experience of a traumatic event is a necessary prerequisite for a diagnosis of PTSD, not all individuals who experience one or multiple traumatic events meet the criteria for the disorder. In addition, research has demonstrated that while experiencing childhood abuses and street victimizations was independently associated with negative mental health outcomes, their interaction was not (Bender, Brown, Thompson, Ferguson, & Langenderfer, 2015). Contrary to prior research demonstrating that individuals who experience several abuse types, followed by victimizations, frequently have poorer mental health outcomes (Ford, Elhai, Connor, & Freuh, 2010), recent research has suggested that experiencing street victimization did not exacerbate the relationship between childhood abuse and PTSD (Bender et al., 2015). As traditionally used hierarchical logistic regression models have failed to provide insight into the cumulative effect of traumatic experiences on the presence or absence of PTSD, AI modeling techniques may offer insights that cannot be revealed by linear modeling (Bender et al., 2015).

Machine Learning within the Social Sciences

Machine learning techniques coupled with data mining have been used in different studies to assess PTSD symptoms. Random forest classifiers were used for prediction purposes based on different data sets including psychiatric interview, psychiatric scales (i.e., Clinician-administered PTSD scale, positive and negative syndrome scale, Hamilton anxiety scale, and Hamilton depression scale) and a combination of both of them. This study was conducted on 102 inpatients, i.e., 51 with a diagnosis of PTSD and 51 with psychiatric diagnoses other than PTSD. Applicability of data–mining methods was demonstrated, and group of comorbid diagnoses, including neurotic, stress-related, and somatoform disorders, surfaced as important (Marinić et al., 2007). Also, another rsearch study was conducted using a sample of 1,517 treatment-seeking military veterans to develop a truncated assessment protocol based on the Clinician-administered PTSD scale. Decision tree analysis was used to analyze the most important predictor variables among all items in the Clinician-administered PTSD scale to diagnose PTSD (Stewart, Tuerk, Metzger, Davidson, & Young, 2016). Although decision tree–based models were shown to be accurate in the existing literature, their importance in analyzing PTSD symptoms for homeless youth based on their foster care attributes is still uninvestigated.

Data Augmentation

Generally, machine learning techniques work best with more data (Domingos, 2012). Data augmentation is the collection of techniques used to increase the amount of data points, such that machine learning techniques can train better predictive models. These techniques have become popular in computer vision, speech recognition, and, more recently, natural language processing. In computer vision, data augmentation for image recognition involves applying a transformation to an image, such as a rotation, translation, or flip. The new image depicts the same objects and object relationships as the old image, but the new image is a new data point for the model (Hauberg et al., 2015; Wong, Gatt, Stamatescu, & McDonnell, 2016; Zhang & LeCun, 2016). In speech recognition, examples of transformations include the addition of artificial noise and the manipulation of speech signals (Hannun et al., 2014); in natural language processing, researchers have replaced words and phrases with synonyms (Zhang & LeCun, 2016).

Data augmentation techniques are not generally used in social science research; as social science research outcomes directly affect the well-being of human subjects, analysis from real data is typically used. As such, there is not much prior work on exploring augmentation techniques on human data. In our work, we augment our data sets in order to show the viability of our machine learning techniques if we collected more human data; we do not use data augmentation as a technique to directly influence intervention and treatment policies. In the intersection of AI and social work, it remains unclear if data augmentation is more of a strength or a weakness; on one hand, it could help improve the effectiveness of AI techniques, but on the other hand, the results may not be meaningful from a social work perspective. We experiment with data augmentation in our work to investigate how it could be effective to both disciplines.

Data Samples and Procedures

Two data sets will be utilized for these analyses. The first data set utilized the YouthNet data set, a convenience sample of 352 homeless former foster youth (aged 13–25) from three drop-in centers in Hollywood, Venice, and Santa Monica, CA, collected as part of a panel study of 1,046 homeless youth. Any client receiving services at a participating agency during the data collection periods was eligible to participate. General inclusion criteria for participation in the study included self-identifying as homeless (e.g., sleeping on the streets, in an emergency shelter, at immediate risk of being homeless such as couch-surfing, about to be evicted) and being 13–25 years old. Recruitment was conducted for approximately 1 month at each site; during that time period, recruiters were present at the agency to approach youth for the duration of service provision hours. Youth new to the agency first completed the agency's intake process before beginning the study to ensure they met the eligibility requirements for the agency (and thus the study). Two research staff members were responsible for all recruitment to ensure youth did not complete the survey multiple times during each data collection period per site.

Signed voluntary informed consent was obtained from each participant, with the caveat that child abuse and suicidal and homicidal intentions would be reported. Informed consent was obtained from youth 18 years of age or older and informed assent was obtained from youth 13 to 17 years old. The affiliated institutional review board waived parental consent because homeless youth younger than 18 were unaccompanied minors who may not have had a parent or adult guardian from whom to obtain consent. Interviewers received approximately 40 hours of training, including lectures, role-playing, mock surveys, ethics training, and emergency procedures. The study consisted of two parts: a computerized self-administered survey and a social network interview. The former included an audio-assisted version for participants with low literacy, and both parts of the survey could be completed in English or Spanish. All participants received $20 in cash or gift cards as compensation for their time. The institutional review board approved all survey items and procedures.

The second set (FCHIV) of data utilized a sample of 155 homeless former foster youth, utilizing the same drop-in center and data collection procedures as the YouthNet Study. In this second study, however, additional questions were added to the YouthNet questionnaire. This augmented Foster Care Experiences

Assessment included quantitative measures created from qualitative interviews and questions related to foster care experience. The sample collected was modeled after the YouthNet Study in terms of age range, data collection site, and participant demographics. The only exception is the distribution of race among two populations, which slightly differed between the two datasets.

Data: Selected Variables and Outcomes for PTSD Prediction

To predict PTSD symptoms, the most relevant variables in two datasets are chosen as follows:
YouthNet Data Set:

1. Age
2. Gender
3. Sexual Orientation
4. Race
5. Age at placement in foster care
6. Number of foster care placement
7. Time of homelessness

FCHIV Data Set:

1. Age
2. Gender
3. Sextual Orientation
4. Race
5. Age at placement in foster care
6. Number of foster care placement
7. Foster care placement type
8. Reason for being placed in foster care
9. Their overall opinion of foster care experience
10. Asking whether they were respected while in foster care
11. Asking whether they felt supported while in foster care

The outcome variables assessing for PTSD (included in both data sets) are:
In the past 30 days,

1. Have you had nightmares about a situation or thought about that when they did not want to?
2. Have you tried hard not to think about a situation or went out of your way to avoid situations that reminded you of it?
3. Were you constantly on guard, watchful, or easily startled?

4. Have you felt numb or detached from others, activities, or their surroundings?

The main outcomes of study could be either the total sum of PTSD symptoms experienced or the dichotomized version, i.e., presence or absence of any PTSD symptom.

Methods

Data Preprocessing for Models

Data Sets: To process the data for our models, we filter out individuals without PTSD predictor values, leaving a total of 449 individuals from the YouthNet data set and the FCHIV data set combined, 133 from FCHIV and 316 from YouthNet. We standardize the features "Age at placement in foster care" and "Number of foster care placement" so that the values are binned for both data sets. As mentioned in the previous section, YouthNet Data Set includes 7 predictor features and FCHIV Data Set includes 11 predictor features. So, when these two data sets are combined, some predictor feature values are missing for data samples inherited from YouthNet Data Set.

In the first group of experiments, we combined and preprocessed YouthNet and FCHIV data set, which contains 449 samples. In this case, we enable the existence of missing values for missing predictor features for data samples inherited from YouthNet Data Set, i.e., when some features are present in one data set but not in the other, we use the value "−1" to represent these missing values. In these experiments, 25% of the combined data is held out as the test set to evaluate the results of learning on different training sets. The training data sets are constructed based on (1) 75% of the FCHIV+YouthNet combined data sets, (2) only the YouthNet data set, (3) only the FCHIV data set, (4) variations of the augmented data set, and (5) 75% of the FCHIV data set in conjunction with subsets of the augmented data sets (we experimented with FCHIV combined with different subsets of augmented data as opposed to FCHIV+YouthNet combined with different subsets of augmented data, because FCHIV has more non-missing foster care-specific features that we thought might be interesting to study if we had more data).

In the second group of experiments, we want to see if certain features are more important predictors of PTSD than others. We run a series of experiments where we remove different subsets of features. The intuition behind these experiments is that if removing feature X results in a dramatic decrease of model score, then we know feature X must be an important predictor of PTSD.

In the third group of experiments, we want to examine the FCHIV and YouthNet data sets separately. The motivation is that if the two data sets were collected under slightly different contexts and thus have different distributions of features, it may not be the best idea to combine everything together. In other words, we train models only on one data set at a time and also test only on the corresponding test sets. We also take a common subset of features between FCHIV and YouthNet, create separate data sets for FCHIV-subset and YouthNet-subset, and train and test separate models. The common subset of features used in this group of experiments are gender, age, sexual orientation, race, entry age into foster care, and number of foster care placements. One final data set variation we experiment with is combining FCHIV-subset and YouthNet-subset and training one model on the combined data set.

Augmented Data Sets: We perform data augmentation based on the distributions of values for each feature and the correlations between features. Specifically, we first decide the number of new individual data points we want to generate. We constrain the generation so that half of the individuals will have PTSD symptoms and half will not. Some machine learning techniques are more sensitive to data imbalance, so we ensure our data generation does not skew the population of people with and without PTSD symptoms.

Before generating new data, we calculate the distributions of values for all features based on a simple ratio of observed values for each feature. We also calculate the kappa coefficient (Cohen, 1960) between each pair of categorical features (all data set predictor features excluding age). The kappa coefficient measures the correlation of two categorical variables above chance.

The data augmentation algorithm we use is depicted in Figure 10.1. To generate data for a sample, we first choose if the sample has the presence or absence of PTSD symptoms; we assign a binary 1 or 0 to the dichotomized PTSD outcome variable. Then, we randomly select the next feature X to assign a value to. To choose a value X-value for feature X, we generate a random real number between 0 and 1. If the number is less than or equal to $\frac{1}{|Previously\ selected\ features| + 1}$, then we choose an X-value from the distribution of feature X in the preprocessed data set of 449 samples. Otherwise, we look at all the features that have already been selected for the sample and get the correlation scores between all previously selected features and feature X. We use $\frac{1}{|Previously\ selected\ features| + 1}$ as a basic threshold to decide whether to pick the X-value from feature X's distribution or based on the correlation with previously selected features; in our work, we are interested in observing the general effect data augmentation and not necessarily searching for the best data

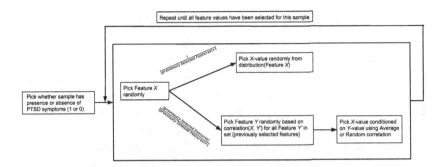

Figure 10.1 Data augmentation algorithm used to generate a new sample

augmentation method. An interesting point of experimentation could involve tuning the threshold value as a hyperparameter.

If "Age" is a previously selected feature, we skip its correlation score because we only calculate kappa correlations for pairs of categorical features. If "Age" is the feature of interest, i.e., feature X, then we simply randomly choose the X-value from the distribution of feature X as described earlier. We normalize the correlation scores across all previously selected features, generate another random real number between 0 and 1, and use the number to select which previously selected feature value Y-value to condition on when choosing the X-value. To choose an X-value given the previously selected Y-value, we take all samples in the preprocessed dataset that have feature Y value of Y-value, and collect a list of the X-values of the aforementioned samples. We experiment with two different approaches to select an X-value from the list of X-values. In what we call the *Average Correlation* approach, we choose the X-value by taking an average over the list of X-values. In our *Random Correlation* approach, we choose a random X-value from the list of X-values. After generating an X-value for feature X, we then repeat the process until we have generated values for all features and thus created a new sample. To generate a value for the predictor PTSD variable that is the sum of the four individual PTSD variables, we constrain the value to be 0 if the dichotomized PTSD variable is 0, and otherwise randomly generate a value from 1 to 4.

For this work, we generate 551 new samples with the Average Correlation method and another 551 new samples with the Random Correlation method. This gives us two separate sets of augmented data to experiment with, which can be used separately or in conjunction with the preprocessed real set of 449 samples.

Modeling Techniques and Evaluations

Evaluation Techniques

Prior to discussing the different machine learning techniques studied in this chapter, we briefly mention the evaluation metrics we used. According to existing machine learning literature, we considered precision, recall, and F1 score to evaluate the prediction results, quantitatively. In more details, *precision* is the fraction of the true positive labeled instances compared to all positive labeled classes predicted by model. *Recall* is the fraction of the true positive labeled instances compared to all actual positive labeled instances in test set. *F1 score* is a score to measure accuracy, which considers both precision and recall. More precisely, F1 score is a harmonic mean of precision and recall defined as $F1 = 2.$ (precision * recall)/(precision + recall). We study various machine learning techniques including Logistic Regression as the baseline, Neural Networks, Decision Tree, and Bayesian Networks. In addition to the evaluation metrics, we also assess the branching rules generated by Decision Tree model from a social science viewpoint to develop insight about the most important factors affecting PTSD experiences for former foster care youths.

Model 0 (baseline): Logistic Regression

We use logistic regression as a baseline technique to predict PTSD from our sample features. Logistic regression is similar to linear regression, though the dependent variable is categorical instead of continuous. This technique allows us to analyze which sample features influence the PTSD variables. The precision, recall, and F1 results are shown in Table 10.1. From the model weights we also observed that the support people received and being placed in a shelter had the largest influence on the PTSD variables. Cox (1958) first proposed this technique, and it has been popular as a general machine learning method. We use this technique as a baseline for our other techniques because we believe more sophisticated methods will let us better examine the relationship between foster care variables and PTSD variables.

In Table 10.1, we observe that for logistic regression, using FCHIV alone as the training set best predicts the presence of PTSD in the test set, which is composed of a subset of FCHIV and a subset of YouthNet. We also see that the augmented data set for training does no better than FCHIV alone, which makes sense, as the augmented data set was created according to feature distributions and correlations in the FCHIV and YouthNet data sets. Table 10.1 also shows that FCHIV and a subset of the augmented data set does no better than just the augmented data set. We also see that the dichotomized PTSD prediction models always outperform the multi-class PTSD prediction models

Table 10.1. *Logistic regression results for models trained on different training data and tested on the same YouthNet+FCHIV test data (first group of experiments)*

Training data	Dichotomized PTSD prediction			Multi-class PTSD prediction		
	Precision	Recall	F1	Precision	Recall	F1
FCHIV	**0.65**	**0.82**	**0.72**	**0.34**	**0.17**	**0.18**
YouthNet	0.57	0.64	0.60	0.19	0.13	0.12
FCHIV+YouthNet	0.55	0.43	0.48	0.23	0.14	0.16
Aug_Rand_Corr-552	**0.65**	0.39	0.49	0.20	**0.22**	**0.19**
Aug_Avg_Corr-552	0.60	**0.82**	**0.69**	**0.29**	0.17	0.16
FCHIV + Aug_Avg_Corr-552	0.58	**0.82**	**0.68**	0.22	0.15	0.12
FCHIV + Aug_Avg_Corr-100	**0.59**	0.81	**0.68**	0.24	0.16	0.14
FCHIV + Aug_Avg_Corr-50	0.51	0.60	0.55	**0.26**	**0.5**	**0.21**

by a significant amount. The low scores of the multi-class PTSD prediction models could be due to the fact that the multiple "classes" of PTSD are the number of predefined symptoms that individuals report having experienced, and that the number of data samples we have is relatively low.

We examine the effects of different features on the logistic regression model more closely in Table 10.2. Taking different subsets of features for all data samples in the combined FCHIV and YouthNet data sets, the best model results are when we use only the foster care–specific features. In general, the scores we get from withholding different subsets of features do not vary by significant amounts, which suggests that we have an insufficient amount of data to be able to meaningfully generalize from the logistic regression model.

We perform additional experiments with models that are both trained and tested on subsets of the same data, e.g., trained on a subset of FCHIV and tested on a subset of FCHIV, to see if models would better be able to predict PTSD for samples from the same data collection; the results are shown in Table 10.3. Although the different test data makes it difficult to compare these additional models, the results do not indicate particularly high precision, recall, and F1 scores for the respective data sets.

Here we present the logistic regression model as a baseline model. We expect that with more sophisticated machine learning techniques that are more tuned to this prediction task, we can get better results. Regardless, if the sparsity of data presents a problem in the simpler logistic regression models, we acknowledge that it might have a larger impact on the more complex models.

Table 10.2. *Results for models trained on FCHIV+YouthNet training set with withheld features*

| | Dichotomized PTSD prediction | | |
Withheld features	Precision	Recall	F1
None (Used all ['gender', 'age','sexori', 'raceall'] and foster care questions)	0.55	0.43	0.48
['sexori'] (Used only ['gender', 'age', 'raceall'] and foster care questions)	0.57	0.54	0.55
['gender', 'sexori'] (Used only ['age', 'raceall'] and foster care questions)	0.54	0.52	0.53
All foster care questions (Used only ['gender', 'age', 'sexori', 'raceall'])	0.54	0.45	0.49
All foster care questions + sexori (Used only ['gender', 'age', 'raceall'])	**0.58**	**0.55**	**0.56**
['gender', 'age', 'sexori', 'raceall'] (Used only foster care questions)			

Table 10.3. *Logistic regression results for models trained on different training data and tested on corresponding test data. FCHIV subset and YouthNet subset use a subset of features for all samples (third group of experiments)*

| | | Dichotomized PTSD prediction | | |
Training data	Features used	Precision	Recall	F1
FCHIV	All	0.78	0.58	0.67
	Subset	**0.79**	0.46	0.58
YouthNet	All	0.65	**0.71**	**0.68**
	Subset	0.59	0.57	0.58
Combined	All	0.55	0.43	0.48
	Subset	0.63	0.54	0.58

Model 1: Neural Networks

A neural network is a powerful machine learning model that can learn a mapping from inputs to outputs using objective function. For binary classification outputs, the most commonly used objective function is binary cross-entropy, which can be considered a continuous extension of prediction accuracy. It has been shown that neural networks are universal function approximators (Csáji, 2001), meaning that they can learn any mapping present in the data given enough data and trainable parameters. Here, we will not only utilize neural networks for our prediction task but also use them as a tool to discover feature importance. A base neural network will be trained with all the features available in the data set. Model complexity of this base model has to be adjusted such that it has a reasonable prediction performance. Then, comparative neural networks will be trained, but with features that are subsets of original set of features. By comparing their prediction performance, we can discover the importance of each feature or a combination of features.

To illustrate the process, let us examine Figure 10.2. The base model to the left is trained with all the features available in the data set. The comparative model to the right is trained with only features X_a and X_b. If the comparative model's prediction performance is significantly worse than the base model's, we infer that feature X_c contributes significantly to the model's prediction performance. It should be noted, however, that this does not imply a direct causation link.

As a rule of thumb, the size of the data set should be comparable to or larger than the number of trainable parameters. Due to the small size of this dataset, we have to design the architecture of the neural networks carefully, making sure that we are frugal with the number of trainable parameters. After experimentation, we selected a model that has four hidden layers with rectified linear activation. The output layer has exactly one node with sigmoid activation. We experimented with dropout technique to reduce overfitting and have found that our data set is too small to effectively utilize dropout in our model.

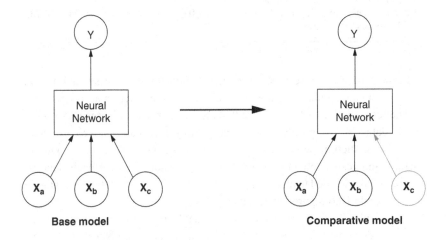

Figure 10.2 Base model versus comparative model

Table 10.4. *Neural network results for models trained on different training data and tested on the same YouthNet+FCHIV test data*

	Dichotomized PTSD prediction		
Training data	Precision	Recall	F1
FCHIV	0.61	0.68	0.65
YouthNet	0.58	0.62	0.60
FCHIV+YouthNet	**0.61**	**0.81**	**0.70**
Aug_Rand_Corr-552	**0.58**	**0.85**	**0.69**
Aug_Avg_Corr-552	0.56	0.72	0.63
FCHIV+Aug_Avg_Corr-552	0.65	0.33	0.44
FCHIV+Aug_Avg_Corr-100	**0.67**	**0.42**	**0.51**
FCHIV+Aug_Avg_Corr-50	**0.67**	0.35	0.47

Table 10.5. *Base model and comparative model results, using YouthNet+FCHIV as training data*

	Dichotomized PTSD prediction			
Withheld features	Accuracy	Precision	Recall	F1
None	**0.59**	**0.61**	**0.81**	**0.70**
['sexori']	0.58	0.60	0.82	0.69
['gender', 'sexori']	0.60	0.60	0.94	0.73
All foster care questions (Used only ['gender', 'age', 'sexori', 'raceall'])	0.58	0.58	1.00	0.73
All foster care questions + sexori (Used only ['gender', 'age', 'raceall'])	0.58	0.58	1.00	0.73
['gender', 'age', 'sexori', 'raceall'] (Used only foster care questions)	0.60	0.60	0.94	0.73

From experimental results, we conclude that for this classification task, having extra augmented data does not help improve prediction accuracy.

The results in Table 10.5 suggest that the neural network learns very poorly in this data set. Using only gender, age, and race as features, we can obtain the same prediction performance as using all the available features. Due to encouraging results obtained from training decision trees on each data set separately, we decided to also train neural a network on each data set separately as well. Table 10.6 reports the results.

The results in Table 10.6 improve markedly over previous experiments. This suggests that the data from the two data sets (YouthNet and FCHIV) was sampled from two significantly different populations. Traditional machine

Table 10.6. *Neural network results when trained and tested on each data set separately*

Training data	Features used	Dichotomized PTSD prediction		
		Precision	Recall	F1
FCHIV	All	0.72	0.96	0.82
	Subset	0.64	0.58	0.61
YouthNet	All	0.62	0.98	0.76
	Subset	0.57	0.85	0.68
Combined	All	**0.61**	**0.81**	**0.70**
	Subset	0.64	0.99	0.78

learning methods will struggle to learn if they are trained on merged data containing such discrepancies. This issue is well known in the machine learning community and has been studied under the name "domain adaptation." Interested readers can take a look at a recent work of interest published by Ganin and colleagues (2015). We left the incorporation of domain adaptation in our model for future work.

Model 2: Decision Tree

A decision tree model is a well-known technique for inductive learning that is comprised of a sequence of branching operations based on the comparisons of existing quantities of specific attributes or features of the data samples. Decision tree classifies instances of data samples by sorting them down the tree to some leaf node, which provides the classification of instances. Each node in the tree represents a test of some attribute of the instance, and each branch descending from that node corresponds to one of the possible values of that attribute. An instance is classified by starting at the root node of the tree, testing the attribute specified by this node, then following the tree branch corresponding to the value of the attribute in the given example. This process is then repeated for the subtree rooted at the new node. Figure 10.3 illustrates a typical learned decision tree. This decision tree classifies a day according to whether it is suitable for playing tennis (Mitchell, 1997). In this study, we learn a decision tree model to predict the presence of PTSD symptoms based on the different variations of the datasets mentioned earlier. The decision tree's attributes are the aforementioned shared variables of the data sets.

Table 10.7 demonstrates the results for the decision tree learned based on the setup for the first group of the experiments. The main outcome is the dichotomized version of PTSD symptoms. Experiment results demonstrate

Table 10.7. *Decision tree results for models trained on different training data and tested on the same YouthNet+FCHIV test data (first group of experiments)*

Train data	Dichotomized PTSD prediction		
	Precision	Recall	F1
FCHIV	**0.65**	0.39	0.49
YouthNet	0.62	0.6	0.6
FCHIV+YouthNet	0.62	**0.75**	**0.68**
Aug_Rand_Corr-552	**0.57**	0.54	0.55
Aug_Avg_Corr-552	0.56	**0.66**	**0.61**
FCHIV +Aug_Avg_Corr-552	0.55	**0.61**	0.58
FCHIV + Aug_Avg_Corr-100	0.61	0.51	0.55
FCHIV + Aug_Avg_Corr-50	**0.62**	0.6	**0.6**

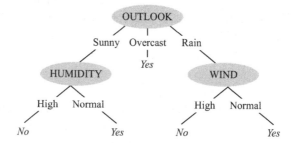

Figure 10.3 A typical learned decision tree

that augmented data sets are dominated by the original data sets in their performance quality. Another important point about Table 10.4 is that the model learned based on the smaller and more specific data set, FCHIV, is not a good representative for a test set that consists of 25% of the combined data set. Most of the specific variables are missing in the combined samples, and that may lead to poor results. Learning based on the YouthNet data set and the combined data set results in nearly similar results; however, the combined version outperforms all other training schemes. This observation led us to conduct the third group of experiments, where we learned and evaluated each data set separately to address the intrinsic differences between two data sets.

It is worth noting that, not only the prediction results are not sufficiently significant, but also the large amount of missing data renders the application of decision tree rules difficult to justify. Figure 10.4 demonstrates the first

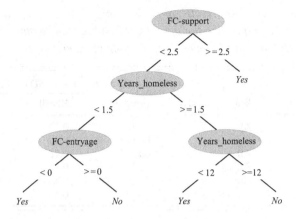

Figure 10.4 The learned decision tree for predicting PTSD symptoms

three layers of the decision tree learned. The root node represents the foster care support attribute of the data set. The first rule indicates that if foster care support attribute is larger than 2.5, there is a high probability of experiencing PTSD – which is counterintuitive. As discussed earlier, the YouthNet data set has a larger number of data samples and a smaller number of variables. Consequently, combining the data sets while enabling missing variables leads to a high level of uncertainty and missing values for major portion of the data points. The presence of a huge imbalance in the distribution of the samples over different categories demonstrates that handling missing data requires a more attentive treatment.

To minimize the adverse effects of missing values and challenges due to combining two data sets, we conducted the third group of experiments discussed in the data processing subsection. According to Table 10.8, evaluation results improve when we study each data set independently. Subset means that we only use gender, age, sexual orientation, race, entry age into foster care, and number of foster care placements to make prediction, rather than using all available features. For both FCHIV and YouthNet, when we reduce number of the variables, accuracy is reduced. Since some of the more specific variables, which had a predicting potential, were removed, accuracy consequently declined. To facilitate comparison, the row for Combined-All is basically borrowed from the previous group of experiments, as it is impossible to disable the missing values and hold all of the available features simultaneously while merging two different size data sets. Since the majority of the data samples are from YouthNet data set, the combined data set is mostly similar to the

Table 10.8. *Decision tree results for models trained on different training data and tested on corresponding test data. FCHIV subset and YouthNet subset use a subset of features for all samples (third group of experiments).*

Training data	Features used	Dichotomized PTSD prediction		
		Precision	Recall	F1
FCHIV	All	0.88	0.96	0.92
	Subset	0.79	0.92	0.85
YouthNet	All	0.82	0.76	0.79
	Subset	0.75	0.85	0.8
Combined	All	0.62	0.75	0.68
	Subset	0.78	0.86	0.82

YouthNet data. So supplementing the YouthNet with data from FCHIV results in improvement in predictions compared to individual YouthNet dataset. This combined version for the subset of features is demonstrated in the last row of the table, which is showing a nearly average performance between two individual data sets.

Results of decision tree model presented in Table 10.8, outperforms all other models. So in addition to the standard metrics for evaluation, we also present the explanation of decision trees learned. Since decision tree is a rule-based model, it provides the opportunity to develop insight about the most important underlying factors in prediction of outcomes. We examine the decision trees rules for the most *general* data set, which is a combination of YouthNet and FCHIV for the common subset of features, and the most *specific* data set in terms of foster care attributes, which is FCHIV including all of its variables, in order to figure out the most important variables for predicting PTSD.

For the *general* data set, age at entry into foster care, number of foster care placements, and gender were found to be the most important factors, which confirms that foster care attributes play a more important role in prediction of experiencing PTSD compared to only demographics. Several traced rules for discovering PTSD symptoms for the *general* data set is outlined below:

- If you have less than 3 placements AND are 22 years old or older
- If you have more than 3 placements AND you are lesbian, gay, or bisexual
- If you have more than 3 placements AND you were placed in foster care before the age of 2 AND you're under 19 years old

- If you have more than 3 placements AND you were placed in foster care after the age of 3 AND you are female or transgender
- If you have more than 3 placements AND you are heterosexual or questioning AND you were placed in foster care over the age of 6 years
- If you have more than 3 placements AND you are heterosexual or questioning AND you were placed in foster care over the age of 6 years AND you had less than 5 placements
- If you have more than 3 placements AND you are heterosexual or questioning AND you were placed in foster care under the age of 5 years AND you are currently under 19 years old
- If you have more than 3 placements AND you are heterosexual or questioning AND you were placed in foster care at 6 years old or older AND you had more than 3 placements AND you are questioning

For the *specific* data set, gender, fc-reason-neglect and fc-opinion were found to be the most important factors. Several traced rules for discovering PTSD symptoms for the *specific* data set are as follows:

- If you were placed in foster care at birth
- If you were placed for parental drug problems
- If you were placed for parental drug problems AND you were not placed in a juvenile detention camp
- If you were placed for and "other" reason
- If you have an opinion of FC that is not entirely positive AND you were placed earlier than 4 years old
- If you have an opinion of FC that is not entirely positive AND you were placed older than 4 years old AND you are female or transgender
- If you have an opinion of FC that is not entirely positive AND you were placed older than 4 years old AND you are male AND you are under 21.5 years old

Model 3: Bayesian Networks

A Bayesian network (BN) is a probabilistic graphical model that represents a set of variables and their conditional dependencies via a directed acyclic graph (DAG). For example, suppose that there are two events that could cause grass to be wet: either the sprinkler is on or it is raining. Also, suppose that the rain has a direct effect on the use of the sprinkler (namely that when it rains, the sprinkler is usually not turned on). Then the situation can be modeled using a Bayesian network (shown to the right). All three variables have two possible values, T

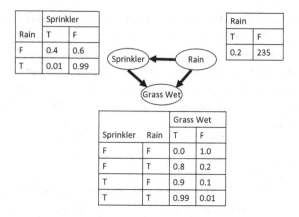

	Sprinkler	
Rain	T	F
F	0.4	0.6
T	0.01	0.99

Rain	
T	F
0.2	235

		Grass Wet	
Sprinkler	Rain	T	F
F	F	0.0	1.0
F	T	0.8	0.2
T	F	0.9	0.1
T	T	0.99	0.01

Figure 10.5 Example of a Bayesian network

(for true) and F (for false). Figure 10.5 represents the network structure of dependencies and the corresponding probabilities.

Based on the network of the dependencies above we can fit that to the data and obtain a set of coefficients in order to build a linear predictive model containing the variables of the network. Such a model then can be used for inferences and and predictions.

Bayesian networks are very intuitive for humans to understand, and one of the main uses of Bayesian network is to find the causality through the dependences in the network.

There are two ways to find the dependency network structure:

1. The network dependencies can be defined by the domain export based on their knowledge of the data and their dependencies of the variables.
2. The dependency network can be learned from the data based on the conditional probabilities. There are different algorithms to use for learning such network.

For our current data we used both data sets separately and also combined from the augmented data set. We tried different multiple learning algorithms for extracting the links from the datasets. The methods used are:

1. Grow shrink and two variations of it
2. Tabu
3. Hill climbing

The best results were from hill climbing algorithm for all data sets. However, in all cases, the PTSD variable had no dependency links. That means that we cannot use our variables to predict the PTSD variable with the Bayesian network dependencies. The reason is that since there are no links at all to the PTSD variable, it is conditionally independent of all other variables, and it reduces to just a probability distribution, since all predictive coefficients are zero.

Nonetheless, learning the links from different data sets can exploit other dependencies. Specifically the links that are common among networks from different data sets indicate a very strong dependency among such variables.

Figures 10.6–10.8 present the dependency links learned for different data sets using the hill climbing method.

As one could imagine, there is a very strong network among variables related to foster care and age in the FCHIV data set. As it is shown in all of the networks, we can see that the foster care age of entry has a direct effect on the number of places for foster care, in all three networks. So even though based on this network we cannot make any predictions for the PTSD variable, we can find the natural dependencies among variables based on the data. Also, the domain knowledge is quite important for the links learned in the network. For example, even though the variables age and gender have a dependency from conditional probability perspective, based on the domain we know that they are

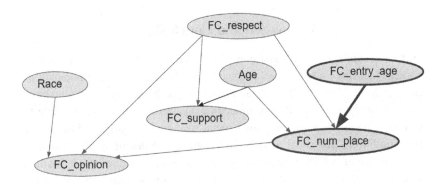

Figure 10.6 The learned network from the FCHIV dataset

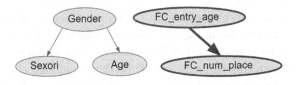

Figure 10.7 The learned network from the YouthNet dataset

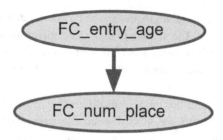

Figure 10.8 The learned network from the Augment_avgcorr dataset

completely independent, which leads us to consider the links of dependency only based on the domain knowledge.

Looking at the data itself, it is observable that the data sets are quite small and the data are very sparse. Both of those qualities cause the BN learning algorithms to suffer a lot and have a difficult time finding the proper dependencies. Given that the data were collected prior to analysis, it would be helpful if future data collection efforts would be mindful of those two qualities for a BN analysis.

Discussion and Conclusions

Artificial intelligence (AI) space models have a great deal to offer social workers focusing on behavioral and mental health outcomes. For populations that can be hard to reach, such as homeless youth, and difficult to sample in large numbers, the predictive modeling capabilities of AI may be able to answer some difficult questions that social workers have struggled to answer using traditional statistical models. In an attempt to determine if AI models may better predict PTSD outcomes among a sample of former foster youth, a series of experiments were run with models such as neural networks, Bayesian networks, and decision trees. Not only were we able to improve the prediction accuracy by using rule-based techniques (i.e., decision tree), but also these methods provided some extremely valuable insight for research within this population. Data augmentation, while not a predictive model, can be extremely useful for generating additional data samples, which can be later used for prediction. Among the specific predictive models tested, neural networks were not found to be effective for predicting PTSD symptomatology when compared to the logistic regression model. These findings were most likely the result of small sample size. However, future work with larger size may prove the use of neural networks to be helpful in predicting outcomes for populations such as homeless former foster youth.

Bayesian networks were also not effective at finding dependency links between foster care characteristics and PTSD symptoms. However, when examining both data sets, dependency links emerged between foster care entry age and number of placements, indicating a relationship between the two. Thus, while this model was not able to predict PTSD symptoms from a sample of former foster youth, it was able to direct our attention to other variables, within the arena of foster care variables, that could be further explored. Future work with Bayesian networks should consider the impact that sparse networks have on the results. Finally, a series of decision trees were used to explore the predictive nature of foster care attributes where PTSD symptoms were concerned. Models for both data sets were run separately as well as combined. Final models utilized only those variables common to both data sets, as they outperformed all other models. Results indicate several important features of these data. For the most general model, utilizing both data sets and only those variables common to both data sets, it was determined that the age at which a youth entered the foster care system, number of placements in foster care, and gender were the most important variables for predicting PTSD outcomes among homeless former foster youth. For the more specific model, utilizing only the foster care data set with all available variables, it was determined that gender, being placed into foster care due to neglect, and one's opinion of foster care (positive or negative) were the most important variables for predicting PTSD symptoms among this population. Overall, the decision tree results outperformed the other models, with an F1 score 20% larger. More specifically, decision tree models and neural networks outperformed logistic regression in terms of accuracy of predictions and standard evaluation metrics (e.g., F1 score), but decision tree modeling was more helpful in terms of explanation compared to neural networks. Potential hindrances to the performance of decision trees may be differences between the data sets. While the smaller FCHIV data set intended to model its gender and race demographics, differences, such as race, do vary between the data. These differences make comparison between the data much more difficult.

These results highlight several important aspects of this population. Modeling based on both data sets and more general variables yielded highly different results compared to the more specific data set with a larger number of variables but smaller sample size. Thus, depending on the individuals of the population being considered, different models should be used. Alternatively, modeling techniques that explicitly handle population difference can be explored, such as domain adaptation. Additionally, results indicate important information for working with youth with PTSD symptoms. For the more general model, in predicting PTSD symptoms, youth's age of foster care placement, number of placements, and gender should be considered when attempting to intervene in the development of PTSD symptoms. For the more specific model, gender, reason for foster care placement, and opinion of foster care should be considered. These results could prove to be extremely important in the development of screening tools and interventions aimed at reducing the burden of PTSD symptoms, as it directs practitioners on specific characteristics and experiences that would likely impact the development of PTSD. Future work combining social work constructs and AI methods should consider the importance of the type of data collected and needed, both to capture all necessary aspects of a population, but also to meet the specific data requirements needed for AI predictive models. Nevertheless, the future of AI and social work has proven to be full of potential, leveraging the powerful predictive techniques of AI to solve real-world social work problems.

References

Badeau, S., & Gesiriech, S. (2004). *A child's journey through the child welfare system.* Washington, DC: The Pew Commission on Children in Foster Care.

Bender, K., Brown, S. M., Thompson, S. J., Ferguson, K. M., & Langenderfer, L. (2015). Multiple victimizations before and after leaving home associated with PTSD, depression, and substance use disorder among homeless youth. *Child Maltreatment, 20*(2), 115–124.

Bender, K., Thompson, S. L., Ferguson, K. M., Yoder, J., & Kern, L. (2014). Trauma among street-involved young adults. *Journal of Emotional and Behavioral Disorders, 22,* 53–64.

Breslau, N., Wilcox, H. C., Storr, C. L., Lucia, V. C., & Anthony, J. C. (2004). Trauma exposure and posttraumatic stress disorder: A study of youths in urban American. *Journal of Urban Health: Bulletin of the New York Academy of Medicine, 81*(4), 530–544.

Bruskas, D. (2008). Children in foster care: A vulnerable population at risk. *Journal of Child and Adolescent Psychiatric Nursing, 21*(2), 70–77.

Cohen, J. (1960). A coefficient of agreement for nominal scales. *Educational and Psychological Measurement, 20*(1), 37–46. doi:10.1177/001316446002000104.

Courtney, M. E., Piliavin, I., Grogan-Kaylor, A., & Nesmith, A. (2001). Foster youth transitions to adulthood: A longitudinal view of youth leaving care. *Child Welfare, 80*(6), 685.

Cox, D. R. (1958). The regression analysis of binary sequences (with discussion). *Journal of the Royal Statistical Society B. 20,* 215–242.

Domingos, P. (2012). A few useful things to know about machine learning. *Communications of the ACM, 55*(10), 78–87.

Dworsky, A., Dillman, K. N., Dion, R. M., Coffee-Borden, B., & Rosenau, M. (2012). *Housing for youth aging out of foster care: A review of the literature and program typology.* Washington, DC: U.S. Department of Housing and Urban Development.

Ford, J. D., Elhai, J. D., Connor, D. F., & Freuh, C. B. (2010). Poly-victimization and risk of posttraumatic, depressive, and substance use disorders and involvement in delinquency in a national sample of adolescents. *Journal of Adolescent Health, 46,* 545–552.

Ganin, Y., Ustinova, E., Ajakan, H., Germain, P., Larochelle, H., Laviolette, F., Marchand, M., & Lempitsky, V. (2015). Domain-adversarial training of neural networks. *Journal of Machine Learning Research, 17,* 1–35.

Hannun, A., Case, C., Casper, J., Catanzaro, B., Diamos, G., Elsen, E., ... Ng, A. Y. (2014). Deep speech: Scaling up end-to-end speech recognition. *arXiv preprint arXiv:1412.5567.*

Hauberg, S., Freifeld, O., Larsen, A. B. L., Fisher III, J. W., Hansen, L. K., Pudwell, L., ... Pechenot, B. (2015). Dreaming more data: Class-dependent distributions over diffeomorphisms for learned data augmentation. *arXiv preprint arXiv: 1510.02795.*

Hudson, A., & Nandy, K. (2012). Comparisons of substance abuse, high-risk sexual behavior and depressive symptoms among homeless youth with and without a history of foster care placement. *Contemporary Nurse, 42*(2), 178–186.

Keller, T. E., Salazar, A. M., & Courtney, M. E. (2010). Prevalence and timing of diagnosable mental health, alcohol, and substance use problems among older adolescents in the child welfare system. *Children and Youth Services Review, 32*(4), 626–634.

Lette, J., Colletti, B. W., Cerino, M., McNamara, D., Eybalin, M. C., Lavasseur, A., & Nattel, S. (1994). Artificial intelligence versus logistic regression statistical modeling to predict cardiac complications after noncardiac surgery. *Clinical Cardiology, 17*(11), 609–614.

Marinić, I., Supek, F., Kovičć, Z., Rukavina, L., Jendričko, T., & Kozarić-Kovčć, D. (2007). Posttraumatic stress disorder: Diagnostic dat analysis by data mining methodology. *Croatian Medical Journal, 48*(2), 185–197.

Merikangas, K. R., He, J. Burstein, M., Swanson, S. A., Avenevoli, S., Cui, L., ... Swendsen (2010). Lifetime prevalence of mental disorders in U.S. adolescents: Results from the National Comorbidity Survey Replication – Adolescent Supplement (NCS-A). *Journal of the Academy of Child & Adolescent Psychiatry, 49*(10), 980–989.

McMillen, J. C., Zima, B. T., Scott, L. D., Auslander, W. F., Munson, M. R., Ollie, M. T., Spitznagel, E. L. (2005). Prevalence of psychiatric disorders among older youths in the foster care system. *Journal of the American Academy of Child & Adolescent Psychiatry, 44,* 88–95.

Mitchell, T. M. (1997). *Machine learning.* Burr Ridge, IL: McGraw-Hill Education.

National Alliance to End Homelessness (2012). *An emerging framework for ending unaccompanied youth homelessness.* http://www.endhomelessness.org/library/entry/an-emerging-framework-for-ending-unaccompanied-youth-homelessness.

Pecora, P. J., White, C. R., Jackson, L. J., & Wiggins, T. (2009). Mental health of current and former recipients of foster care: A review of recent studies in the USA. *Child & Family Social Work, 14*(2), 132–146.

Reilly T. (2003). Transition for care: Status and out of youth who age out of foster care. *Child Welfare. 82*(6), 727–748.

Roman, N. P., & Wolfe, P. (1995). *Web of failure: The relationship between foster care and homelessness.* Washington, DC: National Alliance to End Homelessness.

Stewart, A. J., Steiman, M., Cauce, A. M., Cochran, B. N., Whitbeck, L. B., & Hoyt, D. R. (2004). Victimization and posttraumatic stress disorder among homeless adolescents. *Journal of the American Academy of Child & Adolescent Psychiatry*, *43*(3), 325–331.

Stewart, R. W., Tuerk, P. W., Metzger, I. W., Davidson, T. M., & Young, J. (2016). A decision-tree approach to the assessment of posttraumatic stress disorder: Engineering empirically rigorous and ecologically valid assessment measures. *Psychological Services, 13*(1), 1.

Wong, S. C., Gatt, A., Stamatescu, V., & McDonnell, M. D. (2016, November). Understanding data augmentation for classification: when to warp? In *Digital Image Computing: Techniques and Applications (DICTA), 2016 International Conference on* (pp. 1–6). IEEE.

Zhang, X., & LeCun, Y. (2016). Text understanding from scratch. *arXiv preprint arXiv:1502.01710*.

11

Artificial Intelligence to Predict Intimate Partner Violence Perpetration

Robin Petering, Mee-Young Um, Nazanin Alipourfard, Nazgol Tavabi, Rajni Kumari, and Setareh Nasihati Gilani

Introduction

One-third of homeless youth (HY) experience some sort of physical intimate partner violence (IPV), and frequently young people experience bidirectional partner violence. One in four homeless youth have reported being both a victim and a perpetrator in their current or most recent romantic relationship [1]. Programs that address youth IPV frequently focus on victim and survivor support. Although supporting victims/survivors is necessary, offering only this type of support is not only paternalizing, with the underlying assumption that it is the victim's fault or responsibility to prevent IPV; it also does not effectively break the cycle of violence [2]. IPV prevention programs should focus on reducing perpetration. Although "batterer interventions" exist [3, 4], they intervene after the incident of violence has occurred. These programs are typically court ordered, meaning the perpetrator participates in the intervention after there is an arrest or conviction. Additionally, "batterer interventions" have been shown to be ineffective and potentially do more harm than good in reducing IPV [4, 5]. The current study proposes a method to predict the occurrence of adolescent and young adult IPV perpetration using machine learning. Using data from homeless youth, an IPV perpetration "triage tool" will be built that can be implemented in the field to identify young people who are at high risk for engaging in violence perpetration. This tool will encourage targeted services that will buffer the likelihood of engaging in violence, such as mindfulness training to reduce impulsivity or general education in healthy conflict resolution skills. In order to solve the aforementioned problem, different ML techniques will be used to predict the chance of perpetration for an individual and also most effective factors will be identified using statistical approaches and later compared with primary expectations from social work perspectives.

Problem Definition

Violence is a complex phenomenon that impacts adolescents and young adults across the United States. It occurs in multiple ways including interpersonal violence, intimate partner violence, gang violence, and gun violence. Homeless youth experience all types of violence at higher rates than their housed counterparts [6–8]. This is typically the result of many contributing factors including childhood experiences of trauma, subsistence survival strategies, and exposure to perpetrators while living on the streets [9–11]. The consequences of violence are severe: besides the proximal consequence of severe injury or death, violence can also cause nonphysical ailments such as posttraumatic stress disorder, depression and externalizing behavior, delinquency, and aggression. It is clear that reducing violence in the lives of homeless youth is imperative and will contribute to a young person's ability to safely and successfully exit the streets and lead a long a productive life in society. However, public health and social interventions to reduce violence within adolescent and young adult populations are difficult [12], because, again, this phenomenon is complex, with many intrinsic and extrinsic contributing factors.

The public health model recognizes three levels of prevention: primary, secondary, and tertiary [13]. Primary prevention is designed to reduce incidence by preventing the first occurrence of an event. Secondary prevention is designed to decrease the prevalence of a problem after its onset and often includes interventions targeting populations at greatest risk of harm. Tertiary prevention occurs once a problem is clearly evident and causing harm [13, 14].

There are primary IPV prevention mechanisms that are curriculum based, which focus on teaching awareness about violence, promoting healthful behavior, and teaching conflict resolution skills. However, the IPV problem among homeless populations is more complex, given that the youth are not usually going to school and are not a regular part of any community to get access to those primary intervention techniques [12].

Moreover, some primary intervention systems use simplistic and generic methods that might not be particularly effective in the long run. There are several community programs to help the IPV victims, but not many programs are out there that are focused on identifying and counseling the perpetrators and batterers. Often, perpetrators learn their violent behavior by witnessing or being exposed to domestic violence during their formative years. The personal background and upbringing of each perpetrator play a key role in their future violent behaviors. Hence, these might go unnoticed in traditional intervention techniques, which highlights the need for newer and efficient ways to intervene. Most of the intervention and prevention programs for IPV for the homeless have limited funding, and it is important that we use the allocated resources in the most efficient way. AI-supported methods are expected to provide targeted interventions that are more effective.

Currently, there are several organizations that are working on many of the world's hardest problems: combating child exploitation, disrupting illicit networks, delivering humanitarian aid in the wake of conflict and natural disasters, and more. When we talk about AI here, it spans the core AI, machine learning, and data mining using machine learning methods. AI and data mining helps revolutionize the way we use data in pursuit of helping the society. Further, unlike many other proposals to improve society, machine learning tools can be easily scaled to larger demographics depending on the requirements.

Data Set Description

As part of a longitudinal study of Los Angeles area homeless youth, drop-in service–seeking youth completed a self-administered questionnaire. The presented results are from the third panel of data collection (sample size; $N = 452$). The Revised Conflict Tactics Scale (CTS2) was used to assess physical IPV perpetration. The sample was limited to youth who answered the questions related to IPV (99 youth either did not answer the corresponding questions or were never in a relationship, which narrows down the sample size to 353). The research team approached all youths who entered the service agencies during the data collection period and invited them to participate in the study. The selected agencies provided weekday services to eligible HY, including basic needs, medical and mental health services, case management, and referrals and connections to other programs such as housing services. Each youth signed a voluntary consent form, and a consistent pair of research staff members was responsible for all recruitment to prevent youths from completing the survey multiple times during each data collection period per site. The questionnaire asks the respondent about their personal life, their interactions with other people, where and how they live, the quality of their relationship and sexual life if they have any partner, etc. These data are unique in that they include the Revised Conflict Tactics Scale [15], which was to assess physical IPV perpetration in each participant's most recent intimate relationship. The CTS2 is the most widely used instrument in research on interpersonal violence and includes data on perpetration and victimization across various domains of violence (i.e., physical, emotional, relational, sexual, and threatening). The current study's

Table 11.1. *Description of data set variables*

Age	Age at the time of interview
Exchange Sex	Exchanged sex for money or other items
Children	Number of children
Suicide Attempt	Suicide attempt in previous 12 months
Homeless Age	Age of first homelessness
Jail	Ever been in jail
Juggalo	Identifies as a Juggalo (fan of musical group ICP)
Male	Identifies as male
LGBQ	Sexual minority
White	Of Caucasian race/ethnicity
Literal Homeless	Is literally homeless (sleeps on street, park, car, etc.)
Weapon	Carried a weapon in previous month
Violence	Engaged in interpersonal violence (physical fight) in previous 12 months
Gang	Is current or former gang member
PTSD	Has symptoms of PTSD
Depressed	Has symptoms of depression
Community Violence	Witnessed community violence during childhood
Sexual Abuse	Experienced childhood sex abuse
Physical Abuse	Experienced some form of physical child abuse (physical and witness family IPV)
Lonely 1	How often do you feel that you lack companionship?
Lonely 2	How often do you feel left out?
Lonely 3	How often do you feel isolated from others?
Hard Drug Use	Hard drug use in past 30 days
Foster Care	Ever in foster care
Job	Currently has a job
IPV perpetration	In a violent relationship or not? (The outcome variable we want to predict)

primary outcome variable was physical perpetration that includes a range of items from "I slapped my partner" (minor) to "I kicked my partner" (severe). The original data set had more than 1000 variables. The number of variables in comparison with the number of participants is too large for using ML techniques. Therefore, unrelated variables were removed from the data set for analyses, which resulted in decreasing the number of potential predictor variables to 26. The variable name and description are presented in Table 11.1.

Data Analysis

The data analysis occurred in several stages. First, we did an analysis based on what is found in previous social science literature on IPV perpetration. Second, we did a p-value and LASSO technique analysis. Each stage in this analysis phase will be used to identify the most important features that could be included in a IPV perpetration triage tool.

Theoretical Quantitative Analysis

Before performing machine learning analyses, we established a baseline analysis as a comparison. We identified variables in the current data set that correspond with risk factors and predictors that have been found in previous literature. Age, race, and gender were included in the baseline analysis as statistical control variables. For adolescents and youth, IPV experiences are not predicted by gender, which is contrary to adult experiences of IPV [16]. The most common predictor for youth IPV perpetration is experiences of childhood maltreatment or abuse. A large body of literature has suggested that exposure to maltreatment in childhood is related to some form of IPV in later life [17–21]. The link between maltreatment and IPV is often referred to as intergenerational transmission of violence [22, 23], which is derived from Bandura's (1979) social learning theory. This framework suggests that children exposed to violence, either as a victim or a witness, are more likely to use violence as a tactic for conflict resolution because this has been modeled in intimate relationships during childhood. A statistical analysis was performed including: Age, White, Male, Community Violence, Sexual Abuse, and Physical Abuse.

Statistical Analysis

Multiple methods were used to uncover the most important features. *P*-value is described here; AI algorithm techniques, such as SVM and random forest, are described in the Methodology section later in the chapter.

P-value

The p-value is used in the context of null hypothesis testing in order to quantify the idea of statistical significance of evidence [24]. We calculated this value for each feature to achieve a ranking of the most influential ones.

LASSO

A method that is useful in determining the most important features is LASSO [25]. LASSO is a regression analysis method that performs both variable selection and regularization in order to enhance prediction accuracy and interpretability of the statistical model it produces. In other words, it will give us the variables that are most influential on the target variable. Since we have many variables, using this method will help us reduce the number of features to consider in the final model and in our triage tool at the end, since it is not feasible to consider all the features that we have now.

Support Vector Machines (SVM)

SVM is a well-known predictive model. Assuming features form the dimensions in space (in this way each data point would be a point in our space), SVM finds the hyperplane or a set of hyperplanes that best separates the data points of different classes. Best separator for an SVM model is the one with the largest margin (distance of the hyperplane to the nearest data point of any class). Having the trained model, a previously unseen data point is mapped into the same space, and based on its position relative to the hyperplane, it is marked as positive or negative (in a binary classification). For some data sets, different classes are not linearly separable, so to generate nonlinear classifiers, kernels are introduced. Different kernels and also different parameters for each kernel are among parameters we tune to get the best model. The best SVM model for our data set is an rbf kernel. Though this model is clearly a predictive model, its other features lead us to try it to find the most effective features. The hyperplane constructed by SVM gives a weight to each feature in space. These weights or coefficients can be used to determine which features had a bigger impact in separating the positive and negative values and which features were irrelevant [26].

Random Forest

Random forest is a popular algorithm for feature ranking. In the structure of decision trees, leaves represent class labels, or "IPV_perpetration" in our data, and branches represent conjunctions of features that lead to those class labels.

Final Rankings

In Table 11.2, seven most effective features based on each algorithm are given. LASSO and T-test are described in the previous subsections; SVM and Random Forests are described in the Methodology section. The repetitive features in algorithms are used as important features. With this approach, the most important features are: "PTSD", "depressed", "violence", "hard_drug_use", "lonely3", "exchange_sex".

After removing "ptsd" from variables set, we run the ranking algorithms again on the data. By removing "ptsd," other variables can increase their power in the data. Based on the results, most important features are: "depressed", "hard_drug_use", "violence", "gang", "physical_abuse", "lonely 3".

Table 11.2. *Ranking of the features in the decreasing order of importance*

	SVM	Random Forest	T-test	LASSO
1	**lonely2**	**depressed**	**ptsd**	**violence**
2	**hard_drug_use**	**ptsd**	**depressed**	**ptsd**
3	**ptsd**	homeless_age	**hard_drug_use**	**depressed**
4	**exchange_sex**	Age	**violence**	**hard_drug_use**
5	juggalo	**violence**	**lonely3**	**gang**
6	**lonely3**	weapon	physical_abuse	**exchange_sex**
7	sexual_abuse	**hard_drug_use**	suicide_attempt	**LGBQ**

Table 11.3. *Ranking of the features, after excluding PTSD, in the decreasing order of importance*

	SVM	Random Forest	T-test	LASSO
1	**hard_drug_use**	**depressed**	**depressed**	**depressed**
2	exchang_sex	homeless_age	**hard_drug_use**	**hard_drug_use**
3	**gang**	**violence**	**violence**	**violence**
4	lonely2	Age	**lonely3**	**gang**
5	juggalo	**hard_drug_use**	**physical_abuse**	**physical_abuse**
6	**lonely3**	**lonely3**	suicide_attempt	**LGBQ**

Methodology

In this section, we will describe the final features we used in our ML techniques, our baseline model with which we will compare our results, and a short description of all the ML algorithms that we used.

Features

As discussed in the section describing the data set, we have 26 features in our data set. In the data analysis part, we were trying to find the most important variables that we have. Based on the results, we found out that "ptsd" is a major contributor to determining the target value. But in fact, this is a controversial issue, because the direct correlation of this variable with perpetration is unclear. There is an immense research body that shows that PTSD is a direct consequence of violence [27], and without longitudinal data there is no way to confirm this is not what is happening. Therefore, PTSD was excluded from the predictive modeling. In order to see the importance of this variable and to determine if we can perform as good as we did when we are not considering this variable at all, we are defining three feature sets with which to explore our ML algorithms. The first feature set includes all the features. The second one is just considering the most important ones based on the results of our data analysis. And the third feature set is using the most important features when we remove the "ptsd" from the initial feature set and then rank the other features based on their importance. Results of running our algorithms on these three distinct feature sets are reported in the "Results" section.

Baseline

Due to lack of prior work in the domain of our problem, we define literature-based baseline. We used logistic regression algorithm for the following variables: age, white, male, community_violence , sexual_abuse, physical_abuse.

Learning Algorithms

Predictive models use known results to develop (or train) a model that can be used to predict values for unseen data. Modeling provides results in the form of predictions that represent a probability of the target variable based on estimated significance from a set of input variables. Using the previously described features, we tried several approaches by using different ML algorithms to build our classification models. Some of the supervised ML system that we explored were: Logistic Regression, Support Vector Machines, Random Forest, Neural Network, Deep SVM. We trained and tested these models using K-fold (fivefold) cross-validation, and in order to evaluate the models we used metrics such as precision, recall, F1-score, ROC AUC (Area Under Curve) and accuracy.

Neural Networks

Artificial neural networks are a computational model used in several computational techniques in computer science and other research disciplines. They are analogous to biological neurons where connections between neurons carry activation signals of varying strengths. If the combined strength of the incoming signals is large enough, the neuron becomes activated and is passed on to the next layer [28]. We chose neural networks for our model because they have an ability to generalize and respond to unexpected inputs and patterns. But at the same time neural nets usually need massive amounts of data to train, which might be the reason we are not getting the best results. For our model we are using 10 layers and 10 hidden nodes.

The structure of a decision tree gives a good overview of important features; thus, beside classification, we use random forest for feature ranking.

Logistic Regression

Logistic regression is a linear classifier that finds the hyperplane that can best describe the data (by mapping the data points onto that hyperplane) and then separates the data points by a threshold on that hyperplane, which again best separates the data points of different classes [29].

Deep Support Vector Machine

The next model we used for classification is two-class locally deep support vector machine. It is a supervised learning method and is available as part of the Microsoft Azure Toolkit. It creates a two-class classification model and uses nonlinear support vector machine (SVM) optimized to achieve higher efficiency in cases of larger training sets [30]. Use of a local kernel function enables the model to learn arbitrary local feature embeddings, including high-dimensional, sparse, and computationally deep features that introduce non-linearities into the model. The kernel function that is used for mapping data points to feature space is designed to reduce the training time while maintaining the classification accuracy. LD-SVMs are best used when we have a complex data such that linear models (viz. logistic regression) perform poorly and data is very complex.

Results

We performed our experiments with several algorithms. To standarize the experiments we used 10-fold cross-validation of handling the test and training sets. The following metrics were used to determine which algorithms worked best for our experiments.

1. Accuracy – Accuracy is the proportion of true results to the total number of examined data.
2. Precision – Precision is the probability measure that a retrieved information is relevant.
3. Recall – Recall is the probability measure relevant information is retrieved in a search.

Table 11.4. *Results of prediction of classification algorithms for all variables (feature set 1)*

	Deep SVM	Neural Net	Random Forest	Logistic Regression	SVM(RBF kernel)	Baseline
Accuracy	0.65	0.62	0.66	0.61	0.66	0.55
Precision	0.5	0.47	0.46	0.42	0.48	0.36
Recall	0.48	0.45	0.34	0.56	0.6	0.52
F1	0.48	0.44	0.44	0.48	0.53	0.42
ROC_AUC	0.64	0.6	0.64	0.62	0.69	0.54

4. F1-score – A measure that combines precision and recall in the harmonic mean of precision and recall, the traditional F-measure or balanced F-score:

(2*(Precision*Recall)/(precision+recall)

5. ROC AUC – Area under the curve

Since we have imbalanced data, the best measures for comparing different algorithms are F1-measure and ROC AUC. As shown in Table 11.4, both F1-score and ROC AUC measure of the SVM classifier (with RBF kernel) have the highest value and produces the best results, so this is the model we propose for our problem.

For defining the most important factors, we find factors that are more common in our four rankings available in Table 11.2. The most important variables are "ptsd", "depressed", "violence", "hard_drug_use", "lonely3", and "exchange_sex".

As mentioned before, after removing "ptsd" from features, we then extracted the most important features from the rest of the features. Hence we got a new feature set: "depressed", "hard_drug_use", "violence", "gang", "physical_abuse", "lonely3". Table 11.6 shows the results using this feature set.

To summarize the data presented in Table 11.4 and Figure 11.1, Table 11.5 and Figure 11.2, and Table 11.6 and Figure 11.3, we observe that SVM gave us the best results in two of our feature sets. When using all the variables as our feature set, we got the highest ROC and F1-score (ROC = 0.69, F1 = 0.53) using SVM with RBF kernel. SVM with linear kernel gave us the best ROC and F1-score when we used the significant variables (after removing PTSD from our initial variables) (ROC = 0.67, F1 = 0.51). When exploring with the significant variables including PTSD, we got the highest ROC using the logistic regression method (ROC = 0.69). In this case, SVM with RBF kernel

Table 11.5. *Results of prediction of classification algorithms for important variables including PTSD (feature set 2)*

	Deep SVM	Neural Net	Random Forest	Logistic Regression	SVM(RBF kernel)	Baseline
Accuracy	0.69	0.71	0.62	**0.66**	**0.58**	0.55
Precision	0.49	0.6	0.41	**0.48**	**0.43**	0.36
Recall	0.36	0.42	0.43	**0.63**	**0.9**	0.52
F1	0.41	0.47	0.42	**0.54**	**0.58**	0.42
ROC_AUC	0.64	0.71	0.67	**0.69**	**0.67**	0.54

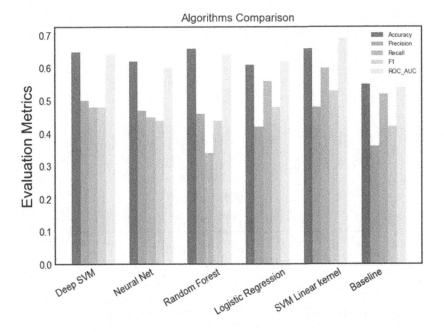

Figure 11.1 Comparison of different algorithms for feature set 1

gave us the highest F1-score of 0.58. In general, we didn't get great results in terms of F1 measure and ROC curve. However, these might have resulted from our limited and sparse data set. We had too many variables compared to the size of our data set; we also had a lot of missing values for some variables.

Table 11.6. *Results of prediction of classification algorithms for important variables excluding PTSD (feature set 3)*

	Deep SVM	Neural Net	Random Forest	Logistic Regression	SVM(Linear kernel)	Baseline
Accuracy	0.66	0.66	0.61	**0.63**	**0.63**	0.55
Precision	0.43	0.5	0.41	**0.45**	**0.46**	0.36
Recall	0.26	0.36	0.41	**0.58**	**0.58**	0.52
F1	0.3	0.4	0.41	**0.51**	**0.51**	0.42
ROC_AUC	0.67	0.64	0.63	**0.66**	**0.67**	0.54

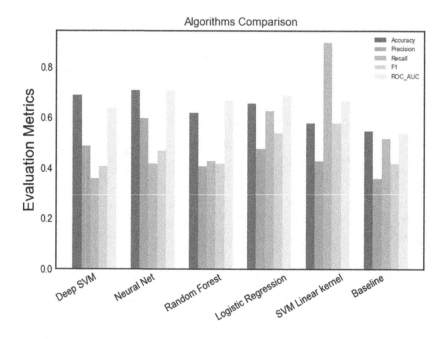

Figure 11.2 Comparison of different algorithms for feature set 2

Conclusion

Violence experienced during adolescence is related to experiences of violence in adulthood, as a result of developing ineffective coping strategies in situations of conflict within relationships [31]. Additionally, it is known that children who witness intimate partner violence between their parents are at increased risk of becoming perpetrators themselves. There is a broad understanding that violence is not only learned, but there is a "cycle of violence," meaning violent victimization only perpetuates more violence interpersonally and

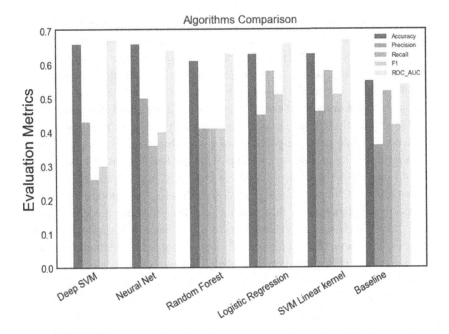

Figure 11.3 Comparison of different algorithms for feature set 3

intergenerationally. To break this cycle of violence, it is imperative that we shift the narrative from "victim" to "perpetrator." Although victim support services are necessary, solely focusing on victim services perpetuates an underlying "victim-blaming," misogynistic, and oppressive service system. As noted before, perpetrator programs exist but they are ineffective and happen after the incident of violence. Additionally, by switching the narrative from "victim" to "perpetrator" we are not proposing a "perpetrator-blaming" model. To that end, our study aimed to build a triage tool that could help us predict perpetrator behaviors among homeless youth populations before they start showing such behaviors. Our study results indicated that experiencing physical abuse during childhood, being a current or former gang member, and engaging in a recent physical fight were significantly associated with IPV perpetration. Machine learning techniques allowed us to gain better insights into the data set, which traditional techniques used in social sciences could not have alone.

IPV perpetration is the result of negative early-life experiences and other life stressors. Holding the individual accountable does not take into consideration a life-course or systems model that is the framework that defines social work research and practice. To stop the cycle of violence, primary prevention services are necessary. IPV can affect youth regardless of race, culture, or socioeconomic status. However, certain groups, including homeless youth, are at greater risk of experiencing IPV when compared to the general youth population (O'Keefe, 1997). Healthy relationship and conflict resolution skills building programs should be offered widely but in particular within at-risk populations. Given limited resources, which is the unfortunate reality of social service settings, a tool that could triage those that are at risk for perpetrating violence toward their partner could be extremely useful in reducing overall violence in adolescent and youth populations. This triage tool could be used as brief screening or assessment and provide targeted supportive services that would improve an individual's skills in coping with stress and conflict in a relationship. It is important that predictive models for social good come from a supportive approach rather than punitive one. The predictive model and triage tool that we are building will not claim that an individual *is* a perpetrator; it will only identify those that are *at risk*. This is an important distinction, especially since our model intends to prevent violent incidents before they occur.

It is important to note some potential limitations of our study. All survey data rely on individual's reports of abuse perpetrated, and their experiences of violence may be subject to response bias. Despite extensive interviewee training and efforts to ensure privacy, individuals might not have felt able to disclose their experiences of perpetrating violence on their intimate partners. Although our study provides important insight on what factors are the most important in perpetration of violence, we might have limited details about the degree of violence or the conditions in which the violence occurred, lack of some of which might change our results drastically. Also, the data set we had was too small to verify the correct applicability of machine learning and data mining algorithms and to build a model based on that. In social sciences a data set with more than 300 observations with rich behavioral data is applauded, but in computer science it is not. This modeling was also only done within a sample of homeless youth in Los Angeles. In the future, we can have more generalized versions of the data set that span the demographics, living conditions, and age of the individuals. Hopefully, we are able to predict and help the pepetration even better in the coming future with using better data sets and better data mining algorithms.

References

[1] Petering, R., Rhoades, H., Rice, E., and Yoshioka-Maxwell, A. (2015). Bidirectional intimate partner violence and drug use among homeless youth. *Journal of Interpersonal Violence*, 32(14):2209–2217.

[2] Meyer, S. (2011). Seeking help for intimate partner violence: Victims' experiences when approaching the criminal justice system for IPV-related support and protection in an australian jurisdiction. *Feminist Criminology*, 6(4):268–290.

[3] Feder, L. and Wilson, D. B. (2005). A meta-analytic review of court-mandated batterer intervention programs: Can courts affect abusers' behavior? *Journal of Experimental Criminology*, 1(2):239–262.

[4] McGinn, T., Taylor, B., McColgan, M., and Lagdon, S. (2016). Survivor perspectives on ipv perpetrator interventions: A systematic narrative review. *Trauma, Violence, & Abuse*, 17(3):239–255.

[5] Murphy, C. M. and Baxter, V. A. (1997). Motivating batterers to change in the treatment context. *Journal of Interpersonal Violence*, 12(4):607–619.

[6] Petering, R., Rice, E., and Rhoades, H. (2016). Violence in the social networks of homeless youths: Implications for network-based prevention programming. *Journal of Adolescent Research*, 31(5):582–605.

[7] Heerde, J. A., Hemphill, S. A., and Scholes-Balog, K. E. (2014). "Fighting" for survival: A systematic review of physically violent behavior perpetrated and experienced by homeless young people. *Aggression and Violent Behavior*, 19(1):50–66.

[8] Eaton, D. K., Kann, L., Kinchen, S., Shanklin, S., Flint, K. H., Hawkins, J., et al. (2012). Youth risk behavior surveillance-united states, 2011. *Morbidity and Mortality Weekly Report. Surveillance Summaries (Washington, DC: 2002)*, 61(4):1–162.

[9] Milburn, N. G., Rotheram-Borus, M. J., Rice, E., Mallet, S., and Rosenthal, D. (2006). Cross-national variations in behavioral profiles among homeless youth. *American Journal of Community Psychology*, 37(1–2):63.

[10] Robertson, M. J. and Toro, P. A. (1999). Homeless youth: Research, intervention, and policy. In *Practical lessons: The 1998 national symposium on homelessness research*. Washington, DC: US Department of Housing and Urban Development and US Department of Health and Human Services.

[11] Whitbeck, L. B. and Hoyt, D. R. (1999). *Nowhere to grow: Homeless and runaway adolescents and their families*. Piscataway, NJ: Transaction Publishers.

[12] Petering, R., Wenzel, S., and Winetrobe, H. (2014). Systematic review of current intimate partner violence prevention programs and applicability to homeless youth. *Journal of the Society for Social Work and Research*, 5(1):107–135.

[13] Wolfe, D. A. and Jaffe, P. G. (1999). Emerging strategies in the prevention of domestic violence. *The Future of Children*, 9(3):133–144.

[14] Limbos, M. A., Chan, L. S., Warf, C., Schneir, A., Iverson, E., Shekelle, P., and Kipke, M. D. (2007). Effectiveness of interventions to prevent youth violence: A systematic review. *American Journal of Preventive Medicine*, 33(1):65–74.

[15] Bandura, A. (1979). The social learning perspective: Mechanisms of aggression. In H. Toch (Ed.), *Psychology of crime and criminal justice* (pp. 198–236). Prospect Heights, IL: Waveland Press.

[16] Johnson, W. L., Giordano, P. C., Manning, W. D., and Longmore, M. A. (2015). The age–IPV curve: Changes in the perpetration of intimate partner violence during adolescence and young adulthood. *Journal of Youth and Adolescence*, 44(3):708–726.

[17] Delsol, C. and Margolin, G. (2004). The role of family-of-origin violence in men's marital violence perpetration. *Clinical Psychology Review*, 24(1):99–122.

[18] Eriksson, L. and Mazerolle, P. (2015). A cycle of violence? Examining family-of-origin violence, attitudes, and intimate partner violence perpetration. *Journal of Interpersonal Violence*, 30(6):945–964.

[19] Franklin, C. A. and Kercher, G. A. (2012). The intergenerational transmission of intimate partner violence: Differentiating correlates in a random community sample. *Journal of Family Violence*, 27(3):187–199.

[20] McKinney, C. M., Caetano, R., Ramisetty-Mikler, S., and Nelson, S. (2009). Childhood family violence and perpetration and victimization of intimate partner violence: Findings from a national population-based study of couples. *Annals of Epidemiology*, 19(1):25–32.

[21] Widom, C. S., Czaja, S., and Dutton, M. A. (2014). Child abuse and neglect and intimate partner violence victimization and perpetration: A prospective investigation. *Child Abuse & Neglect*, 38(4):650–663.

[22] Widom, C. S. and Wilson, H. W. (2015). Intergenerational transmission of violence. In *Violence and mental health* (pp. 27–45). New York: Springer.

[23] Widom, C. S. (1989). The cycle of violence. *Science*, 244(4901):160.

[24] Wasserstein, R. L. and Lazar, N. A. (2016). The ASA's statement on p-values: Context, process, and purpose. *The American Statistician*, 70(2):129–133.

[25] Tibshirani, R. (2011). Regression shrinkage and selection via the LASSO: A retrospective. *Journal of the Royal Statistical Society: Series B (Statistical Methodology)*, 73(3):273–282.

[26] Press, W. H., Flannery, B. P., Teukolsky, S. A., Vetterling, W. T., et al. (1989). *Numerical Recipes, Vol. 3*. Cambridge: Cambridge University Press.

[27] Silverman, J. G., Raj, A., and Clements, K. (2004). Dating violence and associated sexual risk and pregnancy among adolescent girls in the united states. *Pediatrics*, 114(2):e220–e225.

[28] Russell, S. J. & Norvig, P. (1995). *Artificial intelligence: A modern approach*. Englewood Cliffs, NJ: Prentice Hall.

[29] James, G., Witten, D., and Hastie, T. (2013). *An introduction to statistical learning: With applications in R*. New York: Springer.

[30] Jose, C., Goyal, P., Aggrwal, P., and Varma, M. (2013). Local deep kernel learning for efficient non-linear svm prediction. In *International Conference on Machine Learning*, pp. 486–494.

[31] Flannery, D. J., Singer, M. I., and Wester, K. L. (2003). Violence, coping, and mental health in a community sample of adolescents. *Violence and Victims*, 18(4):403–418.

12

SHIHbot

Sexual Health Information on HIV/AIDS, chatbot

Joshua Rusow, Jacqueline Brixey, Rens Hoegen, Lan Wei,
Karan Singla, and Xusen Yin

Motivating Social Problem

Human immunodeficiency virus (HIV) is an incurable virus that leads to chronic illness – and the potentially fatal disease, acquired immune deficiency syndrome (AIDS) [1]. HIV is currently incurable because the human immune system has not adapted to completely rid the body of the virus after it takes hold, and neither medicine is available that can completely eradicate it, nor has a vaccine been developed. HIV uses the body's immune system as its mechanism of attack, infecting and reducing the number of CD4 cells (also called T cells), leaving infected individuals at risk for other infections that would otherwise be easily fought off [1]. These so-called opportunistic infections are potentially fatal, and lead to the distinction between HIV and AIDS. While no cure exists, there are several effective prevention techniques available at reducing or eliminating the rates of future HIV infection [2]. However, for many prevention techniques to work, individuals need to know if they are currently HIV-infected, to select the most appropriate prevention strategy. The only way to know for certain if one is HIV-infected is to be tested for HIV antibodies [1].

HIV/AIDS develops in the body of most people in a similar way, regardless of gender, sexual orientation, or racial/ethnic identity. However, the prevalence of HIV among the general US population is uneven. For example, while gay, bisexual, and other men who have sex with men (hereafter referred to as MSM) make up approximately 2% of the US population, in 2013 they made up 55% of individuals living with HIV [2]. In terms of new diagnoses in 2014, MSM accounted for 83% of new diagnoses among males over the age of 12 years, 67% of all new diagnoses, and 92% of diagnoses of male youth ages 13–24 years [2]. Stark racial/ethnic differences also exist, with black MSM accounting for the highest number of new diagnoses in 2014, despite their

211

relatively lower makeup of the general population, and Hispanic/Latino MSM showing the greatest *increase* in new diagnoses when compared to rates in 2010 [2].

These figures show that the highest HIV burden in the United States falls on gay, bisexual, and other MSM. Since this group is somewhat insular when it comes to finding sexual partners, gay and bisexual men are also at an increased chance of HIV exposure. Overall estimates place the prevalence of HIV infection among gay and bisexual men in the United States at 15%, or around 1-in-7; however, only approximately 73% of those infected actually are aware of their HIV status through diagnosis [2]. Without diagnosis information, HIV-infected people are unable to access medication that can vastly improve their health, while also reducing their risk of passing HIV on to their sexual partners. HIV-negative individuals can also take a daily medication called pre-exposure prophylaxis (PrEP) to prevent becoming HIV-infected, but again, medical intervention is required. Since anal intercourse with an HIV-infected person when condoms or proper medication are not present is the most likely way to acquire HIV in this group, knowledge about transmission and prevention methods is paramount. Condoms, in particular, can prevent other STDs like chlamydia, gonorrhea, and syphilis, for which MSM are also at increased risk [2]. However, stigma and/or discrimination, particularly in the form of homophobia, may prevent MSM from accessing providers for support in these areas.

As HIV is a chronic, lifelong illness, and the rates among gay, bisexual, and other MSM are most pronounced in youth aged 13–24 years, reaching these young men who have sex with men (YMSM) with prevention and treatment options at a young age is vital. Despite efforts to prevent early sexual debut, nearly two-thirds (64.1%) of American youth have had sex by the 12th grade [3]. Additionally, of the approximately 20 million newly diagnosed sexually transmitted infections each year, half occur among individuals between the ages of 15 and 24 [4]. The behaviors that put youth at risk for these unintended consequences are further pronounced among sexual- and gender-minority (i.e., lesbian, gay, bisexual, transgender, questioning and queer [LGBTQ]) youth [5, 6].

Many schools implement some form of sexual health education, but when asked, youth indicate that these programs do not meet their needs [7]. Students report that sex education often provides technical but not practical information, causing them to seek out additional resources to supplement the gap [7]. Many students report being uncomfortable discussing sensitive topics with their teachers in the classroom, who play an ongoing role outside of sexual health education instruction, or who might inform their parents about their inquiries [7]. Access to medically accurate information and/or confidential, individual counseling has been shown to decrease negative consequences by increasing condom and contraception use and delaying sexual debut while encouraging abstinence [8, 9].

Students and other youth may respond better to culturally competent [10] and confidential sexual health counseling if it were made available on demand and throughout the year. Youth may not be currently sexually active [11], or may not have developed questions about sexuality, during the prescribed times that sexual health education classes are offered (if they are offered at all). Perhaps some LGBTQ youth are concealing their sexual or gender identity because of victimization [12] fears and thus may not be comfortable discussing their unique sexual health needs in a group setting.

Disseminating sexual health information is key in curbing the spread of HIV, but youth may be embarrassed to seek information from sources that they would normally go to for medical or other advice. A plethora of information exists online, but the quality can be very hard to assess, particularly for young people who might not have much exposure to the topic. A chatbot that utilizes artificial intelligence (AI) to train on only information vetted to be medically accurate can provide information to users in an anonymous fashion, while keeping anonymized logs that can be used to further improve the usability of the virtual chat agent. This chapter goes on to explain the conceptualization and implementation of the *sexual health information on HIV/AIDS chatbot*, or *SHIHbot*. First, we discuss the architecture of SHIHbot, followed by the strategy we used to collect medically accurate information, as well as some example questions from actual users to train the system. We then describe *NPCEditor*, which selects the best response to user questions, after which we discuss our deployment and evaluation strategies.

Overview

In order to inform our target group of YMSM with reliable information on HIV/AIDS, we propose a system that employs a chatbot to dispense this information. The benefit of using a chatbot is that people often feel less judged when interacting with a virtual agent than with a real person [13]. The system will also be readily available to users all the time, allowing users to receive answers faster than seeking answers from a professional. We hypothesize that a system using a virtual agent in the form of a chatbot will be an efficient way of informing YMSM on a subject that is often considered taboo.

Although a lot of the information can be obtained by simply searching the Web, some of this information might contain factual errors, such as information coming from open forums. Therefore, a second benefit of using a more closed environment like the chatbot is that this system can be programmed to use only data from reliable sources.

In the following sections we provide explanations of the general architecture of the system (Figure 12.1). Starting by describing our data-gathering process, we then present how this data is preprocessed and formatted. The

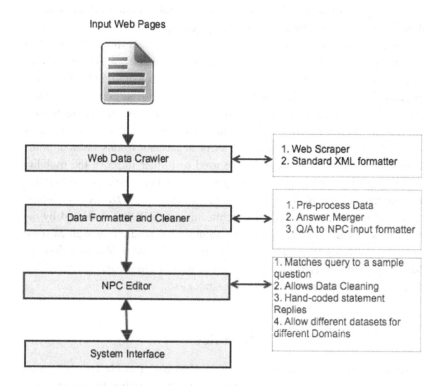

Figure 12.1 High-level overview of the architecture. We first find Web sources that have correct answers to generally asked questions about HIV/AIDS for YMSM. Data crawler automatically extracts data from various sources and brings them to the standard XML format. Data formatter and cleaner further cleans and prunes the repetitive data according to question topics. Data are then fed to NPCEditor, which learns to interpret queries given by the user and interacts with the system and then to select an appropriate response. The end user only interacts with the system interface to get answers to their questions related to HIV/AIDS.

preprocessing also involves merging semantically similar questions into one topic. In the following section, we describe the use of NPCEditor and then talk about the interface provided to the end user. NPCEditor also allows the system to improve based on user questions and statements. Finally, we describe deploying *SHIHbot* on Facebook Messenger, and our offline evaluation results.

Data Gathering

To build an AI model for answering questions about HIV/AIDS, a database containing proper questions and answers should be available for reference. The sources for both the questions and answers are critical. The qualities of the questions will directly affect the understandability of this model for all potential questions asked by our users. The answers provided through our model should be verified for accuracy. It is preferable that the interaction created by our model does not make our users feel uncomfortable.

The question sources provide coverage for potential questions coming from the ultimate service users. The database of questions will focus on three perspectives: professional knowledge, language habits, and synonyms.

First, users come to our platform in need of professional knowledge (e.g., "whether or not AIDS can be cured"; "what is the relationship between hepatitis and HIV infections?"). The questions should cover a range of profession keywords for the model to capture the most effective information, such as "relationship," "hepatitis," "HIV/AIDS," "cure," etc.

Second, users of the platform have different habits when it comes to asking questions, e.g., some users will not invert the subject and the verb when asking questions. Some users tend to ask very subjective questions, so instead of asking "Is AIDS curable?" they might ask, "Am i going to die because i am infected with AIDS?" There are any number of ways to ask questions that might lead to the same correct answer.

Third, users of the platform might be of different cultural backgrounds, different ages, or have differing levels of knowledge about medication, health care, or diseases. For example, people with medical research backgrounds will refer to the white blood cells that send signals to activate the body's immune responses as *CD4 cells*, but other people might call them *T cells*, or *T-helper cells*. Another example is that users may refer to *semen* as *sperm* or vice versa, or some of them will not recognize *semen* but use *cum*. By increasing the number of questions relating to an answer we can address the variety in language habits of users.

To achieve the professional knowledge coverage for HIV/AIDS information, we use questions and answers organized by federal agencies and institutes
and departments of health from states. Since these organizations focus on
developing and applying HIV/AIDS control and prevention nationally or
within a whole state for a large range of different population over years,
we trust them to be a credible source of information. Two example question
sources we use are the HIV/AIDS question and answer section of Centers for
Disease Control and Prevention (CDC; https://www.cdc.gov/actagainstaids/
basics/whatishiv.html) and New York State Department of Health (https://
www.health.ny.gov/publications/0213.pdf).

To improve the source of different forms of questions considering the
different habits of language use, we also use sources from non-government
or non-federal institution. In smaller forum sites built by volunteers and
researchers, the questions asked are more personal and very likely to appear
when users are chatting with a chatbot. At the current phase, we collect these
personal questions from forums like i-base (http://i-base.info/qa).

To identify relevant synonyms and similar phrases for key terms, we uses
sources from CDC and other credible institutions' records. These records
usually use parentheses to mark a word or a phrase with different usages,
such as, *Polyurethane (**plastic**) or polyisoprene (**synthetic rubber**) condoms
are good options for people with latex allergies, but plastic ones break more
often than latex ones.*

The sources of our answers all come from credible institutions like the CDC
and the New York State Department of Health. We have made this a limited
source to make sure the answers will not harm or distress the users. In future
iterations we may add information from other trustworthy sources.

To obtain the data from our resources, we used Web-scraping techniques.
Using a Web crawler to crawl the websites for the required data and then format
it to specifically formatted comma-separated values (CSV) files containing
question-answer pairs to be used by the chatbot. In addition to the professional
information websites of the CDC and the New York State Department of
Health, we obtained data from the i-base website. We obtained over 3,000
question-answer pairs from these websites, allowing us to address a wide
variety of topics on HIV and AIDS.

NPCEditor

To drive our chatbot responses we used NPCEditor, a response classifier
and dialogue management system [14, 15]. NPCEditor employs a statistical

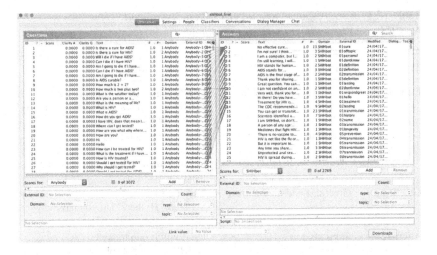

Figure 12.2 Example of potential input statements and responses. The connecting lines between the question panel and the answer panel indicate to which responses in the answers an input in the questions list is connected.

classifier that is trained on linked questions and responses; these links are visualized in Figure 12.2. For each new user utterance, the classifier ranks all the available responses; the full details of the computations can be found in Leuski and Traum [14]. We trained the classifier on our QA corpus, which is augmented by questions and responses about the chatbot itself and utterances that maintain dialogue flow such as greetings and closings (Table 12.1).

The dialogue manager functionality within NPCEditor chooses which response generated by the classifier to give to the user. Typically it will choose the response that was ranked highest by the classifier, but it may choose a lower-ranked response in order to avoid repetition. In the event of multiple responses scoring above the threshold, the returned response will be the one not given most recently, and/or the response with the most relevant answer words in the response. Examples of scores can be seen in Figure 12.3. If the score of the top-ranked response is below a predefined threshold that is determined during training, the dialogue manager will instead select an off-topic response that indicates non-understanding (such as "please repeat that").

The classifier also has special tokens to recognize when a user asks the chatbot to repeat an answer or elaborate on a previous answer, and when such a token is identified, the dialogue manager will repeat or elaborate, based on the topic annotation of the responses. For example, should a user ask for more information after receiving an answer tagged with "transmission," the

Table 12.1. *Each response was tagged with a "type" and "topic" in NPCEditor to help direct the dialogue manager*

Type	Purpose	Example dialogue
Don't know	No relevant response in domain above threshold	User: What is the weather in LA? SHIHbot: I am not confident on an answer for that question.
Personal	Questions about the chatbot	User: are you a robot? SHIHbot: I am a computer, but I have lots of human colleagues who helped make me so smart.
Greeting	Greetings and pleasantries	User: hello SHIHbot: Hi there! Do you have any questions about HIV/AIDS?
Alternative	Suggests a new conversation topic after 3 off-topic inputs from user	User: will it rain today? SHIHBot: I'm not sure on that. I would be happy to answer any questions you have about HIV/AIDS though.
Say more	Gives a random response with the same topic as the previous response	User: Should I get tested even if I do not have symptoms? SHIHBOT: If you think that you may have been exposed to HIV, you should get tested as soon as possible. Someone can have HIV and have no symptoms for many years. User: tell me more about this topic. SHIHBot: The CDC recommends that everyone between the ages of 13 and 64 get tested for HIV at least once as part of routine health care. About 1 in 8 people in the United States who have HIV don't know they have it.
Repeat	Repeats previous response	
QR	In-domain responses annotated with topics	

system would then give the next highest scoring answer with that same topic. A counter keeps track of the number of consecutive times the chatbot has failed to provide a direct answer, and on the third instance, an "alternative" response is given to suggest returning to the HIV/AIDS domain. The counter restarts after giving an "alternative" response (Figure 12.4).

Previous applications of NPCEditor have been used to drive interactive characters in various domains such as interactive museum guides [16], entertainment experiences [17], and interviews with Holocaust survivors [18].

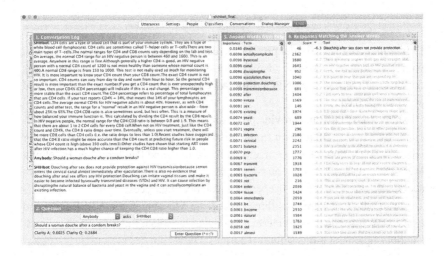

Figure 12.3 Example of how potential responses while chatting are scored based on input from the user. Panel 6 (the rightmost panel) shows the total score of the response chosen (in this case above the threshold for an acceptable response to return). Panel 5 (the middle panel) shows which words in the response led to the overall score and gives insight into which words were most important for the response being chosen.

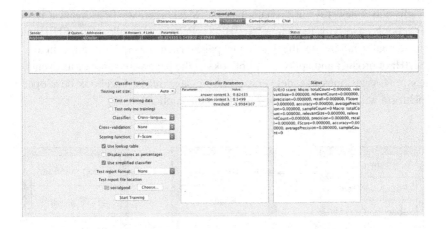

Figure 12.4 Example of a classifier's performance in NPCEditor

NPCEditor was applied to the HIV/AIDS domain in the development of a virtual reality application designed for HIV-positive young men who have sex with men (YMSM), to practice disclosing their status to intimate partners in an immersive, nonjudgmental environment [19].

Deployment

Deployment of the SHIHbot provides a real-world platform for users to interact with it. Through it we can also collect more questions to expand the Q&A database and further train NPCEditor. A version of SHIHbot was demonstrated at Sigdial 2017 [20].

Many Web platforms provide programming interfaces for third-party developers to integrate their own applications. Among of them, several popular ones include Facebook Messenger, Slack, Twitter, and PandoraBots. Facebook Messenger was selected as our deployment platform as it currently has more active and age-appropriate users and developed interfaces.

Our deployment involves three layers: the Messenger, the NPCEditor, and a proxy Web service as an intermediate layer to isolate the user interface with chatbot implementations (Figure 12.5).

Messenger as the User Interface

To deploy a chatbot on Facebook, we needed first to register a developer account on Facebook, then add a new product, which we called SHIHbot, to start our deployment.

To add a new role of a chatbot in the Messenger, we first create a new Facebook page with the name "SHIHbot." People who talk to the SHIHbot are actually talking to the Facebook page. Then we add the page in our SHIHbot product and apply for webhooks to the page with some of its events, e.g., messages, message_deliveries, and message_reads. Facebook developer platform will forward all applied events to the application.

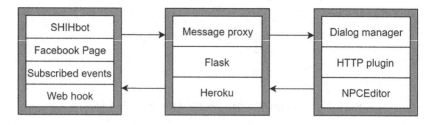

Figure 12.5 SHIHbot deployment architecture. Users interact with the chatbot via the Facebook page. Typed messages are passed via a message proxy to the HTTP plugin within NPCEditor. Once the message has been received by NPCEditor, the dialogue manager determines an appropriate response. The message is then passed back through the proxy to show up as a response on Facebook messenger.

Intermediate Web Service as the Proxy

To receive the events mentioned above, we need to build a Web service with a URL, which can accept RESTful requests as a callback. Then we register the URL as a callback URL in the webhook product of the Facebook developer platform. After this registration, the Facebook developer platform will forward all events applied to the Web service. We use the Python Flask package to build a test purpose Web service and hold it in the Heroku platform, which provides a fast way to deploy a Web service. The intermediate layer can either reply to simple questions from Messenger, like "what is your name" and reply with "I'll be back in a moment" if the backend chatbot is down, or forward messages it received to any kind of chatbot backends.

NPCEditor as the Backend

The NPCEditor has many plugins to provide versatile interfaces for users. For example, the e-mail plugin supports interacting with the NPCEditor via e-mail, while http plugin provides RESTful interface. It also contains phone plugin, Jabber plugin, and so on.

We use its http plugin to connect with the intermediate layer. First we create a new user in the NPCEditor with a name "SHIHbot," then we add a http account for the user with a port number. After that, we can interact with the SHIHbot user via the URL http://localhost:port/SHIHbot/[1] to post questions to it, e.g., http://localhost:port/SHIHbot/?q="what is your name"&from= "user-id"

Broken down, the above URL shows the user "user-id" asking the question "what is your name" to the user "SHIHbot." We use JSON to compose the question and user id content in the intermediate layer, then forward the message to the NPCEditor. After receiving the reply from NPCEditor, the intermediate layer then forwards the response back to Messenger.

Evaluation Metrics

We measure the performance of SHIHbot to better serve users in three aspects: the real-time interaction, the long-term engagement, and the learning and improvement of SHIHbot over time. Accordingly, we use linguistic-driven, online-driven, and social-driven metrics to measure our bot.

---

[1] A public URL is needed for the NPCEditor for connecting it with the intermediate layer.

Linguistic-Driven

Given the huge range of possible user input, chatbots often misinterpret or are unable to understand what a user wants. The times when a bot responds with a version of "I don't understand" highlights the bot's interpretation ability and a potential lack of responding item in the database. Such incidences might upset users.

However, there is no absolutely versatile chatbot, so to test the percentage of "I don't understand," the question test set must be selective of reasonable questions. A robust chatbot serves reasonable "I don't understand" to unreasonable questions.

Conversation steps represent another metric for interpretation. A single back-and-forth exchange between a user and a bot marks one conversation step. For example, if a user asks one question, and the chatbot asks two subquestions and then delivers the final answer, it means there are three conversations steps.

The definitions are as follows,

Confusion Trigger Rate (CTR): The percentage of answers returned as "I don't understand," which happens when the bot fails to find any appropriate reply to a question.
Conversational Steps: Number of subquestions raised by bot following an original question. This shows the bot's robustness in engaging a user in a more natural conversation and giving an appropriate answer.

Online-Driven

As with all online services, we expect to measure the retention: the ratio of long-term users to registered users for our chatbot.

Also, we measure the engagement rate for each user. Each time a user responds to the chatbot is considered an engaged session.

Social-Driven

A customer satisfaction questionnaire is planned for our chatbot when users do not respond with the chatbot but leave the website open. A prompt will ask the user a concluding question, such as, "Was I able to answer your questions today?" Users will be prompted to send feedback through the chatbot if they wish.

To research on correctness and social acceptability, we can ask human annotators to annotate each answer for a question in terms of user acceptability.

Each annotator marks a reply for a question in terms of two metrics, **Comfort** and **Trust**. Both will be measured on a Likert-like scale of 0 to 5, where 0 is "not at all" and 5 is "completely." Comfort pertains to whether or not the answer provided is sensitive to the way the question was asked; trust is whether or not the answer provided was accurate. Meanwhile, further research can determine if SHIHbot is effective in reducing HIV-exposure risk.

Alpha Test

The current version of evaluation is a test of the alpha version of SHIHbot, which means it is only open to insiders offline. We expanded the Confusion Trigger Rate (CTR) into the a scale from 0 to 5 (see Table 12.2). We use human experts available to rate our question data set. The question data set we use is from a government source; in this way, we make sure all these questions are already supplied with a credible answer that our human experts can evaluate.

Data

We use two different data sets to evaluate the alpha version of SHIHbot. The first data set, which we call "va38q," consists of 38 questions extracted from the Frequency Asked Questions section of the US Department of Veterans Affairs (https://www.hiv.va.gov/HIV/patient/faqs/index.asp). The second data set consists of 100 questions on the subject of HIV/AIDS, published by the New York State Department of Health (https://www.health.ny.gov/publications/0213.pdf), which we call "ny100q." Feeding these questions into the SHIHbot, we get 138 answers related to these questions. Then we evaluate our Q&A pairs using the rubric provided in Table 12.2.

Observations

Figures 12.6 and 12.7 show three consistent cumulative distribution results from our four human experts. For both data sets, the distribution of scores does not differ greatly between the human experts, implying agreement in interpretation of the overall performance of SHIHbot. We see in Figure 12.6 that human expert 2 has a slightly different scoring distribution than the other three, which can be attributed to the smaller sample size of questions in that dataset. Figure 12.7, which has nearly three times the sample size and the same human experts, has much more consistent scoring.

Table 12.2. *Explanations and examples of rating*

Rating	Explanation	Case (Q&A pairs from ny100q)
0	returns "I don't understand," "I'm still learning," or similar answers	question 17: Does sexual contact with many partners increase my risk of getting HIV? answer 17: I'm not sure! I think Google might have a better answer.
1	returns an answer other than "I don't understand," but unrelated to the topic of the question	question 21: Can a person with HIV who has an undetectable viral load pass HIV to someone else? answer 21: It is okay for HIV-positive people to date anyone positive or negative. There are no additional risks if you are both positive. Sometimes it means you have a shared understanding about HIV, and this can be good.
2	returns a misleading answer	question 7: Where can I find updated statistics on HIV and AIDS? answer 7: There are a number of resources you can use to find this information. The first resource is our guide to ARVs. The guide lists ARVs currently available. It also provides a one-page summary on each drug. This includes information such as generic and brand drug names, and brief characteristics and potential side effects of each drug. If you would like information on managing side effects of the different drugs, please follow this link to our guide on HIV and your quality of life. Other resources you can use are: The European Medicines Agency website. The site provides information in two formats. The first is patient information in nontechnical language and the second is more technical drug product information. The European Medicines Compendium Website. This site provides a concentrated technical summary on each drug. Also know as the SPC [Summary of Product Characteristics], it includes information on how the drug works; how it was studied; side effects; contraindications (when it should not be used); and why it was approved.

The NHS (National Health Service) website.
The American National Institute for Health website.
The third and most personal option is to talk to your HIV clinician or pharmacist. This option is a good opportunity to ask direct questions on anything you're not too clear about.

question 1: Who is at risk for getting HIV?
answer 1: Case reports of female-to-female transmission of HIV are rare. The well-documented risk of female-to-male transmission shows that vaginal fluids and menstrual blood may contain the virus and that exposure to these fluids through mucous membranes (in the vagina or mouth) could potentially lead to HIV infection.

question 9: Is it easy to get HIV?
answer 9: It sounds as if you would benefit from some professional counseling about why you are so concerned about getting HIV. With today's modern drugs, someone with HIV can lead a normal life with a near-normal life expectancy so there is really nothing to worry about. HIV is not that easy to catch, especially in the UK where the prevalence is very low and where HIV-positive people have access to treatment making them noninfectious. You cannot get HIV from handling a parcel and you cannot get it from a needle that has been lying around for 4 hours.

question 4: Is there a cure for HIV or AIDS?
answer 4: No effective cure currently exists for HIV or AIDS. But with proper medical care, HIV can be controlled.

3	returns an answer that only partially answers the question
4	returns an answer covering most of the question
5	returns an exactly correct and related answer

225

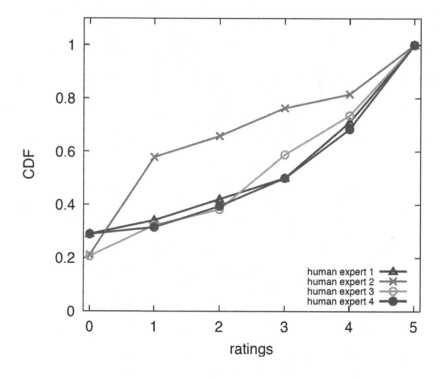

Figure 12.6 CDF of ratings of the va38q

Based on rating standards in Table 12.2, the start points of lines in Figures 12.6 and 12.7 mean the experts giving the 0 rating, which shows there is a lack of knowledge for SHIHbot to return the good answers. The current results show that there are about 20–50% answers for which SHIHbot has no related records. This lack of information will be addressed after SHIHbot is activated online, and information can be added according to collections of unsolved questions.

If we exclude the starting points from Figures 12.6 and 12.7, both graphs show a greater slope from rating 4–5 than from rating 2–3, which indicates that when SHIHbot has information about the questions that users are asking in the referral database, it uses it to create a satisfactory answer.

Future Work and Directions

Currently, SHIHbot is only in its first iteration. Although SHIHbot is a fully functional chatbot capable of answering questions on HIV and AIDS,

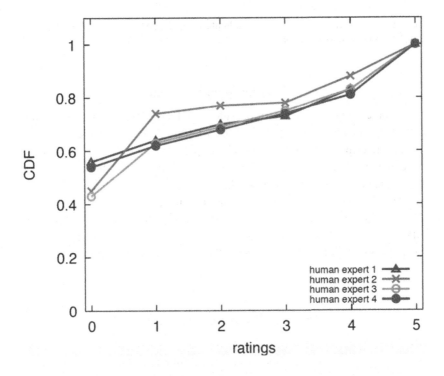

Figure 12.7 CDF of ratings of the ny100q

we envision the following improvements that will improve its capability of reaching its target audience and providing information.

Support for Additional Platforms

SHIHbot currently supports the Facebook Messenger platform. Although Facebook is widely used, having the chatbot deployed on only one platform will limit the number of people we can reach. Additionally some people might not want to use the chatbot on Facebook, as the platform technically allows us to gather personally identifiable information. Although we do not track or store any of these data, it is hard to convince skeptical users of this.

One additional platform to deploy SHIHbot on is Twitter. Users could privately send direct messages to the chatbot. Another option is to build our own website that allows its users to interact with the chatbot. That would enable users without a Facebook or Twitter account to interact with the bot. Similar to a separate website would be to build an app for the iOS and Android operating systems giving users a dedicated app for obtaining information on HIV/AIDS on their smartphones.

Obtain Additional Information

SHIHbot currently provides information on HIV/AIDS using information obtained from the Centers for Disease Control and Prevention (CDC), the New York State Department of Health, and the Q&A section of the i-base website. We can improve the bot by obtaining new information from additional websites (e.g., aids.gov, Scarleteen, Go Ask Alice).

We also can broaden our search for information on sexual health in general. The current version of SHIHbot only answers questions directly relating to HIV and AIDS. However, it would make sense to create additional question categories on topics such as other STDs, sexual orientation, and gender identity.

Add Additional Functionality

SHIHbot is currently only capable of answering a single question. This means that it does not keep track of the entire conversation it has been having with the user. We can improve this behavior by tracking the history of a conversation. History would allow SHIHbot to give more appropriate answers and also to allow its users to ask follow-up questions on some topics. By doing this, chatting with SHIHbot will feel more natural, perhaps enticing the user to also spend more time and ask more questions.

Analyze User Data to Improve SHIHbot

SHIHbot can be continuously improved by analyzing the anonymized user data. A review of the questions being posed to the system and the answers provided offer a metric of how well the system is performing and also indicate areas that need to be strengthened. By gaining a better understanding on what users are interested in, it will be possible to better address their questions and concerns. In addition to the anonymous user data within the system, users will also have the ability to provide feedback directly to the system, or through usability questionnaires and feedback forms available on the platform they are using.

Overall, the system can be iteratively developed and improved to provide a satisfying user experience. While the topics tackled by the system are potentially sensitive, they also have great public health and social justice implications. It is our hope that SHIHbot will move online and provide the most vulnerable – or the otherwise curious – the best information to reduce HIV transmission.

References

[1] US DHHS (Department of Health and Human Services). (2016). HIV/AIDS 101: What is HIV/AIDS? Retrieved from www.aids.gov/hiv-aids-basics/hiv-aids-101/what-is-hiv-aids/

[2] CDC (Centers for Disease Control and Prevention). (2017). HIV among gay and bisexual men. Retrieved from www.cdc.gov/hiv/group/msm/index.html

[3] Kann, L., et al., Youth risk behavior surveillance – United States, 2013. *MMWR Surveill Summ*, 2014. **63**(Suppl 4): 1–168.

[4] Centers for Disease Control and Prevention. Incidence, prevalence, and cost of sexually transmitted infections in the United States. 2013; Available from: www.cdc.gov/std/stats/.

[5] Robinson, J. P. and D. L. Espelage, Peer victimization and sexual risk differences between lesbian, gay, bisexual, transgender, or questioning and nontransgender heterosexual youths in grades 7–12. *American Journal of Public Health*, 2013. **103**(10): 1810–1819.

[6] Mojola, S. A. and B. Everett, STD and HIV risk factors among US young adults: Variations by gender, race, ethnicity and sexual orientation. *Perspectives on Sexual and Reproductive Health*, 2012. **44**(2): 125–133.

[7] DiCenso, A., V. W. Borthwick, and C. Creatura, Completing the picture: Adolescents talk about what's missing in sexual health services. *Canadian Journal of Public Health*, 2001. **92**(1): 35.

[8] Kirby, D., et al., School-based programs to reduce sexual risk behaviors: A review of effectiveness. *Public Health Reports*, 1994. **109**(3): 339.

[9] Underhill, K., D. Operario, and P. Montgomery, Systematic review of abstinence-plus HIV prevention programs in high-income countries. *PLOS Medicine*, 2007. **4**(9): e275.

[10] Hoban, M. T. and R. L. Ward, Building culturally competent college health programs. *Journal of American College Health*, 2003. **52**(3): 137–141.

[11] Cavazos-Rehg, P. A., et al., Age of sexual debut among US adolescents. *Contraception*, 2009. **80**(2): 158–162.

[12] D'Augelli, A. R., N. W. Pilkington, and S. L. Hershberger, Incidence and mental health impact of sexual orientation victimization of lesbian, gay, and bisexual youths in high school. *School Psychology Quarterly*, 2002. **17**(2): 148.

[13] Gratch, J., Lucas, G. M., King, A. A., and Morency, L. P. (2014, May). It's only a computer: the impact of human-agent interaction in clinical interviews. In *Proceedings of the 2014 International Conference on Autonomous Agents and Multi-Agent Systems* (pp. 85–92). International Foundation for Autonomous Agents and Multiagent Systems.

[14] Leuski, A., and D. Traum, NPCEditor: Creating virtual human dialogue using information retrieval techniques. *Ai Magazine*, 2011. **32**(2): 42–56.

[15] Leuski, A., and D. R. Traum, NPCEditor: A tool for building question-answering characters. Proceedings of the Seventh conference on International Language Resources and Evaluation. L'REC 2010. pp. 2463–2470.

[16] Swartout, W., et al. Ada and Grace: Toward realistic and engaging virtual museum guides. *International Conference on Intelligent Virtual Agents*. Springer Berlin Heidelberg, 2010.

[17] Hartholt, A., J. Gratch, and L. Weiss, At the virtual frontier: Introducing Gunslinger, a multi-character, mixed-reality, story-driven experience. *International Workshop on Intelligent Virtual Agents*. Springer Berlin Heidelberg, 2009.

[18] Traum, D., et al. New dimensions in testimony: Digitally preserving a Holocaust survivor's interactive storytelling. *International Conference on Interactive Digital Storytelling*. Springer International Publishing, 2015.

[19] Knudtson, K., K. Soni, K. Muessig, M. Adams-Larsen, R. Artstein, et al. Tough talks: Developing a virtual reality application to support HIV status disclosure among young MSM. *21st International AIDS Conference (AIDS 2016) Abstract Book*, 2016.

[20] Brixey, J., R. Hoegen, W. Lan, J. Rusow, K. Singla, X. Yin, R. Artstein and A. Leuski. SHIHbot: A Facebook chatbot for Sexual Health Information on HIV/AIDS. *Proceedings of the 18th Annual SIGdial Meeting on Discourse and Dialogue*, 2017.

13

Ethics and Artificial Intelligence in Public Health Social Work

David Gray Grant

Introduction

As demonstrated by a number of chapters in this volume, autonomous software agents based on artificial intelligence (AI) have many potential applications at the intersection of public health and social work, known as public health social work. These applications are enormously promising, but often pose novel ethical problems for researchers that can be difficult to assess, much less to resolve. The aim of this chapter is to show how analytical tools from moral philosophy and theoretical computer science can be combined to better understand these problems and to develop strategies for addressing them in practice.

I will focus on a specific set of problems that arise in the development of public health social work interventions based on AI. Specifically, I will focus on a class of problems that I call *beneficence problems* (the rationale behind the name will become clear further on). Beneficence problems occur in the context of public health social work interventions that are partially planned, in the field, with the help of an artificially intelligent autonomous software agent (call these *AI planning interventions*).

Consider cases such as the following. Suppose that researchers are developing a public health social work intervention to be conducted by some intervention team with some target population. The goal of the proposed intervention is to provide some specific set of benefits to the target population, such as (for example) reducing the incidence of HIV in the population. In the field, a software agent will assist the intervention team by recommending an intervention plan, consisting of some sequence of actions to be performed by the intervention team. The agent's goal is to identify and recommend the intervention plan that, if carried out, would benefit the target population in the intended way to the greatest extent possible. The intervention team believes that the intervention plans that will be recommended by the agent are likely to benefit the target population, considered as a whole, to a greater extent than would alternative interventions they could perform. However, they also believe that the software agent may, under some foreseeable conditions, recommend a plan that, while well-suited to maximizing benefits to the target population, will also pose a significant risk of harm to some of that population's members. Moreover, they have the capability to predict the individual- and population-level expected benefits and harms of particular intervention plans the agent considers. What should the researchers do?

The answer is far from obvious. Cases such as this one pose a dilemma between two moral duties whose importance is widely recognized in the fields of both public health and social work. The first is the duty not to conduct interventions that are expected to harm others, otherwise known as the *duty of non-maleficence*. The second is the duty intervention teams have to conduct interventions that they expect will provide the greatest possible benefits to the populations they work with, otherwise known as the *duty of benefit maximization*. The challenge posed for the design of the autonomous agents involved in such interventions is how to ensure that the intervention plan that is eventually conducted by the intervention team will demonstrate appropriate respect for both duties. Call the problem of meeting this challenge in a particular AI planning intervention a *beneficence problem*, and call an AI planning intervention that poses a beneficence problem an *AI intervention**. (The asterisk next to this term throughout the chapter indicates that it is different from a standard AI planning intervention.)

As we shall see, it can be difficult in practice to modify the software agent used in interventions of this kind so that there are reasonable guarantees that both duties just mentioned will be respected. That is, it can be difficult to ensure that the intervention plans the agent recommends will both (1) minimize the expected risks of the intervention to a degree compatible with the duty of non-maleficence and (2) maintain the expected benefits of the intervention at a level consistent with the duty of benefit maximization. On the one hand, if the balance researchers strike between minimizing expected harms and maximizing expected benefits weights expected benefits too heavily, favoring the duty of benefit maximization, then the risks posed to particular individuals may be too significant to be morally justifiable. On the other hand, if the balance struck weights expected harms too heavily, favoring the duty of non-maleficence, then the intervention may be rendered ineffective enough to obligate researchers to abandon the proposed intervention in favor of a more beneficial alternative. Either kind of failure would render the proposed intervention morally impermissible to conduct, in the absence of further modifications.

My ultimate objective in what follows is to provide practical guidance about how to approach designing the software agents used in AI interventions* so that both extremes are avoided. The plan for the chapter is as follows. To make the discussion more concrete, I begin in the next section by setting out a real-world beneficence problem currently being faced by researchers at the Center for Artificial Intelligence in Society at the University of Southern California. In the third section, I provide a more formal definition of beneficence problems and set out some necessary technical background. Since implementing appropriate safety constraints requires a working understanding of the moral duties involved, the fourth discusses the duties of non-maleficence and benefit maximization in more detail. The penultimate section proposes a framework, offered in a tentative spirit, for addressing conflicts between the two duties in public health social work interventions. I conclude in the final section by sketching some potential strategies for operationalizing this framework in the context of AI planning interventions.

Case Study: Adapting TND Network for Homeless Youth

Researchers at the Center for Artificial Intelligence in Society (CAIS) are in the process of adapting a drug abuse prevention program called TND (Towards No Drug Abuse) Network for use in residential shelters for homeless youth. The program divides participants into small groups of approximately five members. The goal of the program, which relies heavily on peer interaction, is to use the power of peer influence to help participants develop the attitudes, skills, and confidence required to resist drug abuse. This program has been demonstrated to be effective in schools with at-risk youth – an important result, given how difficult drug abuse has proven to address – but current versions have a significant downside. In a recent large-scale trial of TND Network, Valente et al. (2007) found that particularly at-risk participants failed to benefit from the program. In fact, the program seemed to place them at even higher risk of future drug abuse. Valente and colleagues hypothesized that this increased risk was the result of *deviancy training*, a well-documented phenomenon that occurs when individuals are encouraged by their peers to adopt harmful or antisocial behaviors.[1] When such high-risk youth are placed together in an intervention group, Valente and colleagues concluded, they are likely to influence each other to use substances more, not less.

234   Ethics and Artificial Intelligence in Public Health Social Work

Researchers at CAIS are currently attempting to modify the program in two ways.[2] The first is to make it more suitable for homeless youth at high risk of serious drug abuse living temporarily in residential homeless shelters. The second is to address its deviancy training effects. To achieve the second goal, CAIS developed an autonomous software agent to help improve how the program divides intervention participants (the current residents of a medium-term residential shelter for homeless youth) into groups. The agent's goal is to maximize the intervention's positive effects of peer influence on participants' future drug use, and to minimize its negative (deviancy training) effects.

To do this, the agent uses a peer influence model (and more specifically, a linear threshold model; see Kempe et al., 2003) to predict how attitudes about drug abuse will spread from person to person as a result of the intervention. (The model first predicts changes in participants' social networks that will occur as a result of participation, based on who is assigned to their participation group.) The intervention team conducts interviews with each participant in order to acquire information about their past drug use, who is in their personal (or "egocentric") social network, how strongly they are related to those individuals, and to what extent those individuals are known by the participant to have used drugs, currently or in the past. The agent's influence model is then updated based on this information, allowing it to make predictions about how various choices of intervention groups will affect participants' future drug use behavior. The agent then attempts to identify and recommend the "optimal" set of intervention groups – the set of intervention groups predicted by its model to result in the greatest aggregate (or population-level) reduction in future drug abuse by all participants.

Researchers hope that this modification to TND Network, which we can call *TND Network-SA* ("SA" for "Software Agent"), will render the program even more effective at reducing drug abuse by minimizing potential deviancy training effects. This is particularly important given that their target population, homeless youth, has an unusually high proportion of individuals who currently abuse or have abused drugs in the past, which increases the risk that the intervention will lead to deviancy training by strengthening participants' social ties to other youth who view drug abuse favorably.

On early tests on sample data, however, researchers discovered a potential beneficence problem. Researchers fed previously collected data about the social networks of members of a particular population of homeless youth in Los Angeles, California (where the center is based) into the agent's influence model, and then instructed the agent to recommend intervention groups for a hypothetical set of participants in that population. The agent made a surprising recommendation: it recommended that the intervention team put the youth currently at highest risk of drug abuse into one group, and divide the youth at lower risk among the remaining groups. The agent's model, it turned out, had predicted that grouping the hypothetical participants in this way would result in a substantial reduction in aggregate future drug abuse for the lower-risk youth – at the cost of a substantial predicted *increase* in future drug abuse for the higher-risk youth. The expected decrease in risk for the lower-risk youth was great enough that, despite the increased risk for the higher-risk youth, the resulting grouping was optimal from the point of view of minimizing risk at the population level.

CAIS researchers judged that the model's predictions here were reliable enough for the risk of significant harm here to be genuine if the hypothetical intervention were actually conducted. As a result, the intervention poses a beneficence problem, as defined earlier.

Beneficence Problems

In this section, I provide a more formal definition of beneficence problems in general. In the field of artificial intelligence, a *planning problem* is the problem of identifying the sequence of actions that is best suited for achieving some goal. A particular planning problem can be defined by specifying the following:

1. An *agent* of some kind (e.g., a human, a software agent, a robot, or a team consisting of some combination thereof);
2. A *goal* to be achieved by that agent;
3. A set of possible *states* of the world – particular ways for the world to be;
4. A set of possible *actions* that the agent could perform in order to achieve that goal;
5. The agent's *beliefs* about the starting state of the world, e.g., in the form of a probability distribution over the states referenced above;
6. An optional set of *constraints* on how the goal can be achieved, used to rule out as possible solutions to the problem actions or sequences of actions known to be infeasible or otherwise undesirable for the agent to perform.[3]

In a *beneficence problem*, the agent in question includes both (a) a human team that is planning a public health social work intervention and (b) a software agent that will assist that team in planning the intervention. The goal to be achieved is the goal of maximizing benefits of a particular kind for some target population. The states are various possible features of the intervention context that are relevant to predicting the intervention's effects. Both the intervention team and the agent have relevant beliefs about the starting state of the world prior to the intervention. The intervention team has information about the starting state and supplies that information to the software agent in the form of input. This input is used to generate a formal representation of the starting state in terms that the agent is capable of understanding. There may or may not be any preexisting constraints on how the team achieves the relevant goal. The software agent and the intervention team will plan different aspects of the intervention, depending on what planning tasks are being offloaded to the software agent.

We need to specify two further features of the planning problem to complete our definition of beneficence problems. The first is that it has an explicitly moral constraint on how the goal of maximizing benefits for the target population can be achieved: that it be reasonable to expect that the intervention plan that the intervention team conducts based on the agent's recommendations will appropriately respect the duties of benefit maximization and non-maleficence. Call this the *beneficence constraint*. The second is that the agent is capable, or could be made capable, of providing useful predictions about the expected benefits and harms of the intervention for particular members of the target population.

This last feature is what distinguishes AI planning interventions that pose beneficence problems (AI planning interventions*) from other public health social work interventions that generate similar conflicts between the duties of benefit maximization and non-maleficence. With the greater ability to assess individual-level effects that AI interventions* offer comes a greater responsibility to minimize potentially harmful effects. This leads to difficult questions about how to resolve the associated dilemma between beneficence and non-maleficence.

Moral Duties and Beneficence Problems

A *moral duty*, as I use the term here, is a relatively general moral obligation that applies across a range of possible contexts. As I have mentioned, beneficence problems pose a dilemma between two different and sometimes conflicting moral duties that public health social work professional have: maximizing the benefits of interventions they conduct and avoiding causing harm to particular individuals. These two duties are combined in a foundational principle of human subjects research ethics, the principle of beneficence. The Belmont Report states the principle as follows:

> Persons are treated in an ethical manner not only by respecting their decisions and protecting them from harm, but also by making efforts to secure their well-being. Such treatment falls under the principle of beneficence. The term "beneficence" is often understood to cover acts of kindness or charity that go beyond strict obligation. In this document, beneficence is understood in a stronger sense, as an obligation. Two general rules have been formulated as complementary expressions of beneficent actions in this sense: (1) do not harm and (2) maximize possible benefits and minimize possible harms.[4]

As the last sentence brings out, there are really two principles here. The first, "do not harm," is ancient in its origins[5] and is commonly referred to as the principle of non-maleficence. The second, "maximize possible benefits and minimize possible harms," is a version of the utilitarian injunction to bring about "the greatest good for the greatest number." I refer to it as the principle of *benefit maximization*. The duties of non-maleficence and benefit maximization are widely accepted in public health and social work, whether or not human subjects research is involved, though there is significant controversy over how to address conflicts between the two duties.[6]

It is worth emphasizing that the benefits the duty of benefit maximization refers to are expected benefits, net benefits, and aggregate benefits. They are *expected benefits* because there is uncertainty involved. The intervention could have various possible effects, and researchers are really only in a position to estimate how beneficial or harmful those effects might be under various possible conditions, and assess the expected value or disvalue of the intervention across the full range of possible ways things could turn out. They are *net benefits* because benefits are allowed to compensate for harms in determining the total benefit provided, at least for some types of harms and benefits. (The harms might be greater than the benefits, in which case the net benefit would be negative, a net harm.) And they are *aggregate benefits* because they are calculated by summing the expected benefits for each individual to produce an aggregate score representing the total expected net aggregate benefit for the population as a whole. We can also call them *population-level* benefits for this reason, as opposed to *individual-level* benefits.

The duty of non-maleficence refers to expected harms in the same sense that the duty of benefit maximization refers to expected benefits. Since an intervention's effects cannot be predicted with certainty, public health social work professionals are enjoined to avoid risks that they are in a position to foresee, and weigh those risks both by their severity and by how likely they are to occur. The level of expected risk an intervention poses is therefore a function of both the likelihood and severity of the relevant risks. However, the relevant harms are neither net nor aggregate: the duty directs public health social work professionals to avoid expected harms to particular individuals, regardless of whether they are compensated for by benefits to those same individuals or to others.

It will simplify the discussion in what follows to confine our attention to cases where the expected harms and benefits of an intervention are different sides of the same coin: the benefits alleviate some potentially harmful condition a person can be in (e.g., being disposed to abuse drugs), whereas the harms make that condition worse. This is true in TND Network-SA: the relevant type of harm is being influenced to increase future drug abuse behaviors; the relevant type of benefit is to decrease future drug abuse behaviors. Restricting our attention in this way will let us set aside issues of intrapersonal compensation, such as determining whether a person is harmed on balance when they are made more likely to abuse drugs but less likely to contract HIV.

Some further distinctions between the two duties will also be helpful for our purposes. One such distinction that is worth making explicit (even though it is obvious) is that the duty of non-maleficence requires that specific individuals be treated in certain ways, whereas the duty of benefit maximization requires that larger populations be treated in certain ways. Call moral duties of the former kind *individual-oriented duties* and moral duties of the second kind *population-oriented duties*. One thing to notice right away is that the agent used in an AI intervention* will need the capability to predict both individual- *and* population-level effects in order to help the intervention team make determinations about whether the duties of non-maleficence and benefit maximization are satisfied.

Another crucial distinction between the two duties for our purposes is that the duty of non-maleficence is what is sometimes known in moral theory as a perfect duty, whereas the duty of aggregate benefit maximization is an imperfect duty. At least one way of understanding the distinction is that *perfect duties* specify types of actions that are morally required or morally prohibited. The duty of non-maleficence, then, is a perfect duty because it prohibits us from performing any action that would harm another person. *Imperfect duties*, by contrast, require us to pursue certain goals. The duty to maximize benefits is most naturally understood as an imperfect duty, as it requires those designing and conducting public health social work interventions to make reasonable efforts to maximize the expected aggregate benefits of those interventions. However, the duty does not specify what kinds of means should be used to achieve this goal: it does not require or prohibit actions of any specific kind, except to say that the interventions in question should be well-suited to promoting the goal of maximizing population-level benefits.

There are also imperfect/individual-oriented duties and perfect/population-oriented duties, some of which are highly relevant for thinking about researchers' obligations with respect to beneficence problems. Space constraints prohibit more than a cursory discussion of these and other duties, but it is worth mentioning a few in particular. First, social workers are generally understood, as acknowledged by the National Association of Social Work's code of ethics, to have a general duty to promote the interests of their clients, at least in certain respects.[7] This includes ensuring that services provided to clients – such as enrolling them in a public health intervention – are reasonably expected to be of benefit to them, except under special circumstances. This duty is both imperfect and individual-oriented.

Second, public health social work professionals are generally understood to have a moral duty to ensure that the burdens and benefits of the interventions they conduct are fairly distributed among various subpopulations.[8] This is a perfect and population-oriented duty. Researchers should take special care, then, when designing AI interventions* that may impose unfair burdens on some subpopulation. In AI interventions* as I have described them, the information about social status necessary to determine whether this duty is satisfied by particular intervention plans may well not be represented in the formal model the agent uses to plan the intervention. Building this information into the model can help the researchers developing the intervention determine whether the agent is like to recommend plans that may distribute benefits unfairly, and could potentially be used by the agent itself as it assists attempts to identify and recommend potentially desirable plans.

I will set aside these further duties in what follows, and confine my attention to the duties of benefit maximization and non-maleficence. However, these other moral obligations are worth keeping in mind, and it is important to note that public health social workers have other moral duties that will eventually need to be factored in as well when beneficence problems are addressed.

One reason the distinction between imperfect and perfect duties is useful for our purposes is that it maps roughly onto the distinction between goals and constraints in the literature on AI planning. Imperfect duties specify moral goals that human agents should pursue; perfect duties specify moral constraints that human agents need to observe as they pursue these goals and others. The similarity here is not just superficial: it mirrors the way that perfect and imperfect duties typically interact with one another. Insofar as the two conflict, perfect duties are generally understood to have priority over imperfect duties. The constraints on action imposed by perfect duties, that is, restrict the range of actions an agent is morally permitted to perform as she pursues the goals imposed on her by imperfect duties. Ordinarily at least, an agent is not permitted to violate a perfect duty for the sake of better promoting the goal an imperfect duty obligates her to pursue. We will consider some potential exceptions to this general rule further on.

This suggests a natural strategy for accommodating perfect and imperfect duties in the design of AI interventions*: accommodate imperfect duties through planning goals; accommodate perfect duties through planning constraints. In an AI intervention*, the software agent assists the intervention team by planning certain aspects of the intervention on their behalf. In order to help the intervention team avoid violating imperfect duties, appropriate changes can be made to the goals of the planning problem the agent seeks to solve on their behalf. In order to help them avoid violating perfect duties, changes can be made to the planning problem's constraints.

I'll talk more about how this might work in the "Operationalizing the Framework" section, but first we should consider what obligations public health social work professionals have when the duties of non-maleficence and benefit maximization conflict.

A Framework for Resolving Conflicts

Ethicists working in a variety of fields have long recognized that the duties of beneficence and non-maleficence can come into conflict in ways that generate difficult ethical dilemmas. The Belmont Report acknowledges this possibility early on:

> [The] role of the principle of beneficence is not always so unambiguous. A difficult ethical problem remains, for example, about research that presents more than minimal risk without immediate prospect of direct benefit to the children involved. Some have argued that such research is inadmissible, while others have pointed out that this limit would rule out much research promising great benefit to children in the future. Here again, as with all hard cases, the different claims covered by the principle of beneficence may come into conflict and force difficult choices.[9]

A beneficence problem presents researchers with a dilemma with exactly this structure: in some foreseeable intervention contexts, the software agent may recommend an intervention plan that maximizes expected aggregate benefits for the target population by generating expected benefits for some of its members and expected harms for others. The duties of non-maleficence and benefit maximization appear to conflict in these cases, posing the question of how to resolve the conflict.

I mentioned earlier in the chapter that perfect duties typically place stringent constraints on how imperfect duties may be pursued. Given this, a natural first thought is that these conflicts are easy to resolve: researchers are simply prohibited from imposing expected harms on particular individuals for the sake of producing greater aggregate benefits for the larger population. However, there are good reasons to think that there will be many exceptions to this general rule in the context of public health in general and social work in particular.

There are various ways to defend the claim that public health social work interventions may sometimes violate the duty of non-maleficence, consistent with being morally justifiable on balance, but one standard (if not uncontroversial) argument is as follows.[10] The moral justification for particular public health interventions is often understood to derive from the justification of the public health system as a whole. What justifies the sum total of interventions conducted by a public health system, in spite of the fact that particular interventions impose net costs (including harms and other kinds of costs) on some individuals, is that each individual has a strong reason to prefer living under a public health regime that allows individual interventions to trade off costs for some individuals to achieve comparatively greater benefits for others. That reason is that a system prohibited from intervening to improve the health of a population at a cost to some of its members would be far less effective overall. Provided that the system is designed to ensure that the burdens an individual is subjected to from any given intervention are compensated for by benefits from other interventions, the net result should be that everyone experiences greater benefits on balance from systems that allow such trade-offs to be made than those that do not.

Excise taxes on cigarettes, for example, improve aggregate well-being in a population by reducing the incidence of various diseases, but accomplish this at a cost to those smokers who are not persuaded to reduce their intake. Similarly, access restrictions on performance-enhancing drugs such as Ritalin benefit populations by reducing their abuse, but leave some individuals who would benefit from them worse off. What makes these trade-offs morally acceptable? According to the foregoing argument, these trade-offs are justifiable because those individuals who are negatively affected nonetheless have good reason to prefer living under a public health regime that allows them to be made – provided that there are restrictions on how significant the expected burdens can be in particular cases. Call this argument the *higher-order justification argument*.

This argument is at least initially plausible as it applies to public health social work interventions in particular. The individual members of the populations served by public health social workers have a reason to prefer being served a system that allows public health social work interventions to make the kinds of trade-offs just described, provided that safeguards are in place to ensure that the end result is that each individual expects to benefit more if those trade-offs are allowed in some cases than if they are not. This justifies relaxing the requirements of the duty of non-maleficence as it applies to individual interventions to at least some degree, allowing for net expected harms to individuals in some cases.

Suppose, then, that this argument, or another one with the same conclusion, is correct. If so, then some exceptions to the principle of non-maleficence as it applies to public health social work interventions can be justified. It remains to be seen how public health social work professionals should go about determining whether the expected harms imposed by a specific public health intervention are morally justifiable. This is of course a complex question requiring extensive treatment, but a few preliminary points can be made. I will briefly sketch a framework, based on existing work in public health ethics,[11] that offers a useful and at least initially plausible proposal about how public health social work professionals should go about negotiating conflicts between the duties of non-maleficence and benefit maximization.

The framework posits three moral duties that it takes to apply to public health social work interventions where the duties of non-maleficence and benefit maximization conflict. The first two duties apply to interventions considered in isolation; the third applies to interventions considered in light of available alternative interventions.

First, the duty of necessity. Suppose an intervention is believed to offer certain magnitude of expected benefit to the target population and a certain magnitude of expected harm to some of its individual members. The duty of necessity requires that the expected harms of the intervention be necessary to achieve its expected benefits. If the intervention can be modified in ways that reduce those expected harms while maintaining a comparable level of expected benefit, then the intervention must be modified accordingly. Doing so reduces the severity of the intervention's violation of the duty of non-maleficence. It also increases the degree to which the duty of benefit maximization is satisfied by the intervention, since expected harms for individual members of the target population entail reduced aggregate expected benefits for the population considered as a whole.

Second, the *duty of proportionality* requires that the expected benefits of an intervention be great enough to justify the expected harms involved—that the two be suitably "proportional" to one another. The idea here is that sufficiently great benefits can outweigh comparatively minor harms. We can see this logic at work in an argument mentioned in the second quote from the Belmont report cited earlier (my emphasis added):

> A difficult ethical problem remains, for example, about research that presents more than minimal risk without immediate prospect of direct benefit to the children involved. Some have argued that such research is inadmissible, while *others have pointed out that this limit would rule out much research promising great benefit to children in the future.*

The implicit argument here is that the expected benefits of research of this kind for future children is so great that it justifies the uncompensated risks posed to the children that will be enrolled as research subjects, because the relevant risks and benefits are "proportional" given the relative importance of those two moral considerations.

Why should we accept the duty of proportionality as a necessary condition on permissible interventions? Here is one argument. That an intervention is expected to generate substantial benefits for the target population counts in its favor, from a moral point of view, relative to alternative options. Other things being equal, it is better to perform interventions that produce greater aggregate benefits, as recognized by the duty of benefit maximization. Further, that an intervention poses a significant expected risk of harm to some of the target population's members counts against it, again from a moral perspective. But the two kinds of moral considerations just mentioned are not equally important. Expected risks count more against an intervention than expected benefits of a comparable magnitude. This way of thinking about the comparative moral importance of expected risks and expected benefits recognizes the fact that the duty of non-maleficence imposes a meaningful constraint on the way expected benefits can be pursued by public health professionals. If the two were not weighted differently, in this way, then the duty of non-maleficence would not impose a meaningful constraint.

Third, the *duty of trade-off optimization*. Unlike the first two duties, this duty requires that the expected benefits and harms of an intervention be compared to those of viable alternative interventions. Suppose an intervention team is faced with a choice between possible interventions that all satisfy the duties of necessity and proportionality – various versions of their own intervention, perhaps – and other alternative interventions they could perform. How should they choose among these possibilities? According to the duty of tradeoff optimization, researchers are obligated to choose the intervention from the set that strikes the best balance between expected benefits and expected harms – the expected benefit/expected harm profile that best satisfies the duty of proportionality.[12] The thought here is that the elements of a set of interventions can each satisfy the duty of proportionality, consistent with it being true that the expected benefits and harms are more "proportional" for some of the interventions in the set than for others. More proportional interventions strike a more morally desirable balance between the conflicting demands of the duty of non-maleficence and benefit maximization, and so should be preferred.

The tentative proposal I am offering here is that AI interventions* that satisfy all three of these duties – of necessity, of proportionality, and of trade-off optimization – are morally justifiable insofar as the duties of non-maleficence and benefit maximization are concerned. This is just a first step and requires much further refinement and assessment in light of other ways of approaching conflicts between the two duties. Moreover, other moral duties, such as those mentioned earlier, are not yet taken into account by the framework. However, I think the framework is at least initially plausible as far as it goes, and – despite its partial nature and the complexity of the issues involved – we can use it to draw a number of tentative conclusions about how AI interventions* should be designed.

We need to introduce one final element into the mix before we get down to brass tacks and consider how to operationalize the framework just described. As I mention earlier, autonomous agents such as those considered here make it possible to make more accurate individual-level predictions about an intervention's benefits and risks than was previously possible. One question researchers need to consider as they attempt to satisfy the foregoing three moral duties is to what extent they are obligated to use these tools to improve their estimates of those individual-level risks. This question is important because the goal of achieving a more accurate and comprehensive estimate of the expected individual-level harms of an AI intervention* is to some extent in tension with the goal of maximizing expected benefits for the population as a whole. One reason for this is that there is only so much research time that can be spent improving an intervention in the variegated respects that are morally desirable. Another reason is that many ways of improving a software agent's estimates of expected individual-level effects for particular intervention plans introduce additional computational complexity, which can in itself reduce the agent's ability to optimize population-level benefits.

Operationalizing the Framework

We can now return to the question of how researchers should proceed when they believe an AI planning intervention they are developing has a beneficence problem. Assume researchers are designing the software agent associated with such an intervention.

Let's begin by revising our original definition of beneficence in light of the framework I have proposed for resolving conflicts between the duties of benefit maximization and non-maleficence. Specifically, we can remove the beneficence constraint and replace it with a new constraint: that it be reasonable to expect that the intervention plan the intervention team actually conducts, based on recommendations from the agent, will satisfy all three of the moral duties just described: the duty of necessity, the duty of proportionality, and the duty of optimal trade-offs. This in itself is progress, as the redefined problem gives us a better idea of what is required to respect the duties of benefit maximization and non-maleficence when they come into conflict.

As is probably clear by now, it is extremely unlikely that this constraint can be fully operationalized in the design of the agent so that it never recommends plans inconsistent with it. Determining whether the three moral duties involved are satisfied by a particular intervention requires time, experience, consideration of the merits of possible alternative interventions, and open discussion with other professionals and stakeholders (including members of the target population) with a diverse enough set of perspectives to minimize the chances that something important will be overlooked.[13] Formulating general and operationalizable rules that will provide reasonable assurances that they are never violated by the intervention plans that the software agent in an AI intervention* recommends is almost certainly impossible.

What this means is that human judgment will always be required – the intervention team will need to assess the intervention plans recommended by the agent to determine whether it satisfies the duties of necessity, proportionality, and optimal trade-offs. However, the software agent might nonetheless be designed in ways that make it less likely than it would otherwise be that the duties will be violated in the field. I will sketch out three possible strategies.

First, the agent could be designed so that when it recommends a particular intervention plan, it provides the intervention team with supplemental information relevant to determining whether the recommended plan satisfies the constraints of necessity, proportionality, and optimal trade-offs. Call this the *interpretability approach*.

How might the interpretability approach look in practice? Researchers at CAIS are currently redesigning the agent to be used in TND Network-SA to supply the intervention team with more information about the expected individual- and population-level harms and benefits associated with the plans it recommends. With this information in hand, researchers will be in a much better position to assess whether the moral duties associated with beneficence problems are satisfied. An obvious first step here is for the agent to be programmed to calculate the change in expected value predicted to be achieved by conducting a particular intervention plan, relative to conducting no intervention, for each individual member of the target population, as well as for the target population considered as a whole. This would require, inter alia, that the agent's model include what we can call an individual-level value function. Let an *individual-level value function* be a function from pairs of states and individual members of a target population to real numbers on the interval between 0 and 1. The value assigned to a pair is the value for the individual of being in that state.

If the change in expected value for an individual (or population) associated with a particular intervention plan is positive, then the intervention is expected to benefit the individual (population) relative to doing nothing; if it is negative, then it is expected to harm the individual (population). Providing this information to the researchers lets them know how conducting the recommended intervention plan is expected to positively and negatively affect both particular individuals and the population considered as a whole. This would at least put the researchers in a better position to assess whether the proportionality and necessity constraints are satisfied, in conjunction with the information already available to them.

Second, the agent could be redesigned so that it automatically rules out plans with features that can be determined in advance to violate one of the three duties in the framework. This could be accomplished using what AI researchers call safety constraints. Call this the *safety constraint approach.* How might this work? One possibility is to model the planning problem solved by the agent as a constrained partially observable Markov decision process (constrained POMDP). A *partially observable Markov decision process* (POMDP) is a mathematical tool for modeling planning problems where there is uncertainty about the initial state and how it will evolve over time based on actions performed by the agent.[14] This makes POMDPs useful for modeling beneficence problems, where both kinds of uncertainty are present. In a constrained POMDP, the agent's goal is to maximize the value of one function while simultaneously bounding the values of other functions within a specified range.[15] Researchers could determine a level of expected harm that they judge would be impermissible to impose on an individual in the preponderance of foreseeable starting intervention states, and direct the agent to bound the expected change in individual-level value functions associated with each member of the target population accordingly. An advantage of this strategy is that the intervention team would have to reject recommended strategies less often, which could dramatically reduce the amount of time it takes to identify a morally acceptable intervention plan.

Another variant on the safety constraint approach would be to generate recommended intervention plans using a two-step procedure. In the first step, the agent would eliminate all possible end states that exceed a level of expected harm for individuals that they have decided is unlikely to be acceptable. It would then work backward by considering the states that are possible in the preceding step and eliminating any that have a high probability of resulting in one of those end states. This could be repeated until the step immediately following the initial state is reached. Pynadath and Tambe (2001) show how this can be done in planning problems that can be modeled as vanilla Markov decision processes. Whether the strategy could be extended in a computationally tractable way to beneficence POMDPs is beyond the scope of this paper, but is worth exploring.

Third, researchers could implement what Pynadath and Tambe (2001) call safety conditions. *Safety conditions* specify conditions under which the software agent assisting a human team should transfer control to its human operators in order to request more information or a decision of some kind. The general idea behind safety conditions is that the human operators of a software agent designed to solve a planning problem often have important information about the problem that the agent does not. In many cases, this information cannot be reliably captured or processed by the agent as it decides how to act, regardless of how well it is designed.[16] In principle, such conditions could be used to direct the agent in an AI intervention* to present the intervention team with a selection of possible intervention plans, each with a different risk/benefit profile. If feasible, this would put the intervention team in an even better position to determine how to satisfy our three moral constraints, since they will have more information about the effects of different possible intervention plans. Note that, for this to work, the agent will need to choose alternative plans in an intelligence way, by recommending plans that make the trade-off between expected individual-level harms and population-level benefits in meaningfully different ways. Call this the *safety condition approach*.

These three approaches could of course be combined, if computational limitations allow. Various other strategies are also of course possible. In any case, strategies like these have considerable potential to help the intervention teams in AI interventions* select an intervention plan that promises morally desirable expected population-level benefits without imposing morally unjustifiable expected individual-level harms.[17]

Notes

1 Dishion et al., 1999.
2 See Center for Artificial Intelligence in Society (2017) for more information.
3 Russell and Norvig, 2010.
4 National Institutes of Health, 1979.
5 The Hippocratic Oath, for instance, was written as early as the fifth century BC, and requires physicians to swear as follows: "I will utterly reject harm and mischief" (Wikipedia, 2017). The more familiar phrasing, "first, do no harm," appears to have been coined by the English surgeon Thomas Inman in the 19th century (Sokol, 2013).
6 On the public health side, see, for instance, Mann (1997) and Childress et al. (2002). On the social work side, the NASW's Code of Ethics explicitly endorses a version of benefit maximization ("The primary mission of the social work profession is to enhance human well-being and help meet the basic human needs of all people, with particular attention to the needs and empowerment of people who are vulnerable, oppressed, and living in poverty") and repeatedly enjoins social workers to avoid activities that would harm clients. See National Association of Social Workers (2017).
7 National Association of Social Workers, 2017.
8 See Faden and Shebaya (2016) regarding the field of public health. The NASW code of ethics makes clear that social workers are obligated to promote social justice, including the fair distribution of resources of various kinds, in their work (National Association of Social Workers, 2017).
9 National Institutes of Health, 1979.
10 My presentation of the argument presented later in the chapter owes much to Faden and Shebaya (2016), section 2.1.
11 The framework I develop is based in large part on the framework proposed in Childress et al. (2002), though it differs in important respects.
12 How to understand "best" in the preceding sentence is a further question that I will set aside here, but it will almost certainly depend on the nature of the argument that is given for allowing exceptions to the duty of non-maleficence.
13 There are also independent reasons to consult stakeholders in particular. See Childress et al.'s (2002) discussion of a principle they call "public justification."
14 See Russell and Norvig (2010), chapter 17, section 4.
15 See Isom et al. (2008).
16 Pynadath and Tambe, 2001.
17 The research for this paper was supported by the Center for Artificial Intelligence in Society (CAIS) at the University of Southern California (USC) over the course of a summer research fellowship in 2017. Thanks to Eric Rice, Milind Tambe, and Hailey Winetrobe at CAIS, Robin Petering and Mee-Young Um at the USC Suzanne Dworak-Peck School of Social Work, Aida Rahmattalabi and Bryan Wilder at the USC Viterbi School of Engineering, and Hau Chan at Harvard University for their insight and helpful discussion. Thanks also to the other 2017 summer fellows at CAIS and the members of the Teamcore research group at USC for many useful conversations that contributed to my understanding of the issues discussed in this essay. Special thanks to Lyndal Grant at the Massachusetts Institute of Technology for detailed comments on previous drafts.

References

Center for Artificial Intelligence in Society. 2017. *Social Network-Based Substance Abuse Prevention for Homeless Youth*. Available at: https://www.cais.usc.edu/ projects/social-network-based-substance-abuse-prevention-for-homeless-youth/. Accessed August 15, 2017.

Childress, James F., Faden, Ruth R., Gaare, Ruth D., Gostin, Lawrence O., Kahn, Jeffrey, Bonnie, Richard J., Kass, Nancy E., Mastroianni, Anna C., Moreno, Jonathan D., and Nieburg, Phillip. 2002. Public health ethics: Mapping the terrain. *The Journal of Law, Medicine & Ethics*, **30**(2), 170–178.

Dishion, Thomas J., McCord, Joan, and Poulin, Francois. 1999. When interventions harm: Peer groups and problem behavior. *American Psychologist*, **54**(9), 755–764.

Faden, Ruth, and Shebaya, Sirine. 2016. Public health ethics. In: Zalta, Edward N. (ed.), *The Stanford Encyclopedia of Philosophy*, winter edn. Stanford, CA: Metaphysics Research Lab, Stanford University.

Isom, Joshua D., Meyn, Sean P., and Braatz, Richard D. 2008. Piecewise linear dynamic programming for constrained POMDPs. *AAAI-2008*, **1**, 291–296.

Kempe, David, Kleinberg, Jon, and Tardos, Éva. 2003. Maximizing the spread of influence through a social network. *KDD*, 137.

Mann, Jonathan M. 1997. Medicine and public health, ethics and human rights. *Hastings Center Report*, **27**(3), 6–13.

National Association of Social Workers. 2017. NASW Code of Ethics (Guide to the Everyday Professional Conduct of Social Workers). Available at: https://www .socialworkers.org/LinkClick.aspx?fileticket=ms_ArtLqzeI%3d&portalid=0

National Institutes of Health. 1979. *The Belmont Report: Ethical Principles and Guidelines for the Protection of Human Subjects of Research*. Available at: https://www.hhs.gov/ohrp/regulations-and-policy/belmont-report/read-the-belmont-report/index.html

Pynadath, David V., and Tambe, Milind. 2001. Revisiting Asimov's First Law: A response to the call to arms. *8th International Workshop on Intelligent Agents VIII*, 307–320.

Russell, Stuart, and Norvig, Peter. 2010. *Artificial Intelligence: A Modern Approach*. Upper Saddle River, NJ: Pearson Education.

Sokol, Daniel K. 2013. "First Do No Harm" Revisited. *BMJ*, **347**(October), f6426.

Valente, Thomas W., Ritt-Olson, Anamara, Stacy, Alan, Unger, Jennifer B., Okamoto, Janet, and Sussman, Steve. 2007. Peer acceleration: Effects of a social network tailored substance abuse prevention program among high-risk adolescents. *Addiction*, **102**(11), 1804–1815.

Wikipedia. 2017. *Hippocratic Oath*. Available at: https://en.wikipedia.org/wiki/ Hippocratic_Oath. Accessed: August 15, 2017.

Glossary

Elizabeth Bondi and Mee-Young Um

Alters: An individual described by the **ego** as a person with whom the ego has some type of relationship; the alters surround the ego in an egocentric analysis and network map.

Binary: In the context of modeling (as opposed to binary numbers), a variable can take one of two possible values. For example, information could be propagated along an **edge** or not.

Categorical data: Also known as nominal data, can be divided into groups based on a particular qualitative property. These data cannot be ordered. Some examples of categorical data include race, gender, and education level.

Continuous data: Data that have an infinite number of possible values. Some examples of continuous data include height and weight.

Dichotomize: To make a variable into a **binary** variable.

Dyads: Pairs of **egos** and their **alters**.

Edges: The connections between vertices in graph theory, which can be directed or undirected. In sociometric network analysis, equivalent to **ties**.

Egos: The individual under study in an egocentric analysis (occupies the core position in an egocentric network map); data are collected from the ego.

False negatives: In binary classification, instances that are incorrectly classified as the negative class (i.e., they should have been classified as positive). In the case of multiple classes, this would be measured for each class (e.g., dog or not, cat or not).

False positives: In binary classification, instances that are incorrectly classified as the positive class (i.e., they should have been classified as negative). In the case of multiple classes, this would be measured for each class (e.g., dog or not, cat or not).

Feature: Any characteristic that can vary in values (quantity or quality) among individuals in a population or sample. (Same as **Variable**)

Graph: A mathematical structure used to model relations between **vertices**. Relationships can be directed or undirected, meaning the order of the **edges** may or may not matter. For example, friendship may be directed, since one person (vertex) may nominate another person as his/her friend, but the other person may not. (Same as **Network**)

Health Insurance Portability and Accountability Act (HIPAA): A federal law passed by US Congress in 1996. HIPAA requires medical records and other health information of patients to be kept confidential, protects continuity of health insurance coverage for individuals who change or lose their jobs, reduces fraud and abuse of health care, and standardizes electronic transactions that contain health care information.

Homophily: Tendency for people to bond and associate with others who are like themselves.

Institutional Review Board (IRB): A committee or administrative body who reviews, approves, and monitors research activities involving human subjects to ensure that they are conducted in accordance with all federal, institutional, and ethical guidelines.

Longitudinal data: Data resulting from a study design involving data collection at different points in time. Often used interchangeably with **panel** data, but generally has a larger number of participants.

Machine learning: An area of artificial intelligence research in which algorithms are designed to learn from data (e.g., analyze patterns in the data automatically) and use the learned models to make predictions given new data.

Model: A mathematical description of a phenomenon, such as independent cascade to describe how information propagates through a social network, or logistic regression to represent the relationship between two variables.

Network: A mathematical structure used to model relations between **vertices**. Relationships can be directed or undirected, meaning the order of the **edges** may or may not matter. For example, friendship may be directed, since one person (vertex) may nominate another person as his/her friend, but the other person may not. (Same as **Graph**)

Observations: Experiences in the real world that help build a new social theory or test an existing theory.

Ordinal data: Data with ordered categories that do not have a numeric distance between each category. The Likert scale is a typical example of ordinal data, where ordered categories can be strongly agree, agree, neutral, disagree, and strongly disagree.

Panel of data: Data can be collected at different points in time (**wave**, panel, or **snapshot**) to repeatedly examine the same variables and their changes over time for the same participants. Variables can be added or removed from one wave/panel to another. (Same as **Waves of data** and **Snapshot**)

Planning: An area of artificial intelligence research that involves reasoning about a sequence of actions to achieve a goal, often involving uncertainty.

Policy: A (mathematical) description of what should be done in certain situations, often associated with planning.

Precision: A number between 0 and 1 that can be calculated as the number of **true positives** divided by the total number of instances classified as positive, or the sum of true positives and **false positives**. In other words, it measures whether those instances that were classified as positive are correctly classified or not, or said another way, if there were mistakes while classifying instances as positive. The closer to 1, the closer to correctly classifying all instances predicted to be positive, the fewer mistakes made while classifying instances as positive. Note that some **false negatives** would not affect this measure because it does not take into account how many positive instances were missed.

Qualitative data: Information that cannot be expressed in numerical forms, such as anecdotes or interviews.

Quantitative data: Information that can be expressed in numerical forms or quantified, which is generally collected through surveys.

Recall: A number between 0 and 1 that can be calculated as the number of **true positives** divided by all actual positives, or the sum of true positives and **false negatives**. In other words, it measures the degree to which the classifier is correctly classifying all positive instances, or said another way, whether any positive instances are missed. The closer to 1, the closer to classifying all positive instances as positive, the fewer positive instances missed. Note that some **false positives** would not affect this measure because all positive instances could still be correctly classified even if there were extra positive instances. (Same as **Sensitivity**)

ROC curve: A plot that can be used to evaluate the performance of a classifier. The **recall** is plotted along the y-axis, and the false positive rate (the number of **false positives** divided by the sum of false positives and **true negatives**, or 1 − **specificity**) is plotted along the x-axis. To generate a plot, and not simply two numbers, the confidence threshold of the classifier is varied. For example, the classifier may classify an instance as positive with 80% confidence. This instance would be counted as correct when using a confidence threshold of 40%, but not for a confidence threshold of 90%, which would change the measures used to generate the curve. A well-performing classifier would have a curve close to lines at y = 1 for all x 0 to 1, and x = 1 for all y 0 to 1, meaning there is perfect recall for all false positive rates and vice versa. The ROC curve can also be used to select the optimal confidence threshold for the classifier. ROC curve Stands for Receiver Operating Characteristic curve.

Sample: A subset of a population used to represent the entire population of interest.

Sensitivity: A number between 0 and 1 that can be calculated as the number of **true positives** divided by all actual positives, or the sum of true positives and **false negatives**. In other words, it measures the degree to which the classifier is correctly classifying all positive instances, or said another way, whether any positive instances are missed. The closer to 1, the closer to classifying all positive instances as positive, the fewer positive instances missed. Note that some **false positives** would not affect this measure because all positive instances could still be correctly classified even if there were extra positive instances. (Same as **Recall**)

Snapshot: Data can be collected at different points in time (**wave, panel,** or snapshot) to repeatedly examine the same variables and their changes over time for the same participants. Variables can be added or removed from one wave/panel to another. (Same as **Panel of data** and **Waves of data**)

Specificity: A number between 0 and 1 that can be calculated as the number of **true negatives** divided by all actual negatives, or the sum of true negatives and **false positives**. This can be thought of as the "opposite" of **recall**, in that it measures the degree to which the classifier is correctly classifying all negative instances, or said another way, whether any negative instances are missed. The closer to 1, the closer to classifying all negative instances as negative, the fewer negative instances missed. Note that some **false negatives** would not affect this measure, because all negative instances could still be correctly classified even if there were extra negative instances.

Ties: The relationship between nodes in a sociometric network (also known as an **edge**); ties can be derived from a variety of social relationships, such as friendships, sexual contacts, persons with whom an individual uses drugs, or collaborative networks among social service agencies.

True negatives: In binary classification, instances that are correctly classified as the negative class. In the case of multiple classes, this would be measured for each class (e.g., dog or not, cat or not).

True positives: In binary classification, instances that are correctly classified as the positive class. In the case of multiple classes, this would be measured for each class (e.g., dog or not, cat or not).

Unstructured data: Textual data, such as anecdotes or interviews.

Variable: Any characteristic that can vary in values (quantity or quality) among individuals in a population or sample. (Same as **Feature**)

Vertices: Also known as nodes in graph theory, a set of fundamental points connected by edges. These points are called **egos** in sociometric network analysis.

Waves of data: Data can be collected at different points in time (wave, **panel,** or **snapshot**) to repeatedly examine the same variables and their changes over time for the same participants. Variables can be added or removed from one wave/panel to another. (Same as **Panel of data** and **Snapshot**)

Index

Printed in the United States
By Bookmasters